IN THE WAKE OF THE WAR

A STIRRING RECORD OF FORTY YEARS' SUCCESSFUL
LABOUR, PERIL & ADVENTURE AMONGST THE
SAVAGE INDIAN TRIBES OF THE PACIFIC
COAST, AND THE PIRATICAL HEAD-
HUNTING HAIDAS OF THE QUEEN
CHARLOTTE ISLANDS, B.C.

BY THE
VENERABLE W. H. COLLISON
ARCHDEACON OF METLAKAHTLA

WITH AN INTRODUCTION BY
THE LORD BISHOP OF DERRY

WITH 24 ILLUSTRATIONS & A MAP

TORONTO
THE MUSSON BOOK COMPANY
LIMITED

A MORTUARY TOTEM

The carving represents a bear, and was erected in memory of a chief of the Bear crest. This totem still stands in front of a chief's house at Massett, Queen Charlotte Islands.

TO
THE GLORY OF GOD
IN THE
EXTENSION OF HIS KINGDOM
EVERYWHERE

PREFACE

BY THE RIGHT REV. THE LORD BISHOP OF
DERRY AND RAPHOE

This is the record of a wonderful triumph of the Cross. Foremost and throughout it is this. But even for a reader quite indifferent to religion it ought to have an absorbing interest. In the simplest and least pretentious language it records a career of the most romantic adventure. Captain Marryat never recorded such experiences for the delight of schoolboys.

To be landed with one's wife in northern regions from the last ship of the season, among savages, and to be told as the farewell word of civilisation, "You will all be murdered"; to be chased in an open canoe by sea lions and narwhals, into whose dense masses a disobedient sailor had fired; to be chased again by a shark so huge that his dorsal fin overtopped the stern of the canoe, and so menacing that in despair they struck at his head with a pole, and he dived down and left them; to be prostrated with fever, and to have the pagan medicine men whooping and dancing around your bed, conscious that if you die they will be rid of you, and if you live they will claim the cure, these and storms at sea, and the wars of Indian tribes, and conflagrations, and earthquakes make up a fine catalogue of adventures.

Then there is the most interesting story of the natives, absolutely barbarous in many respects and ready for murder and piracy on the slightest provocation, but with a sort of very real civilisation as well, with a remarkable cere-

BISHOP OF DERRY'S PREFACE

monial for the ratifying of treaties, with a language of fine inflexions, and, as their friend assures us, the finest boat-builders in the world.

We read admirable specimens of native shrewdness, as when a tribe refuses a native catechist because another tribe no better has got a white man. "Listen," said the authority. "Would you refuse a good dinner because I sent it by a native?" "No," said the chief, "I would eat it, and I know that the native teacher would bring us the same feast, but the white man would cook it better." All this should make of the book the most popular Sunday School premium of the season.

But all this is only a by-product. We read of his first overtures to these heathens, and their answer, "Why did you not tell us all this before? Long ago the white man brought us the small-pox; now we have grown old we like our own ways; it is too late."

And says the admirable Archdeacon, "I felt as if I were upon my trial." We are told how there came to him first the sick and those who loved them, and then the old and unhappy, until the battle is won and the chief medicine man renounces his art, and the tribe is Christianised.

It is a wonderful story of devotion and faith triumphant over every conceivable hindrance and difficulty. There are people who talk as if missionaries have a very easy time; there are people who profess to think that religion makes milksops; and there are people who declare that the Cross has lost it power.

Henceforward it will be an excellent answer to all these to refer them to the work of God by His servants in the Queen Charlotte Islands.

GEO. A. DERRY.

AUTHOR'S PREFACE

AFTER over forty years' labour among the Indian tribes of the North-West of British Columbia, including the Queen Charlotte Islands, at the urgent request of many friends I have been induced to write this account of my experiences. The fact that I was privileged to be the pioneer missionary on the Queen Charlotte Islands both at Massett and Skidegate, as also on the Skeena River, and at Giatlaub on the head of Gardiner's Inlet and Tongas in South-Eastern Alaska, and other places, has imparted an additional interest to my record. Many more chapters might have been added, but sufficient has been written to convey an idea of the early history of the country, the Indians, and the Mission.

We are thankful for the measure of success granted to our efforts among the Tsimsheans, Haidas, Nishkas, and Giatiksheans, as well as amongst remnants of other tribes, notably the Zitz-Zaows. And we rejoice to know that all those tribes, as also many others, not only in British Columbia but in Alaska, have been evangelised before the inrush of a new population. In this work we gladly acknowledge the labours and successes of the messengers and missionaries of the several Churches engaged. May the records of what has been achieved in the past prove a stimulus to the yet greater work to be done in the future, so that this northern portion of our Province may not only deserve its new title of the "Garden of British Columbia," but may it prove to be the "field which the Lord hath blessed."

I desire to express my indebtedness to the following pub-

AUTHOR'S PREFACE

lications for extracts and notes, viz. *Captain Meares' Voyages of 1788, 1789, from China to the N.W. Coast of America; The History of the Northern Interior of British Columbia*, by the Rev. A. G. Morice, O.M.I., for his delineation of the location of the Dinne Nation of Indians, and also for his description of the "Pe Ne" craze amongst the Indians of the interior about the years 1847–48; also to the late Captain Walbran's volume of *British Columbia Place Names* for the description given of the last night of the Hudson's Bay Company at their Fort on the Nass River; and to Lieutenant Emmons, late U.S. Navy, for an illustration from his artistic and exhaustive work on "the Fahltan Indians as published by the University of Pennsylvania"; also for photographs to several friends who have supplied me with same.

W. H. C.

CONTENTS

CHAPTER I
THE COUNTRY AND THE MISSION . . . . PAGE 17

CHAPTER II
METLAKAHTLA 33

CHAPTER III
THE MISSION CHURCH 50

CHAPTER IV
THE NASS FISHERY 65

CHAPTER V
STRIFE AND PEACE 75

CHAPTER VI
THE HAIDAS OF QUEEN CHARLOTTE ISLANDS . . 88

CHAPTER VII
LAUNCHING OUT INTO THE DEEP 98

CHAPTER VIII
ARRIVAL FROM THE QUEEN CHARLOTTE ISLANDS BY CANOE 109

CHAPTER IX
OVERCOMING DIFFICULTIES 118

CONTENTS

CHAPTER X
SICKNESS AND TRIAL 129

CHAPTER XI
IN PERILS BY WATERS 142

CHAPTER XII
A CANOE CATASTROPHE 154

CHAPTER XIII
RETURN TO QUEEN CHARLOTTE ISLANDS . . . 162

CHAPTER XIV
FIRST VISIT TO SKIDEGATE 171

CHAPTER XV
THE CONFLICT DEEPENING 188

CHAPTER XVI
MAKAI 198

CHAPTER XVII
INTRODUCTION OF LAW 215

CHAPTER XVIII
A TOUCHING PARTING 226

CHAPTER XIX
THE HAIDAS AS MARINE HUNTERS 244

CHAPTER XX
THE FIRST BISHOP OF CALEDONIA 252

CONTENTS

CHAPTER XXI
The Nass River 267

CHAPTER XXII
Ankidā Encampment 276

CHAPTER XXIII
The Skeena River Mission 288

CHAPTER XXIV
The Zitz-Zaow Tribe 307

CHAPTER XXV
The Nishka Indians as Hunters 315

CHAPTER XXVI
A Revival 325

CHAPTER XXVII
The Lakgalzap Mission 338

INDEX 349

LIST OF ILLUSTRATIONS

A Mortuary Totem	*Frontispiece*	
Ascending a River	To face page	56
Indian Women	,,	72
Olachan-curing	,,	72
Canoe-making	,,	88
Haida House	,,	88
Interior of Haida Chief's House . .	,,	104
A Haida Indian	,,	120
A Haida Chieftainess	,,	120
An Indian Sub-chief in Full Dress .	,,	136
Indian Weapons	,,	144
Indian Chief's Dress	,,	144
Haida Tomb	,,	160
Haida War Canoes	,,	160
Totem Poles	,,	176
Indian Medicine Men	,,	176
Medicine Man's Rattle	,,	184
Indian Masks	,,	184

LIST OF ILLUSTRATIONS

Haida Tombs	*To face page*	216
Tomb of Indian Chief	,,	216
Indian Handiwork	,,	248
On the Nass River	,,	272
On the Nass River—Fishing through the Ice	,,	280
Indian Bridge	,,	296
Map of British Columbia . . .	,,	16

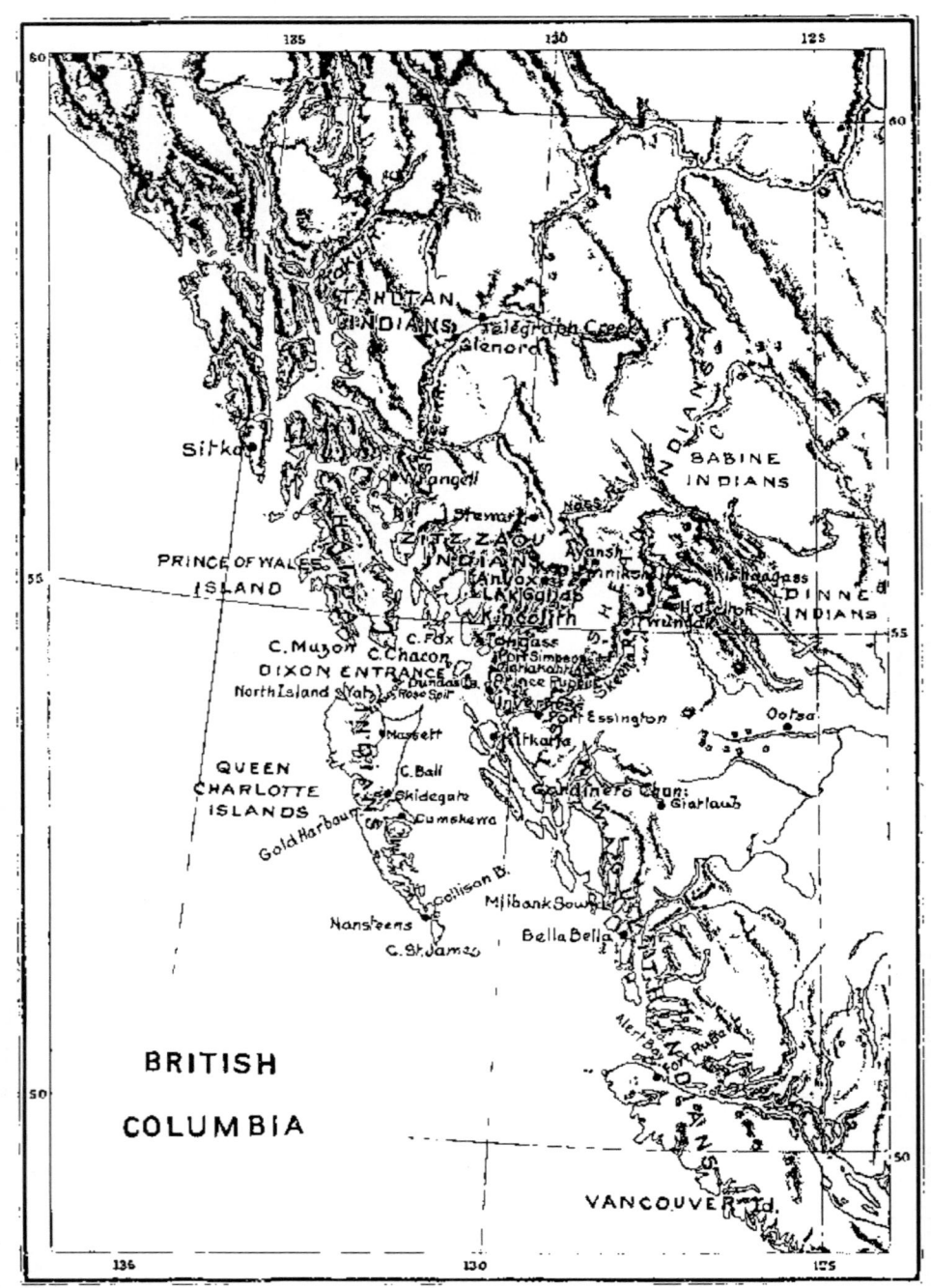

MAP OF BRITISH COLUMBIA.

IN THE WAKE OF THE WAR CANOE

CHAPTER I

THE COUNTRY AND THE MISSION

"God's in His heaven,
All's right with the world."—BROWNING.

IT is interesting to note how British Columbia was first discovered. Other navigators had touched at various points along the coast; but it was Vancouver who first sailed round the island which now bears his name, and in his search for a north-west passage sailed up many of the inlets along the coast. While he was thus engaged in investigating the coast line another intrepid discoverer was forcing his way through difficulties and dangers from Eastern Canada to the coast. This was Alexander Mackenzie, whose discoveries have also been perpetuated by the noble river named after him.

It was befitting that the country destined to become the maritime province of the Dominion on the Pacific should thus be discovered by two of Britain's sons, the one by sea and the other by land; and whilst the one represented her maritime power and research, the other represented her commercial enterprise. Without knowing aught of one another, they had almost clasped hands, both as to time

THE COUNTRY AND THE MISSION

and place, so near were they to meeting on the coast. Mackenzie had urged his way onward across the Rocky Mountains, which had hitherto proved such a barrier between East and West, and when unable further to use his bark canoe, he and his men packed their provisions and other necessaries on their backs, and pushed onward for the coast.

His progress was opposed by tribe after tribe of Indians, few of whom had ever seen a white man before. But by caution and patience, accompanied by courage and perseverance, he overcame every obstacle, and at length emerged from the forest on the tidal waters of the Pacific, at the head of the inlet now known as Bentinck Arm. More than once his men attempted to turn back, but the courage and determination of their leader restrained and re-assured them, and he succeeded in fighting and forcing his way to the coast. Here, he recorded his exploit in the only way possible. Mixing a little vermilion with melted grease, he wrote on the face of a rock, "Alexander Mackenzie from Canada by land, the twenty-second day of July, One thousand seven hundred and ninety-three." The Indians there informed him that a great war canoe had just visited the Channel, and they exhibited some presents which the white chief of the great canoe had given them. This was Vancouver and his ship. These Indians had not been so affrighted by the visit of Vancouver's vessels as the Giatkatla Indians, a tribe near the mouth of the Skeena.

When they first sighted the ships which were approaching under sail, the Indians, who were fishing off shore for halibut, cast their lines overboard and fled. Leaving their canoes, they rushed into the forest, from which they watched the arrival of these strange sea monsters. They too, had been sighted from the ships, which came to anchor, and put off a boat to open communication and to interview them. But nothing would induce the Indians to come out from their concealment.

THE COUNTRY AND THE MISSION

At length the white men kindled a fire, and proceeded to boil some rice in an iron pot. Their proceedings so interested the Indians that some of the more courageous approached to examine why the vessel, though placed on the fire, did not burn. They had never seen an iron vessel before, as all their cooking was done in cedar boxes with heated stones. When they saw the rice, they believed it was maggots, and when the white men proceeded to mix the rice with molasses, they concluded that it was the blood of their enemies whom they had slain. When invited to partake of it, they all fell back filled with astonishment. Then one of Vancouver's men raised a gun and fired at a flock of ducks which flew over the bay, one or two of which fell. At the report of the gun, with the flash of the powder and the fall of the birds, the Indians again fell to the ground in astonishment. They believed that these strange visitors were from the skies, as they could thus make thunder and lightning obey their will.

But the Indians who announced Vancouver's visit to Mackenzie were not so impressed. Probably they had heard of the white man's great flying canoes with their command of the thunder and lightning, as news of such moment would spread quickly from tribe to tribe. Vancouver's ships had been anchored within forty miles of the inlet when Mackenzie had struck the coast, and while his ships were at anchor, he and his officers, in their boats, had examined the neighbourhood, including the channel where Mackenzie so soon afterwards recorded his name and his success. This Vancouver had named Cascade Channel only a few days previously. He weighed anchor and sailed from this vicinity on the tenth of June, and on the twenty-second of the following month Mackenzie reached the spot. Thus both the coast and the interior of the country were discovered by Mackenzie, whilst at the same time Vancouver was surveying the coast. Yet, strange to say, it does not appear that either of them had given the newly discovered

THE COUNTRY AND THE MISSION

country a name. This is all the more singular when we remember that Vancouver named numerous places along the coast, and, together with Quadra, a captain of the Spanish navy, named the largest island on the coast as "Quadra and Vancouver," now, however, known only as "Vancouver's Island."

It remained for Simon Frazer, who was also an officer of the North-West Fur Trading Company, thirteen years afterwards, to make another journey of discovery to the coast from the interior, and to give a name to the country thus discovered. He encountered even greater difficulties than Mackenzie, as he did not follow the same route, but descended the river that now bears his name, which he mistook for the Columbia. That "history repeats itself," was illustrated in Frazer's adventure. At the period of the Roman invasion of Britain, the southern Britons called the inhabitants of the northern part of the island " Caoilldaoin," or the people of the woods. Hence the latinised name of Scotland—Caledonia. Frazer's parentage was of Scotland, and though he had never himself seen the rugged beauty of his fatherland, yet, from what he heard of it, he believed this new country, with its lofty mountains, mighty rivers, and expansive lakes resembled it, and hence he named it "New Caledonia."

But New Caledonia and Vancouver's Island, with the Queen Charlotte group, and all the coast islands, were included in the title of "British Columbia," which was given to it by "Victoria the Good," in a letter addressed by her Majesty to Sir E. Bulwer Lytton in 1858. This appears in the letters of Queen Victoria, which were published a few years ago, and runs as follows: "The Queen has received Sir E. Bulwer Lytton's letter. If the name of 'New Caledonia' is objected to as being already borne by another colony or island claimed by the French, it may be better to give the new colony, west of the Rocky Mountains, another name. New Hanover, New Cornwall, New

THE COUNTRY AND THE MISSION

Georgia, appear from the maps to be the names of subdivisions of that country, but do not appear on all maps. The only name which is given to the whole territory in every map the Queen has consulted is 'Columbia,' but, as there exists also a Columbia in South America, and the citizens of the United States call their country also 'Columbia,' at least in poetry, 'British Columbia' might be, in the Queen's opinion, the best name." Her gracious Majesty's decision was hailed with enthusiasm, and thus the western province of the Dominion will ever bear this honoured name.

British Columbia, the country thus discovered and named, lies between the forty-eighth and sixtieth degrees of north latitude, and is bounded on the east by the Rocky Mountains, and on the west by the Pacific Ocean and Alaska. The coast line is fringed by numerous islands, which form an almost continuous breakwater to the inner channel, and afford a safe and smooth passage for navigation along the coast for over six hundred miles. The principal islands are Vancouver's to the south, and the Queen Charlotte group of islands to the north. The latter, which were so named by Captain Dixon in 1787, are distant from the shores of the mainland about one hundred miles on the south, and about half this distance on the northern island. The country is very mountainous on the coast line, which is fringed by the coast range, whilst, further inland, rises the Cascade Range of mountains. Between the mountain ranges and the interior are numerous valleys, which offer excellent prospects for future settlements.

This, then, is the country and its coast, to which the attention of the Church Missionary Society was drawn in 1856. Numerous tribes of Indians were encamped along the coast, and on the islands, as well as on the lakes and rivers of the interior, where they had dwelt from time immemorial. The attention of the Society had been directed to the state of these Indian tribes thirty-six years

THE COUNTRY AND THE MISSION

previously, when the Red River Mission was begun, but the distance and inaccessibility of the country at that time deterred them from entering upon it.

Now, however, the call was clear, as a naval officer, Captain J. C. Prevost, who had been in command of H.M.S. *Virago*, had just returned from the British Columbian coast, where he had been engaged in connection with the settlement of the boundary line between British Columbia and the United States. Whilst there, he had witnessed enough to convince him of the necessity for a Mission among these too long neglected tribes. They were almost constantly warring, tribe against tribe, and had attacked ships and schooners, killing or capturing their crews, so that the services of this officer, with his command, had been called into requisition on several occasions to punish them.

He first communicated his report to the Editorial Secretary of the Church Missionary Society, at a meeting in Tunbridge Wells. This Secretary, the Rev. Joseph Ridgway, whilst sincerely sympathising with the officer in his appeal on behalf of the Indians, informed him that the Society had no funds in hand to enable them to undertake the proposed Mission, but requested him to write a report on the state of the Indians and their need, which he proposed to insert in the Society's publications. This was done, and the article appeared in the *Intelligencer*, with the result that, in the next monthly issue of this magazine, the sum of five hundred pounds was acknowledged, "from two friends," for the proposed Mission. Even with this sum in hand, which was probably supplemented by smaller contributions, the scheme might have been postponed yet longer had not a further stimulus been given. This was from the same naval officer, who informed the committee that he had been again commissioned by the Admiralty to proceed to the North Pacific coast, in command of H.M.S. *Satellite*, to sail in ten days, and that he was

THE COUNTRY AND THE MISSION

empowered to offer a free passage to a missionary, should the Committee be prepared to send one.

The Hon. Secretary of the Society at that time, the Rev. Henry Venn, at once proceeded to the Society's College at Highbury, where young men who had been accepted by the Committee were under training for the mission field. Here, a young man was found named William Duncan, who at once volunteered for the new Mission. In ten days he was ready, and having received his official instructions from the Committee, embarked as the messenger of the Gospel of Peace, on board a vessel of war, for his distant destination. This was on the twenty-third of December 1856, and nearly six months afterwards, on the thirteenth day of June 1857, the *Satellite* cast her anchor in Esquimalt harbour, near Victoria, Vancouver's Island. Here he remained, awaiting an opportunity to proceed northward to Fort Simpson, near to the Alaskan border, where he had been instructed to establish the Mission.

There were then over thirty thousand Indians [1] in British Columbia, speaking as many as eleven different languages, of which six were spoken by the Indians of the coast and islands, and the remaining five by the tribes of the interior. Of these languages, there are many dialects. Perhaps in no part of the world is the confusion of Babel so remarkably evidenced. The tribes in the vicinity of Fort Simpson are known as the Tsimshean. Their language is divided into three dialects, viz. the Tsimshean, the Nishka, and the Giatikshean. The Nishka is spoken by the tribes on the Nass River, whilst the Giatikshean is the language of the Indians on the Skeena River. There were three thousand Tsimshean Indians encamped around the fort.

Whilst waiting at Victoria, Mr. Duncan's time was not lost, as he made the acquaintance of the Governor, Sir

---

[1] Some reports represent the Indian population as double this number. They were certainly much more numerous formerly, and no census had been taken at that time.

THE COUNTRY AND THE MISSION

James Douglas, who was also the Governor of the Hudson's Bay Company in the province. From him, Mr. Duncan received letters of introduction to the officer in charge of Fort Simpson, requesting that accommodation should be given him in the fort. This meant much for the missionary. It secured to him protection and privacy, besides affording him more leisure for the acquirement of the language. He arrived at Fort Simpson on the first day of October 1857. The Indians had heard that he was expected, and they gathered in numbers on the shore to see the white necromancer who could read their hearts. But they did not see much more of him that winter, as he at once applied himself to the study of the language, having secured the assistance of a young man, a Tsimshean, named Clah, who knew a little English, being employed in the fort. As Mr. Duncan failed to appear, a report spread amongst the Indians that the white Shaman had gone to sleep, as the bears did, during the winter.

The missionary had not been long in the fort, before he was enabled to witness some shocking scenes, which revealed to him something of the character of the natives amongst whom he had been called upon to labour. The first was the murder of a slave woman on the beach in front of the fort. After her body had been thrown in the sea, two bands of medicine men, some of them in a state of nudity, came rushing to the spot, howling like wolves, and having found the body, they rushed on it, and tore it to pieces, the two naked leaders each rushing off with half of the body which they had torn asunder. A few days afterwards, a man was shot close to the gates of the fort. In this case, it was the act of a chief who had been irritated whilst partly intoxicated. He fired the first shot, which failing to kill his victim outright, he ordered two of his men to despatch him, which they did, shooting him as he lay wounded on the shore. Such scenes as these only stimulated the missionary to renewed efforts to acquire their

THE COUNTRY AND THE MISSION

language, and in eight months he was enabled to deliver his first address, which with the aid of his interpreter he preached to every tribe in the encampment.

In the spring of 1860 Mr. Duncan first visited the Nass River. He was well received at the lower villages, where several of the chiefs feasted him and gave him presents of furs. One chief, Kadonāh, received him with a performance of the "Ahlied," much against the missionary's desire, as he feared it would prevent him from delivering the message which he was anxious to proclaim. But it rather opened up the way, and provided him with a large assembly to hear him. In Mr. Duncan's own account of it he states: " I had heard Kadonāh say that they intended to perform me their 'Ahlied,' but I requested him to have no playing, as I wanted to speak very solemnly to them. He promised me they would do nothing bad, but now that the feasting was over, much to my sorrow, he put on his dancing mask and robes.[1] The leading singers stepped out, and soon all were engaged in a spirited chant. They kept excellent time by clapping their hands and beating a drum. (I found out afterwards that they had been singing my praises and asking me to pity them and to do them good.) The chief, Kadonāh, danced with all his might during the singing. He wore a cap which had a mask in front, set with mother of pearl, and trimmed with porcupine quills. The quills enabled him to hold a quantity of white swansdown on the top of his head, which he ejected while dancing by poking his head forward; thus he soon appeared as if in a shower of snow. In the middle of the dance a man approached me with a handful of down and blew it over my head, thus symbolically uniting me in friendship with all the chiefs present, and the tribes they severally represented. After the dancing and singing were over, I felt exceedingly anxious about addressing them, but circumstances seemed so unfavourable on

---

[1] This was their mode of making peace, or of honouring guests, by scattering the swansdown over them from their crestal crowns.

THE COUNTRY AND THE MISSION

account of the excitement that my heart began to sink. What made the matter worse, too, was that a chief who had lately been shot in the arm for overstepping his rank began talking very passionately. This aroused me. I saw at once that I must speak, or probably the meeting might conclude in confusion. I stood up and requested them to cease talking, and every countenance became fixed attentively on me. I began, and was enabled to speak with more freedom and animation than I had ever done before in the Indian tongue. Much to my encouragement, the Indians unanimously responded at the finish of every clause. The most solemn occasion of this kind was when I introduced the name of the Saviour. At once every tongue uttered 'Jesus,' and for some time kept repeating that blessed name, which I hope they will not forget."

Thus the missionary had been well received by the scattering of the swansdown, which was the highest honour they could confer on a visitor. And they were not to be permitted to forget the message they had heard, nor yet the blessed name of Him who had sent it, for already the Church Missionary Society had under consideration the necessity of establishing a permanent Mission amongst the Indians on the Nass River.

But in the meantime a terrible visitation was impending. The smallpox, which had wrought such destruction among the Indians of British Columbia and Alaska years before, was again about to overtake them. Then it had come from the Russians through Sitka. Now it was about to attack them from Victoria, in the south. Thousands of Indians had congregated there from all the tribes on the coast, and when the dreaded disease broke out amongst them, the Governor, Sir James Douglas, issued an order that all the Indians should return to their respective encampments. But it was too late to stay the plague. They fled, but every canoe carried the infection. Along the entire coast of British Columbia and up into Alaska the

THE COUNTRY AND THE MISSION

disease spread. Out amongst the islands and up the rivers the Indians were stricken. The Nishka tribes were not exempted. Years before, when they had fled from the outburst of the lava, from the angry spirit of the mountain, they had escaped. But from this more subtle spirit there was no escape.

The medicine men confessed their inability to expel it from those who were seized with it, and declared it was the white man's disease. And so in dens and caves all along the coast they sought refuge, and many a canoe never returned, because the occupants had been exterminated.

A Tsimshean Indian and his wife, in a small canoe, were amongst those who sought to return. They had not proceeded very far when the woman realised that she had caught the infection. They hastened to find a sheltered camp, and soon she was covered with the dread disease. As the symptoms increased, she begged her husband to shoot her, and thus end her misery. He was perhaps glad of the opportunity to escape, so, loading his gun with a charge of shot, he first placed all his stuff in the canoe, and then, standing on the shore, he took leave of his wife by shooting her.

A few weeks afterwards, as he stood on the shore of his camp one day with some other of his tribesmen watching a canoe approaching from the south, he was astonished to see his wife amongst the passengers. Without waiting further he fled up the beach and concealed himself in his lodge. He probably believed that it was his wife's spirit which he had seen, and hence his terror. But she soon disabused his mind of this mistake, as she followed him up to the lodge, accompanied by a number of her friends, and brought her husband to bay. And to make matters worse for him, she declared the truth: how that her husband had shot her and left her to perish. This he had concealed from her friends, having informed them that she had died of the disease. Nevertheless the fact remained, and she

THE COUNTRY AND THE MISSION

did not deny it, that it was at her own request that her husband had shot her. But the result was just the reverse of what was expected. A number of the pellets of shot had struck her and caused her to bleed freely, which evidently had brought about a reaction. A vessel containing water stood near her, of which she was able to partake, and on the following day another canoe, homeward bound, stopped at the same encampment, and being of the same tribe they remained with her, acting the part of the Good Samaritan towards her until she was sufficiently restored to embark and return with them. This was but one of many strange adventures of this Indian, whom I attended in his last illness some years afterwards.

At length, on July 2, 1864, the Rev. R. A. Doolan, B.A., arrived at Metlakahtla, and it was decided that he should proceed to the Nass River and open the Mission there. Accordingly, he left Metlakahtla on July 20th, accompanied by Mr. Cunningham, a young layman who had been sent out by the Church Missionary Society to assist Mr. Duncan in the secular work of the Mission. A young man, a native Christian of the Tsimsheans, named Robert Dundas, also accompanied them to assist as interpreter and in the school work. The following extracts from Mr. Doolan's first letter to the Church Missionary Society, dated October 26, 1864, relates his experiences and impressions in the opening of this interesting Mission: " On the 20th of July we left Metlakahtla, and on our arrival at Nass took up our residence in the house of one of the chiefs. The Indians seemed very much pleased that we had come, and helped us as far as they could by setting up our tent in the house and by bringing us food in the shape of salmon. Our first step was to look out for a suitable site for a house, hoping that before the winter we might have a small house erected; and as the Indians are divided into three villages, separated from one another by narrow channels of the river, it was a difficult matter to pitch on

THE COUNTRY AND THE MISSION

a spot which should be equally advantageous to all. The Indians, seeing us busy in preparing the ground for the house, then believed we intended remaining during the winter. They could scarcely credit it as the cold is so intense. Our difficulty with regard to a schoolhouse was for the present removed by renting for a year from one of the chiefs an old deserted Indian house built in the most populous of the three villages. To put this in order before the winter was our next step. The chiefs and some of the other men came forward very readily and lent us bark and plank for roofing and flooring the schoolhouse, telling us they did not intend treating us as the Tsimsheans had treated Mr. Duncan. The time of the year when we had arrived was when most of the Indians were away making food, yet from the very first a small band of young men stuck to us, and these with others we employed in cutting wood for the house. To show the anxiety manifested by some among them to learn ' the Book,' as they called the Bible, I will give one instance. Two young men came down from their own village, a distance of thirty miles, and remained with us over two weeks till forced to return by want of food. Their sole motive for coming was to learn. Another lad, the son of a chief, has from the first remained with us. He has been sorely tempted more than once to leave. Four times in one afternoon men came to him as he was working for us, trying to induce him to accompany them to a whisky feast. He refused to go, telling them if he did we should be ashamed of him. I trust he will soon learn to resist temptation from higher motives than these. His father and mother are very angry with him, and have cast him off because he keeps with us. He tells us he constantly prays to God. At present he is here, and at Mr. Duncan's suggestion he is going to remain with him under instruction during the winter. I trust the Spirit is leading him to inquire after the Saviour; and that in the spring, should it be the will

THE COUNTRY AND THE MISSION

of God, he may be ready for baptism, the first-fruits from the Nass.

Polygamy is very prevalent among them. One chief has no less than five wives.

Extracts from Mr. Doolan's Journal

July 24th, the Lord's Day.—A large whisky feast going on. Went to the second village and collected in Kadonāh's house ten men and fourteen children. A short address given. Went to the third village, where we got together fifteen men and ten children.

July 25th.—Engaged all the morning looking out for a site for our house and school. One of our hostesses (as our host has three wives) was busy painting herself before the fire with pitch and a decoction of berries. Above the fire, hung on horizontal sticks, are salmon and salmon spawn drying, as our host went out on Saturday night and brought home as many as thirty large salmon, some weighing thirty pounds. In the chair of state sits the lord of the house. Two little children, one with nothing but a short skirt on, run about the house. Boxes of grease line the sides, and nets hang up here and there. Two old women, wrapt in dirty blankets, squat round the fire. In another corner is our tent and boxes, and near us are three young men learning to read.

August 4th.—Heard this morning that the Indians are having a whisky feast at Lak-Ankidā. Watched them most of the day. I did not think it expedient to go over. Saw the party go from one house to another, and at last they stopped at the house of a young man for whom they were yesterday working. Saw an instance of temptation. An old man led on by Kinzadak, a chief who is doing all in his power to undermine our work. He had his arm around the man's neck, who seemed to be going very reluctantly. When he got within a hundred yards of the

THE COUNTRY AND THE MISSION

house, down he sat. Kinzadak was now joined by another man, and, between the two, the old man was led step by step into the house. I thought of the devil and his agents, and how impossible to resist him but for the grace of God. The drunken feast was carried on far into the night, as at ten o'clock I still heard the drums (or what they use for substitution, simply boxes) beating."[1]

Thus the Nass Mission was fairly established. It will be noted from the above account that intoxicating liquor was even a greater hindrance to the work of the Mission than heathenism. On one occasion Mr. Doolan had a very narrow escape. As he was passing along in front of one of the villages, a drunken Indian attempted to shoot him. He lifted his gun, which was loaded, and, aiming at him, pulled the trigger. Providentially the gun missed fire, and he was disarmed before he could make a second attempt. After some three and a half years' labour, Mr. Doolan was compelled to resign, but not before he was joined in the Mission by the Rev. R. Tomlinson. Together they decided to remove the headquarters of the Mission further down the river towards the mouth. Accordingly they selected the present site, known as "Kincolith," or the "Rock of Scalps," and Mr. Doolan assisted in the removal of the Mission to the new quarters before his departure. The Mission had been commenced at Abanshekques, a village some twenty miles from the mouth, where it was carried on during Mr. Doolan's charge. This village has long since been abandoned, many of the Indians having moved to the new site on becoming Christians. The site has been gradually swept away by the encroachments of the river. One by one the great totem poles, elaborately carved, fell before the advancing tide, and the last two I observed were two years bending over the river before they also fell in.

[1] They are not simply boxes, but the best and soundest cedar wood, of a squared shape and polished; over this dried skin is fastened, on which figures and emblems are painted.

THE COUNTRY AND THE MISSION

Thus the old order of things was passing away—their heathen customs, including the medicine men's evil practices, in the tearing of flesh both human and animal, and their whisky feasts and fights, in which many were killed or injured; and soon the light of the glorious Gospel would illuminate their beautiful river, reminding them of the pure river of the water of life which causeth everything to live whithersoever it floweth.

CHAPTER II

METLAKAHTLA

"God said 'Let there be light.'
Grim darkness felt His might
And fled away."
—EBENEZER ELLIOTT.

AFTER labouring amongst the Tsimshean tribes for five years at Fort Simpson, Mr. Duncan determined to form a Christian settlement at Metlakahtla, some eighteen miles south from Fort Simpson, to which to move the converts and their children, away from heathen influences. Metlakahtla had been the old home of the Tsimsheans, their winter encampment, from which they had moved to Fort Simpson after the Hudson's Bay Company had built the fort there. It was well suited for such a settlement, being sheltered from the coldest winds, surrounded by numerous islands, and plentifully provided with fish and game. To this site Mr. Duncan removed with some fifty Christian adherents, in the spring of 1862. Their departure caused great excitement amongst the numbers thus left behind, and, whilst we cannot but commend the missionary's plan to build up a Christian community, which should be a model and stimulus to all the tribes around, yet we would add, that the Indians in the Fort Simpson camp should not have been left as sheep without a shepherd. Adequate provision should have been made for their continued care and instruction, before undertaking the inauguration of the new settlement. Subsequent events have testified clearly to the correctness of this view, as will be proved in a future chapter.

METLAKAHTLA

Shortly after the arrival of this little band in their new quarters, they were surprised one day, whilst engaged in preparing sites for their dwellings, to see a fleet of canoes, all well filled with Indians and their effects, approaching from Fort Simpson. They were alarmed also, as they had heard that the smallpox, that dread disease, which has long been the Indian's worst enemy, had broken out in the camp, after they had left it. As the new arrivals approached the shore, a parley was held, when it was found that they had no stricken cases amongst them, and, as they asserted, no infection. This tribe, called the Giatlahn, had been encamped by themselves on the farther side of the fort, and had early established a quarantine amongst them. But seeing the disease spreading rapidly amongst the other tribes, and with the invitation of the missionary still ringing in their ears, they resolved to flee, and follow the Christians to the old camping ground. This, then, was the cause of their flight, and, after due consultation, and an agreement to obey the laws of the new settlement, they were permitted to land and take up their quarters on the eastern shore of the site. This new accession added some three hundred to the numbers of the little band. It proved a veritable city of refuge to those who had thus availed themselves of it, as, so rapidly did the affection spread amongst those remaining at Fort Simpson that no fewer than one-fifth of the entire number were swept away by the dread disease.

By establishing a strict quarantine the new settlement was protected from a foe more deadly than ever Indian warrior had met on the war-path. Rules and regulations and sanitary laws were introduced for the benefit of the community, and a sawmill and trading store established to supply their secular needs. As there was no representative of law on this wild northern coast, the missionary found it necessary to accept a commission of the peace, and in order to preserve the peace and protect the settlement he organised and swore in a body of Indian con-

METLAKAHTLA

stables. That this was necessary was clear, when we remember that all the tribes around were as yet heathen, uncivilised, and unevangelised. And, to make matters worse, whisky schooners were beginning to sail up and down the coast laden with the deadly "fire-water," which they bartered with the Indians for their furs. Whisky feasts generally followed the visit of one of these vessels to a camp, and such feasts always ended in a fierce and free fight, where firearms and other deadly weapons were turned by the intoxicated Indians upon their friends and fellow-tribesmen.

Some of the chiefs and medicine men early began to oppose the efforts of the missionary. They were jealous of the influence he was gaining with their people, and realised that their craft was in danger. But the head chief, Legaic, a man of much influence, who had been the leader of the opposition and had threatened the life of the missionary, at length surrendered to the call of the Gospel, and abandoning his position of head chief, came and joined the Christian settlement at Metlakahtla. He was shortly afterwards baptized by the name of Paul. The Mission sustained a loss in its early history by the resignation of the Rev. F. L. Tugwell and his wife, who had been sent out to reinforce the Mission. They had been nearly two years in the work when Mrs. Tugwell's health failed, and they were compelled to return to England, but not before Mr. Tugwell was privileged to baptize nineteen adults and four children, the first-fruits of the Tsimshean Mission gathered into the visible Church of Christ. Mr. Tugwell's resignation left Mr. Duncan single-handed just at the time when he was embarking on the new scheme of establishing a Christian settlement, and the presence of an ordained missionary and his wife was indispensable. Mr. Duncan had come out unordained and unmarried, but with the understanding that when he had acquired the language and otherwise tested his fitness for the climate and the work he should accept ordination. But the necessity for so much secular

METLAKAHTLA

work led him to decide to continue as a lay agent in the Mission, consequently an ordained missionary became a necessity. Several attempts of the Committee to supply this want had failed from one cause or another. And as the openings and opportunities throughout the mission field were many and the labourers were but few, the Committee found it difficult to meet the many calls for men.

It was this condition of affairs which led them to arrange for a day of prayer in 1872, that more men might be led to offer themselves for service in the mission field. As this was in obedience to the Divine command, " Pray ye therefore the Lord of the harvest that He will send forth labourers into His harvest," it was destined to succeed. My attention was attracted to the notice in the columns of a daily newspaper, and it aroused an old desire. I communicated my desire to the secretaries of the Church Missionary Society, and they replied, inviting me to London for an interview. After due examinations I was accepted, and entered the Church Missionary College at Islington. Here I made the acquaintance of the students, many of whom have since become well known through their labours in the mission field. Amongst them were Hill, afterwards consecrated as Bishop of Sierra Leone, who, with his wife, died shortly after their arrival in that diocese, which has well been named " the white man's grave"; Binns, now Archdeacon, who has laboured so long and successfully in East Africa; Lloyd, who continues to reap where he has so successfully sown in China; Bambridge of India, Williams of Japan; Cavalier, now secretary of the Zenana Mission; Keen, who went out first to the North-West America Mission, where he laboured for some seven years, and then, when compelled to return to England on account of his health, took up duty in London for some years. He afterwards volunteered again for the mission field, and, having been appointed to the North Pacific Mission, laboured amongst the Haida Indians of Queen Charlotte Islands

METLAKAHTLA

for some eight years, and then at Metlakahtla amongst the Tsimsheans, where, in recognition of his services, he was appointed a Canon. Hall also, who joined the North Pacific Mission in 1877 and laboured amongst the Quagulth tribes for some thirty-two years, reducing their language to writing and making translations. All these and many others were in the Church Missionary College during my time, and, though far sundered afterwards in the mission field, yet we have always rejoiced in one another's successes, and sympathised with each other in times of trial.

At length, the period arrived to which the outgoing men had long been looking forward, when we should each receive his commission in the valedictory instructions, prior to embarking for our respective fields of labour. The rule of the Church Missionary Society in regard to young men proceeding to the mission field is, that they shall go out single and ascertain their fitness for the climate and the work, and also acquire the language, before receiving permission to enter the state of matrimony. But, in my case, this rule was reversed. The secretaries intimated to me that, as there was no lady missionary at Metlakahtla, it would be advisable that I should find a helpmeet to accompany me to the field. But little was known then of British Columbia in the mother country, much less of the most northerly part of the province. This was illustrated when, advised by the Secretary of the Church Missionary Society to have my life insured, I applied to a leading insurance company, and, though approved by their own medical officer, yet the directors declined to insure me, as they knew nothing of the country to which I was proceeding. Fifteen years afterwards, the same company's agent met me in Victoria, and urged me to take out a policy.

On the 1st of July 1873, at a public valedictory meeting held in London, the Hon. Secretary, the late Rev. Henry Wright, read the Committee's instructions to the outgoing missionaries. Some of my former fellow-students were

METLAKAHTLA

commissioned to proceed to Africa, some to Palestine, India, China, Ceylon, and Japan. I was the only missionary whose instructions were to proceed to the western shores of "the great lone land," as Captain Butler had termed it in the volume of his travels just then published.

My instructions were as follows: "You, Brother Collison, have been appointed to the North Pacific Mission. Though last upon our list, it is not least in our hearts' affections. God Himself has marked it out as a field of special interest. We trust you will regard it as no small proof of the confidence the Committee have been led to repose in you, that you have been selected for this field. . . .

"The Committee cannot refrain from expressing their satisfaction, that you are to be accompanied by one who, from all that they have heard, they have reason to believe will prove a true helper to you in your work, and a true mother to the infant church at Metlakahtla. . . .

"They would only add that they look for the blessing of our faithful God to accompany you both on your way, and to bless you. You are not going to one of the dense populations of the earth, but you are followers of Him who said, 'What man of you having an hundred sheep, if he lose one of them, doth not leave the ninety and nine in the wilderness, and go after that which is lost, until he find it?' and they pray that you may be abundantly partakers of His Spirit, and sharers in His glory."

Our marriage took place on the 19th of August, and we spent a few days in visiting friends, and arranging and making preparation for our embarkation. My wife, to whom reference had been made in the dismissal instructions, had, as a deaconess, nursed the wounded on the battlefields during the Franco-German war, and was present at the surrender of Metz. She was, together with another lady helper, seized with typhoid fever, which carried off her companion, and well-nigh proved fatal in her own case also. She had also rendered valuable services in taking charge of

METLAKAHTLA

the Protestant patients during the epidemic of smallpox which took place in Cork. She afterwards assisted in the establishment of the first hospital for incurables there. She was thus well prepared to take her part in mission work amongst the Indian women, with whom she soon gained a remarkable influence, and was enabled to correct many abuses, which even those who were Christians still retained amongst them. She was the first white woman to take up her residence amongst the Tsimsheans at Metlakahtla, and afterwards the first amongst the then fierce Haidas of Queen Charlotte Islands, where her skill in ministering to the sick, and in dressing the wounds of those injured, tended in no small degree to bring them under the influence of the teaching of the Gospel of Salvation.

On the 10th of September 1873, we embarked from Queenstown on board the steamship *Idaho* of the Guion Line. We encountered some stormy weather on the Atlantic during the equinoctial gales, and one of the shafts was broken, which occasioned a delay of many hours in substituting a new shaft, which fortunately we had on board. We were some sixteen days in making the passage to New York, which was about as long again as the ordinary time. The Bishop of Zanzibar, the late Dr. Tozier, was a fellow-passenger, taking the trip across the Atlantic for his health. On our first Sunday out, he preached, taking for his text St. James ii. 17, "Honour all men," &c. As the sea was rough, the Bishop was unable to stand alone, and two of the sailors were called to stand, one on either side, to brace up the preacher. But the Bishop, being a tall man, and both the seamen below the average height, it taxed all their efforts to keep him *in statu quo*. It resembled so much an intoxicated man being assisted by two others more sober than himself that I fear the congregation benefited as little as we did from the sermon.

We remained over a Sunday in New York, where we

METLAKAHTLA

enjoyed a pleasant reunion with some friends. I was invited to preach in the evening, in a Brooklyn church, and much interest was manifested in our mission. At an informal meeting held afterwards, a number of young men intimated their desire to offer themselves for the missionary work of the Church, and their names were recorded. They were anxious to obtain my future address, in order to communicate with me, but, as I was unable to inform them of the facilities or dates of mail service in connection with my proposed destination, I could not accommodate them.

We visited Chicago (which shortly after was overtaken by a great fire), and witnessed many interesting incidents there, illustrative of the intense pressure of American life in the cities. The Union Pacific Railroad had but lately been connected with San Francisco, and much of it was as yet in the rough. As the bridge over the Mississippi was only in process of construction, the passengers had to leave the train and walk over a temporary bridge, as it was considered unsafe to remain in the cars. As it was almost impossible to obtain a meal at any of the stations, owing to the rush of passengers, and there were then no dining-cars, I determined to endeavour to procure a little hot water occasionally, with which to prepare some tea.

At a rough-looking station near the Rockies, where the train stopped for ten minutes, I made my way to a wooden structure exhibiting a sign which induced me to believe I should find what I required. Nor was I disappointed, as I was quickly served with a jug of boiling water. But I was scarcely prepared for what followed. A number of hard-looking characters were seated around a table engaged in gambling. With these the man who had served me was evidently in partnership, as no sooner had I paid him than he sprang to the door and, closing it, demanded that I should take part in the game which was being played. The others also joined with him in demanding that I should put down my money, and, as I made a rush for the door, another of them sprang forward to intercept me. I succeeded, however, in opening the door sufficiently to enable me to press my foot between it and the jamb. Failing to dislodge me, one of them then threatened to shoot me, and was drawing his revolver, when I suddenly thought of the boiling water with which they had provided me. Instantly raising the jug, I threatened him with the contents, which threw him off his guard, and, seizing the opportunity, I pulled open the door and escaped. I was followed by a volley of oaths on the "down-easter" who had thus defeated them in their object. This was to detain me till the train left, when I should have been at their mercy. They well-nigh succeeded, as the train was moving when I reached it, and I boarded it with difficulty. There was neither law nor protection in the western wilds in those days, and many a crime was committed of which no account was taken.

We found, on reaching San Francisco, that we should have to wait nearly a fortnight, as there was but one steamer plying to Victoria, Vancouver's Island, which made two sailings monthly. Consequently, we had ample time to see the "City of the Golden Gate" and to study the conditions of life there. It was the month of October, and during the day the weather was excessively warm; but the nights were rather cool. I was struck by the variety and abundance of luscious fruits which were on sale in every street at low prices.

I visited the Stock Exchange, where men appeared to be beside themselves in their keen competition to effect the best bargains. Shouting, jumping, and apparently threatening one another, it sometimes required all the efforts of the salesman to command attention with his hammer. Then, as now, this city was noted for earthquakes, and one large brick building which had been erected for the purposes of a marine hospital was standing split from roof to foundation as the result of one such shock. It had just

METLAKAHTLA

been completed, but they were about to pull it down again as it was unsafe. I did not dream then that in the destruction of the city afterwards by earthquake and fire one of my sons should pass through that terrible ordeal unharmed. But so it happened. He was acting as chaplain to the missions for seamen in that port when it occurred, and he had several narrow escapes.

We embarked on the *Prince Alfred* on October 5th *en route* for Victoria, Vancouver's Island. Our steamer was neither large nor powerful, and as the weather was squally there was quite a swell from the Pacific. As the wind was on our beam the steamer rolled heavily, and most of the passengers were sick. Amongst those who were exempt from sea-sickness there were three young men, who amused themselves by making sport of those who were suffering. On the second day out, when seated at luncheon, it became very rough, so that several who had ventured to take their seats at the table were compelled to retire. Our three heroes were evidently enjoying themselves at the expense of the sufferers, and their laughter rang around the dining saloon. Suddenly the vessel rolled heavily, and one of them lost his balance, and in falling backwards he clutched at one of his party, who in turn, in order to preserve his balance, grasped hold of the third. Instantly all three fell over together, dragging the table-cloth with the soup after them. Amidst peals of laughter from all sides, in which the captain and officers joined heartily, they gathered themselves together and rushed to their rooms, where they secreted themselves for the remainder of the day. When they reappeared they were evidently careful not to make light of their fellow-passengers again.

In six days we reached Victoria, and found on inquiry that there was only one small trading vessel plying north from Victoria, and she was due to sail on the 1st day of November. We were welcomed by the Very Rev. E. Cridge, who was then Dean of Christ Church Cathedral, and Sena-

METLAKAHTLA

tor Macdonald. The Dean invited us to be his guests until the steamer sailed. The trip up the coast occupied nearly nine days. Being the last trip of the year the steamer called at every trading post of the Hudson's Bay Company along the coast. As every such trading post is situated in or near to an Indian camp, we were thus enabled to obtain a fair knowledge of the character and condition of the various tribes. At one encampment to the north of Vancouver's Island a French Roman Catholic Mission had been established for some time, and as our steamer anchored off the village the missionary came on board. Having been introduced by the captain, I inquired from the good father as to what measure of success he had achieved in his Mission.

"Success!" he exclaimed. "Why, I can do nothing amongst them. Only yesterday they stole the blankets off my bed. I have laboured amongst several tribes of Indians in the interior, but I have never found any so bad as these. And," he added, "we are about to abandon the Mission." This they did shortly after, and in 1877 the Church Missionary Society entered on the field amongst the Quagulth tribes, the Rev. A. J. Hall first occupying Fort Rupert as his headquarters, and afterwards Alert Bay.

At some of the encampments we saw the medicine men, in their paint and cedar-bark crowns, performing their incantations over the sick. At Bella Coola a medicine dance was in progress, and a weird scene it presented as they danced around in a large lodge, chanting a wild dirge, in which time was kept by beating as a drum a large cedar chest, over which a dried skin was stretched, whilst the woodwork was decorated by fantastic figures, painted with their colours.

We reached Metlakahtla, our destination, on Sunday at midday, and anchored in the harbour off the village. This was the first Mission station north of Nanaimo along a coast line of over five hundred miles, with the exception above

METLAKAHTLA

mentioned, and there was but another station some fifty-five miles further north, and near to the boundary of Alaska. At each of these two stations there was but one missionary, so that we at once saw there was a wide field of labour awaiting us. Our good captain had informed us that, as it was Sunday, we would probably have to remain on board till the following day, as the rule of the Mission was that no goods or passengers should be landed on Sunday.

After casting anchor, we could see a large congregation of Indians emerging from a rough building standing on the shore, which I afterwards learned was meant to serve the purposes of a guest and market-house, but which was now being used as a temporary church. Shortly afterwards a boat put off from the shore, which on approaching the steamer we saw was manned by two white men. They were on a visit to the Mission, and learning that we were expected by this, which was the last trip of the steamer for the year, they volunteered to come off for us. On reaching the shore we received a hearty welcome from Mr. Duncan, whilst hundreds of the Indians pressed forward to greet us. As they were clean, and dressed in holiday attire, they presented a pleasing contrast to the tribes we had seen in their paint and blankets along the route. There were about four hundred and fifty Indians then at Metlakahtla, many of whom had been baptized; the rest were catechumens. We were present at the evening service, which was well attended.

The language sounded strangely in our ears, and the responses were repeated by all as with one voice. There were no books in the native language, but the hymns and responses were sung and repeated from memory in their own tongue. Many of the Indians possessed English Bibles, and were able to find the text when given out. This was read by the preacher in English, and then translated into the Tsimshean. Though ignorant of the language, the day following our arrival found me hard at work. In a

METLAKAHTLA

long, low blockhouse, constructed of logs, and but poorly lighted, I took up school work—first, in the morning, with over one hundred children of both sexes; and again in the afternoon, with some one hundred and twenty women, including the senior girls, who had been present in the morning; whilst in the evening we had the building well filled with men from seven till nine P.M.

As the cold weather had set in, we had two wood fires some distance apart, on hearths elevated about a foot higher than the floor around. Over the fires, and about five feet above them, were constructed funnel-shaped chimneys of sheet-iron on a wooden framework, but before the draught in these could draw the smoke, the wind blew it through the room, which proved most trying to the eyes.

It was this educational work which enabled me to acquire the language quickly, with the correct pronunciation. At first, the calling of the school roll was always accompanied with considerable merriment at the teacher's expense. The majority of the pupils were as yet unbaptized, and were consequently enrolled by their own old heathen names. As I endeavoured to call these out, "Wenaloluk," "Addaashkaksh," "Tka-ashkakash," "Weyumiyetsk," and scores of other names even longer and more difficult, peal after peal of laughter arose from my pupils. But I did not mind. It served to show me my deficiency, which I made haste to correct. Gradually, this hilarity subsided, and I knew I was overcoming the difficulties of the pronunciation of the language. I also was enabled to undertake a part in the charge and care of the sick, and in this my wife was enabled to render valuable assistance, especially in cases requiring surgical aid, and in female complaints.

Not long after our arrival, an Indian hunter was brought in badly injured by a bear.[1] He had been coasting along

---

[1] This is the hunter "Shu we le haik kum Sakhaha," the "New Great One who stood on high," whose fight with a bear is recorded in Mr. Crosby's book, pp. 278-282. It is there stated that he "got to where

METLAKAHTLA

in his canoe, accompanied by his son, a boy of some ten years old, when suddenly a large black bear was sighted near the shore. Paddling stealthily till well within range, he then took aim and fired, but only succeeded in wounding the bear, which quickly disappeared in the forest. Springing ashore, he hastened in pursuit of the wounded animal, which he tracked by the stains of blood on its trail. He had just succeeded in loading his flint-lock musket, when suddenly the bear sprang upon him from behind a fallen tree, where he lay in wait. The force with which the bear assailed him had dashed the gun from his grasp, so that he was completely at the mercy of the infuriated animal. His son, who had followed his father with axe in hand, rushed to his help on hearing his cries, and together they succeeded in despatching the animal. But what a state he had left the hunter in! His left eyebrow was torn away, and his upper lip ripped open. His left fore-arm was broken, whilst the flesh hung in strips from the shoulder. His thigh was also badly lacerated. We were enabled to dress his wounds by putting in some stitches where necessary, and using adhesive plaster for the lighter wounds. His broken arm was also set, and steps taken to arrest the inflammation. Notwithstanding the high fever which followed, this patient recovered, and appeared grateful for the treatment he had received. He abandoned heathenism, and with his wife and family joined the Methodist Mission at Port Simpson, where, after a course of instruction, they were baptized. But he never completely lost the marks of his life-and-death encounter with Bruin. Many such accidents occurred from time to time amongst the Indians, and as the teachings of the truths of Christianity had led them to abandon their belief in the Shaman or medicine man and his charms, it

---

there was a doctor," where he was cared for and his wounds dressed. It was to Metlakahtla he was brought, where with my wife we set his broken arm, sewed up his wounds and saved his life. Mrs. (Widow) Prevost assisted us then.

METLAKAHTLA

became one of the duties of the missionary to attend to, and endeavour to alleviate bodily suffering and disease.

Mr. Duncan was just then engaged in the erection of the new church, a building designed to accommodate some twelve hundred worshippers. The Indians at Fort Simpson were not wholly neglected, as native evangelists from Metlakahtla sustained weekly services there. In this good work I was also glad to engage, and it was at Fort Simpson that I delivered my first address in Tsimshean, just eight months after my arrival in the Mission. Heathenism was then in possession at Fort Simpson, and sometimes the weird and fanatic cries and howling of the medicine men could be heard miles from the camp, as we approached.

An incident occurred about this time at Fort Simpson which will illustrate the effect of the influence of these Shamans in the Indian camps. An Indian had incurred the displeasure of a medicine man in some way, which caused the medicine man to set his witchcraft in operation against him. So fearful were the Indians of this that, once under its spell, they abandoned themselves to their fate. They became dejected, lost all courage, and usually succumbed under the first attack of sickness. But this Indian was a man of more than ordinary courage and spirit. He determined to obtain the upper hand of the medicine man. One night, when the latter was engaged in performing his incantations over a sick man, this Indian on whom he had cast his spell stole round to the rear of the lodge where he was operating and shot him dead through an opening between the planks of the wall. He was seized by the tribe, delivered up to justice, and taken to Victoria, where, after due trial, he was found guilty and condemned to death.

Knowing well the cause which led this Indian to shoot the medicine man, and that he did so simply in self-defence, we united in signing a petition to the Governor-General of Canada pleading for mercy for the condemned man. I happened to be in Victoria as the time drew near for his execution, and visited the Chief Justice on the arrival of every mail to inquire whether a reprieve had arrived. I had been disappointed several times, when one morning, as I approached his residence, the door opened and the Chief Justice stood in the doorway waving the long-hoped-for document. "A reprieve! A reprieve!" he cried; "it arrived by this morning's mail. Your Indian's life is spared." And then he instructed me to proceed direct to the city prison and inform the governor. I did so, but found this officer unwilling to surrender his prisoner unless the reprieve was lodged with him. Accordingly I returned to the judge, and he accompanied me to the gaol, where, after deliberation, it was arranged that a duly certified copy should be made out and given to the governor of the prison. This was done at the court-house, after which I visited the prisoner. I found him in the condemned cell, an abject picture of misery. When the jailor admitted me, he stood and stared at me as though expecting something.

"Would you like to be free again?" I asked him. "Would you like to see your wife and join your family again?"

He continued to stare at me, and then, as though my words had revived in him memories of his friends, he replied, "Why do you mock me? Don't you know I have only a few days longer to live?"

"Do you believe that the same power which condemned you to die could pardon you and restore you to freedom again?" I replied.

A ray of hope seemed to flash across his mind, and it was reflected from his dark eyes as he sought to read my meaning, but remained silent.

"You are pardoned," I said; "the great chief who speaks for the Queen has sent the paper which sets you free. I have seen it, and that is why I am here. The steamer leaves for the North to-morrow morning, and I shall come for you. You will meet your wife and friends again."

METLAKAHTLA

And as the truth burst in upon him he bowed his head, and the tears fell fast on the stone floor of his cell. His whole frame shook with emotion as I grasped his hand and requested him to be ready in the morning.

I longed to tell him of the greater pardon prepared for him, which only awaited his acceptance, which had been purchased for him at a great price. And silently I prayed that it might be his also.

The following morning at six o'clock I called at the prison. He embarked with me, and on the journey informed me that he would not return to Port Simpson again. He disembarked at Metlakahtla instead, and sent for his wife to join him. Afterwards his brothers also joined him there. This was prior to the establishment of the Methodist Mission at Port Simpson. He eagerly accepted the good news of the great salvation, and was baptized, as also his wife and brothers. But he was seized with pulmonary disease, probably contracted during his imprisonment, and rapidly became weaker. In one of my visits to him at this time he presented me with a swansdown cap which he had prepared with the assistance of his wife from a swan which his brother had shot.

" I cannot give you much," he said, " but I ask you to accept this. You brought me the good news of my pardon when in prison, and now you have taught me of a greater mercy, which I have received. So I am not now afraid to go when the call comes, for I am ready."

Thus he passed away, but not before he had the happiness of seeing his wife and brothers all admitted to the membership of the Church of Christ.

CHAPTER III

THE MISSION CHURCH

" If I take the wings of the morning, and dwell in the uttermost parts of the sea;
" Even there shall Thy hand lead me, and Thy right hand shall hold me."—*Psalm* cxxxix. 9, 10.

THE new church building at Metlakahtla was completed and ready for opening by Christmas 1874. Invitations were accordingly sent out to the tribes around to be present at the dedicatory services. A large number of the Fort Simpson Indians responded, as also a number from our Kincolith Mission of the Nishkas, where the Rev. R. Tomlinson was in charge. Shakes also, the chief of the Giat-kahtla tribe, came in a monster canoe, the largest I have seen, accompanied by nearly one hundred of his tribe. On the occasion of the opening, a large Bible was presented to him, one of a number which had been given by the Society to be presented to such as might be considered worthy of the gift. It lay long in his treasure-chest before he learnt to appreciate its value, but at length the true light illuminated his dark heart, and he renounced heathenism, and was baptized into the Church of Christ by the Rev. F. L. Stephenson, who had been appointed to take charge of that Mission by the C.M.S.

This encampment on Ogden Channel was one of those which I visited when itinerating by canoe in the early years of my work. On my first visit I remained over a Sunday, and was permitted by this chief, Shakes, to conduct services in his large lodge. Some of the leading men of the tribe

THE MISSION CHURCH

feared my influence with him, as they appeared to have arranged that several of them should always be present with him during my stay. Shakes was a bigamist, and after the morning service, his wives roasted some dried salmon before the large fire which burned on the hearth in the centre of the great lodge. Having seated themselves one on either side of the chief, they proceeded to divide up and masticate the salmon for him. Then, withdrawing it from their mouths, they placed it in his mouth, each acting in turn, the one using the right hand, and the other the left. He held a horn spoon himself, from which he occasionally took a sip of olachan grease, renewing his supply from a dish placed before him. At length he intimated that he was satisfied, when they supplied him with a draught of water, after which they proceeded to partake of the dried salmon and grease themselves.

This is the chief of whose conversion Bishop Ridley has written a graphic account under the title of "A Grand Old Chief." As a heathen, he certainly was not worthy of the name, as the above incident will indicate, but when at length, after a long struggle, he divested himself of his paint and feathers, and before the assembled tribe declared his determination to walk in the ways of the Chief of Heaven, he rendered himself more worthy of the title. At his last potlatch, given prior to his embracing Christianity, he gave one hundred dollars for presentation to Her Majesty, the late Queen Victoria. In return he received a handsome engraving of Her Majesty, and a richly coloured rug, which he prized highly while he lived. His predecessor, the once proud and powerful Sebasha, or "Snared Foot," was more worthy of the title "A Grand Old Chief."

As a young man, Sebasha had led the warriors of his tribe as far south as the west coast of Vancouver's Island on marauding expeditions, and to capture and enslave. But at length he was apprehended and conveyed south for trial. A number of his tribe had attacked some white pros-

THE MISSION CHURCH

pectors on their way up the coast, and killed two of them. One of these Indians gave evidence against the murderers and they were executed, but as there was not sufficient evidence to convict the chief, he was sent by order of the Judge, Sir Matthew Begbie, to the Mission at Metlakahtla, to be detained there for five years. It has been publicly stated that he was sentenced to imprisonment, which is incorrect. As he approached the end of his time, it was reported that the men of his tribe were coming in their large canoes to convey him back in triumph. I interviewed him to ascertain his intention, when he informed me that he would not again return to heathenism. Nor did he. He sent a message to the tribe to this effect. Like others of his tribe, he had been a bigamist. He had a slave wife, as also another of his own rank. He put away the former, who obtained her freedom, and after due instruction was baptized, as were also his wife and family. His children by his slave wife went out free, with their mother, and they were also admitted to the membership of the Church by baptism. As a heathen, Sebasha had always been a slave-owner, as indeed all the chiefs were.

It was this same chief from whom Mr. Duncan rescued two slaves on one occasion. One dark night, as he was returning to the Mission-house after a visit to the sick, he was approached in a stealthy manner by two men who appeared to have been lying in wait for him. They were two of Sebasha's slaves, anxious to procure their freedom. Sebasha had arrived on the preceding day, accompanied by a large number of his tribe, and, with them, he was then encamped in the guest-house. Mr. Duncan readily took in the situation, and, inviting the slaves to follow him, he placed them in a log-house, behind the Mission-house. In the morning there was great excitement amongst Sebasha's Indians over the disappearance of the slaves. Suspicion fell upon the missionaries. Soon the chief appeared, and entering the Mission-house with his retainers, he demanded

THE MISSION CHURCH

that his slaves be restored to him. His request was refused, and the reasons given. These slaves belonged to a tribe to the south from which they had been captured, and they had appealed for protection and liberty. This, Mr. Duncan informed the chief, he could not refuse them. Both as missionary and magistrate, he was bound to grant their prayer.

Sebasha became angry and began to threaten. But the native constables had lined up around. There were not many of them in camp; indeed, most of the Indians were away at the time. The chief, it was believed, had a loaded pistol concealed under his blanket, and all his men were ready for action. At this critical moment a number of canoes under sail suddenly appeared, making for the shore under a stiff breeze. Sebasha's look-out passed the word to him and his men. Believing prudence to be the better part of valour, they decamped hastily, and embarked before the arrival of the new-comers. These, however, turned out to be a fleet of Haidas from Queen Charlotte Islands. But their timely appearance saved the situation, as Sebasha would not have surrendered his slaves without a struggle, the result of which would have been doubtful. The slaves were duly restored to their own tribe, and the law of liberty vindicated.

The heathenism of the Giat-kahtla tribe, of which both Sebasha and Shakes were chiefs in succession, was of the darkest and fiercest character. A native teacher, who was a half-breed, had been sent to this tribe, but he returned shortly after and informed us that he could not remain there longer, owing to the vile practices which were carried on nightly in the camp. The flesh of dogs and corpses was torn and devoured by the medicine men in a cannibalistic manner, and even mouthfuls of flesh torn from the arms and shoulders of men and women when passing through the camp. The overbearing character of the Giat-kahtla chiefs is illustrated by an incident recorded of one of Sebasha's

THE MISSION CHURCH

predecessors. This chief was seated in front of his lodge one day in the early spring, when food was scarce. One of the tribe was out fishing for halibut a short distance off shore, in front of the village. At length he succeeded in hauling up a fine fish. On seeing this, the chief immediately called to a slave to launch a small canoe, and to row him out to the successful fisherman. When the latter saw him approaching, he realised at once that his object was to seize the fish. Irritated by the memory of many such acts, he at once resolved to rid himself and his tribe of such an oppressor once for all. So, seizing the bark rope to the end of which a stone was attached, which he had been using as an anchor, he tied it round his waist, and as the chief laid hold of the halibut to transfer it to his own canoe, he seized him securely round the neck and jumped overboard, dragging the chief with him. Unable to free himself from such a death grip, he never rose to the surface again, and thus the oppressed and oppressor died together.

Under the teachings of our missionaries, the Rev. F. L. Stephenson and the Rev. R. W. Gurd, the entire tribe has abandoned heathenism and become Christians. Mr. Gurd, who laboured several years at Metlakahtla, still continues the work at Giat-kahtla, where under his guidance and direction the old village has given place to a new town with well laid out streets and modern dwellings, all crowned by a fine church, erected by themselves. But this great change was not effected without opposition. In 1885 the first Mission church, which had only been erected a short time previously, and for which I selected the site and ordered the lumber, was burnt down by the heathen party, and for a time it appeared as though the little band of Christians must succumb. But they continued to stand firm, and gradually their numbers increased until Chief Shakes at length surrendered, when victory was no longer uncertain. And thus Giat-kahtla also was won for Christ and the truth.

Two names stand out as deserving of honourable mention

THE MISSION CHURCH

amongst the first who cast off the heathen yoke at Giatkahtla and became free men in Christ. They are Stephen Ium-ta-quak and Daniel Lutquazamti. Sebasha survived to see both his successor Shakes and his tribe won to Christianity. He remained faithful through the trials to which the Mission Indians were subjected by the schism which separated the majority of their brethren and fellowtribesmen from them. And when at length he was seized with the illness which proved fatal, during his last hours he gave striking evidence of his faith in Christ. The last words he was heard to utter were a Tsimshean translation of the grand old hymn:

" Rock of Ages, cleft for me,
Let me hide myself in Thee."

It was in the autumn of 1875 that the first inquiry as to the practicability of starting a salmon-canning establishment on the Skeena River was made. I landed at Woodcock's landing, now known as Inverness, from a canoe, accompanied by twelve Indians, where I was introduced by Mr. Woodcock to a gentleman named Colonel Lane, who had just arrived on the H.B. Company's steamer. He informed me that he had come up the coast to ascertain if the salmon abounded in sufficient numbers to warrant the establishment of a cannery. It was a calm evening and sultry as betokening rain, and I had remarked that the salmon were jumping pretty freely, especially up the eastern outlet of the river. So, calling upon the newcomer to follow me, I led him down to the edge of the water where we could see clearly up the channel, and then directed him to look up. "There," I said; "you require no further evidence than that. And just here is about as good a site as you could find for such an establishment."

He was fully satisfied with the outlook, and so impressed with the advantage of the position that he at once entered into negotiations with the squatter for the purchase of the

THE MISSION CHURCH

place. In this he succeeded, and returning to Victoria by the same trip of the steamer, he formed the company which took over Woodcock's landing, and erected the first cannery on the Skeena there, which was renamed by the company " Inverness." And the introduction of this industry on the north-west coast afterwards proved most advantageous to the Metlakahtla Mission.

Mr. Duncan had long laboured to introduce some industrial occupation which would prove profitable to the Indians and the Mission. The manufacture of soap had been tried but proved a failure, owing to the unsuitability of fish oil for the purpose. And even if it had succeeded, it would scarcely have proved profitable, seeing that the fish grease is sold by the Indians who extract it at two dollars to two dollars and a half per tin, containing five gallons, or fifty cents a gallon. Consequently this was abandoned.

The next industry sought to be introduced was that of spinning and weaving shawls and blankets. To this end an instructor was engaged, and machines and wool purchased and procured at considerable cost. But after due trial they only succeeded in turning out an article that none of them would purchase. Had the Indians been taught to manufacture the magnificent robes which are woven by the Chilcat tribe of Alaska from the wool of the mountain goat, and dyed by them with their own peculiar designs, the venture would not have been a failure. And why ? it may be asked. Because it is an Indian design, and as such commands a high price. They are valued at from fifty to seventy dollars at the present time, and are in great demand by tourists and others.

On one occasion when Mr. Duncan was expressing his regret at the failure of his effort to perfect this industry, and at the loss sustained over it, I ventured to introduce a subject which had for some time been on my mind. It was the advisability of introducing salmon canning as an

ASCENDING A RIVER

The canoe, which has been partially emptied, is being forced against a strong current by means of long poles which touch the bottom. The bow is on the right of the picture. The river banks are forest clad.

THE MISSION CHURCH

industry. "You have," I said, "been contending against adverse circumstances. Even supposing your weaving had turned out successful in the manufacture, you could not hope to have competed with the imported article, having to pay freight on the raw material up the coast, whereas the manufacturers in Eastern Canada and elsewhere have the material at hand. No," I added, "why not introduce the salmon canning industry? You have the fishermen ready made and to order. They require no training, as every coast Indian is a fisherman from his youth up, and you have got another important advantage in your sawmill by which you can turn out not only the lumber for the erection of your buildings, but also the material for the salmon cases afterwards. And you are conveniently near to the salmon fishing waters of the Skeena to which the cannery men are now turning their attention." In reply, Mr. Duncan stated that it was impossible to start such an industry without a large capital. I suggested that it could be introduced on a small scale and gradually increased, and urged him on his next journey to Victoria to visit the Fraser River canneries and ascertain just what machinery would be necessary. In the spring Mr. Duncan left on a business trip to the south, and on his return announced his intention to erect a cannery. Not only had he realised his ability to introduce this industry, but he had found friends ready to invest in such an enterprise.

Shortly after the establishment of the first salmon cannery on the Skeena I visited it to conduct evangelistic services for the Indians there, when the manager of the cannery complained to me that the Christian Indians had refused to put out their nets for fish on Sundays. I informed him that I was glad to know that they were faithful to the teaching they had received and to the vows which they had made. At this he was rather indignant, and replied that they should have been taught to obey as their first duty. "That is just what we have endeavoured to do," I replied, "to obey God rather

THE MISSION CHURCH

than man. Would you have us teach them some of the commandments and to set aside the rest? If we teach them, as we have, 'Thou shalt do no murder,' and 'Thou shalt not steal,' we must also teach them to 'Remember to keep holy the Sabbath Day.' And it is this teaching which has civilised and evangelised these men, and prepared them to become docile and industrious, whereas before they were fierce and indolent."

Just then a tall, intelligent-looking Indian approached me. I recognised him as one of our Metlakahtla Indians who had been present at my service. " Oh, sir," he said, in trembling tones, "I want your help; I want you to make peace for me. The white man who escaped when we attacked his party is here, and I long to grasp his hand. I want his forgiveness."

Several years previously a party of three miners, returning from the goldfields on the Upper Stikeen River, had encamped for the night on a small island off the mouth of the Skeena. Early the following morning a canoe, manned by Fort Simpson Indians, emerged from the mouth of the river. The miners had lit their camp fire, and were preparing their breakfast. Attracted by the smoke of the camp fire, the Indians steered for the island. They had been fishing, and had a number of salmon in their canoe. On landing they intimated their desire to sell the miners a fresh salmon. Glad of the offer, one of them inadvertently took out his bag of gold dust, and, taking from it a small pinch, handed it in exchange for the salmon. The Indians embarked, but not to proceed homewards. Their cupidity had been excited by the sight of the gold, and, instead of continuing on their course, they doubled around the further end of the island, which was thickly wooded, and paddled noiselessly until abreast of the camp on the opposite side. Then, creeping stealthily up, they fired a volley on the unsuspecting miners. Two of them fell mortally wounded, whilst the third fled to the off shore. Fortunately he was only dressed in his under-

THE MISSION CHURCH

clothing. Taking his bag of gold from his belt as he ran, he cast it into the deep, and then diving, he struck out for the further shore of a large island near. The Indians fired another volley after him, but he dived on the moment and escaped. Seeing that they had failed to shoot him, they rushed to the canoe, and, jumping in, paddled with all their power in order to intercept him. But it was useless; he was a powerful swimmer, and reaching the shore well in advance, he rushed into the forest and climbed a large tree, where he hid himself amongst the thick branches. As the trees grew thickly together, they failed to find him, and fearing discovery, or perhaps anxious for the plunder, they put off for the camp again to seize what they could, and then fled.

The fugitive remained in the tree that night, and in the morning, famished with cold and hunger, he descended and returned to the shore, where he peered out cautiously. He saw one canoe pass and then another, but they were both manned by men with their faces painted and arrayed as heathen Indians. After a little, a third canoe came in sight. At it drew near he observed that there were women in it as well as men, and from their civilised appearance he concluded they were Christian Indians from Metlakahtla. He therefore ventured out, and, standing on the shore, hailed them. Surprised at the sight of a white man in such a plight, and concluding that he must have been shipwrecked, they took him aboard and brought him to the Mission. He told his sad story to Mr. Duncan, who sent and had the bodies of those who were killed decently interred. Two of the Indians were afterwards seized by a vessel of war, and taken to trial, and one at least was executed. A third, who had formed one of the attacking party, afterwards came and gave himself up at the Mission. He was also taken to Victoria and tried for the crime, but was acquitted, as there was no evidence to convict him.

This, then, was the man who now pleaded to be recon-

THE MISSION CHURCH

ciled to the miner who had so miraculously escaped. Moved by his appeal, I accompanied him. He pointed out the miner to me, who was now engaged in the cannery. He was a man of about equal stature with the Indian, both of them being over six feet.

I saluted him, and informed him of the Indian; who he was, and what his desire. He scrutinised him for a moment. Then he exclaimed with indignation: "Forgive him? No, I will never forgive because I can never forget. That man and those with him shot my friends, and endeavoured to shoot me, and yet he wants my forgiveness. I had gained about five hundred dollars in gold, with which I intended to return to Norway and visit my old father and mother, but, when these Indians made the murderous attack on us, I was compelled to swim for my life. I cast my gold dust into the sea. I was unable to retrieve my loss, and my parents have both died since, and yet this man, who with his party destroyed both my friends and my prospects, asks me to forgive him."

I endeavoured to soften his heart towards the man he regarded as his enemy. I informed him of the great change he had undergone, and also reminded him that the Indians really guilty had been punished, whilst this man had been found not guilty of the crime. But it was useless. I turned to the Indian and explained to him what the miner had said. He felt it deeply, and tears stood in his eyes as I informed him of how he had been prevented from seeing his parents before they died. I sympathised with both these men, as I realised how deeply my white friend had suffered, and I could understand how anxious the Indian was to obtain forgiveness from his fellow-man, having been led to seek and find the Divine forgiveness. He had been baptized, and enrolled as a member of the Church.

Several years afterwards, when at the olachan fishery on the Nass River, a messenger came in breathless haste to call me to see a man who had fainted on the ice. I

THE MISSION CHURCH

hastened to the spot and found it was this same Indian. I felt the pulse and found no sign of life; he had died. The intense cold had touched his heart. He had gone where his plea for forgiveness would not have been forgotten.

Whilst thus engaged in evangelising amongst the tribes on the coast and islands, I visited the fur-seal hunters encamped on Zyass and Bonilla Islands and other points. On both these islands, I had large and deeply interested gatherings of Haidas, Giat-kahtla, and Tsimshean Indian hunters, to whom I preached on the shore, with the waves of the rising or falling tides rolling in on the beach, and blending their music with our voices in the song of praise.

On one of these occasions, whilst passing from Bonilla Island to Giatlaub, at the head of Gardiner's Channel, by canoe, we were caught in Pitt Channel by a strong headwind, which compelled us to lie in shelter on the shore of Banks Island for several days, until our supply of provisions was well-nigh exhausted. Anxious to replenish our stock, as we were on half rations, I called on one of my crew to accompany me, and we started on a hunting trip to the interior of the island. My crew had informed me that there were no deer on the northern part of the island, and certainly I began to believe their report, as we could discern no traces of them. At length we reached a lake, lying near the base of a high range of hills, and, being tired, we sat down to rest on the trunk of a fallen tree. Pulling a blade of grass, I placed it between my thumbs and blew a few blasts. Hardly had I done so when my Indian hunter uttered an exclamation and, with uplifted finger, enjoined caution. He had heard a twig snap, away on the side of the hill. We turned round to scan the vicinity, and, as we did so, we sighted the white flank of a large deer as it turned to flee. Instantly I took aim and fired, and, with a cry of satisfaction, my companion sprang forward, whilst I took another course up the hill to where it

THE MISSION CHURCH

had fallen. Handing me his hat and coat, my Indian hoisted the deer on his back and led the way to the shore. But the load was too heavy, and I took it from him when he showed signs of fatigue. And thus, turn and turn about, we reached the shore. A whoop apprised our crew of our success, and soon all were in the best of spirits, where, only a few hours before, all were depressed and discouraged.

Our evening service was bright and hearty that evening around the camp fire, as all realised how ready Our Father is to supply all our needs. After renewing our stock of provisions, I embarked again, to pay a visit to the Giatlaub Indians at the head of Gardiner's Channel. This tribe, owing probably to its isolation, had suffered greatly from repeated attacks by the Haidas in the past, their object being to enslave all whom they could capture. One of their number, a sub-chief named " Ka-daush," had visited Metlakahtla more than once, and evinced an earnest desire to impart the good news he had received himself to his tribe. To assist him, we had provided him with some large scriptural illustrations and texts, and a C.M.S. banner which I had received from the Missionary Leaves Association. He did what he could amongst his fellow-tribesmen, and at least he awakened a more earnest desire amongst them to know the way of God more perfectly. This desire we recognised by sending them a native preacher—a T'simshean—who had long proved his faith and zeal by his life and conduct. After this man had been there a little time, I paid him this visit to encourage him and those whom he had been able to interest.

I found them encamped at the head of their wonderful channel, on a stream which flows into the head of the inlet. They were engaged in the olachan fishing, for this little fish is found there also, though in but small measure as compared with the Nass River. They are not so rich in grease, either, as those caught on the Nass.

THE MISSION CHURCH

I erected my tent near the camp and remained with them for several days, during which I was enabled to supplement and strengthen the labours of our native teacher. He had succeeded in making a translation from the Tsimshean of the grand old hymn " Rock of Ages," and it was both pathetic and soul-stirring to hear them unite in singing it at a service held outside my tent. Not far from the head of the inlet is the site of their old village, which was destroyed by an avalanche some time previously. It swept down upon the village at midnight before some of them had fallen asleep. As the mountain is very lofty and the avalanche started from the summit, they heard the ominous roar as it increased in force and volume, and had only time to arouse the camp. They seized what covering came to hand and fled almost naked, just in time to save their lives. The immense mass of rocks and debris which the snow carried down completely buried the village, and only the tops of some of the tall totems could be seen when I visited them. Ka-daush was afterwards baptized, the first-fruits of his tribe to Christianity. When the Wesleyan Methodist Missionary Society opened their Mission at Kitamat we withdrew from Giatlaub, as it could more conveniently be worked in connection with the former, and the language is similar.

The mountain scenery up the Gardiner's Channel is most impressive. It is one of the longest inlets on the coast. These fine watercourses so deep and wide, cutting in through the mountain ranges, form one of the natural wonders of the north-west coast. Cataracts shooting over lofty cliffs here and there add to the grandeur of the scene. We passed under one of these about half-way up the inlet, and as we were all heated with paddling in the warm sunshine, we were glad of the cool spray which was blown over us by the breeze.

Our old steersman, who was a Giat-kahtla, related many thrilling adventures which he had in these waters when a

THE MISSION CHURCH

young man. In passing one rocky inlet he informed us that this was formerly a stronghold of his tribe. On one occasion they were attacked by a large fleet of the Stikeen Indians, assisted by other Alaskan tribes. When apprised of their approach, they all fled to this natural fort. There was but one approach to the summit of the rock, and this was defended by sections of thick logs over four feet in diameter, placed in position to roll down on any number of their foes who might be bold enough to endeavour to rush the position. On the occasion referred to a number of the attacking party had been overwhelmed by one of these great logs, which had been rolled down upon them. Then, with stones and arrows hurled upon those within range in their canoes, they were enabled to defend their position and repel the attack. That night, when our little camp was all quiet and we were stretched to rest, I was aroused by the war-whoop. In an instant we were all on our feet; it was from our steersman, who was evidently fighting the old battles over again. We woke him up as he continued to shout at intervals. " Oh ! " he exclaimed, " I have had such a bad dream. We were attacked by the Haidas, and I could not find my gun whilst they were almost upon us." I reminded him that the troubled days of the past had gone and the Prince of Peace had established peace for them both with Himself and towards their fellow-men, and in the consciousness of this blessed peace our camp was soon quiet again.

CHAPTER IV

THE NASS FISHERY

"Wash the war paint from your faces,
Wash the blood stains from your fingers,
Bury your war clubs and your weapons,
Break the red stone from this quarry,
Mould and make it into Peace Pipes,
Take the reeds that grow beside you,
Deck them with your brightest feathers,
Smoke the calumet together,
And as brothers live henceforward."
            LONGFELLOW ("Song of Hiawatha").

THE term "Nass" signifies the "Food Depot," whilst Nishka, properly "Nass-ka," indicates the "People of the Nass," or literally "Nass people." Strange to state, these terms, by which the Indian tribes of this river are known and by which they now even designate themselves, do not belong to their language but are derived from the Tlingit tongue. The early navigators, both Vancouver and Meares, anchored near to the Tongas, an encampment of the Tlingit Indians of south-eastern Alaska. From this point they despatched boats up the Nass Straits, marked on some maps as "Observatory Inlet," and on proceeding some distance up the river from its mouth they found themselves among the sand-bars formed by the river, from which point they returned without reaching the lower villages situated about twenty miles from the mouth. They were then compelled to accept the information given them by these Tlingit Indians by which the tribes on the river, as also the river itself, became known. In their own

THE NASS FISHERY

language, which is a dialect of the Tsimshean and has no affinity whatever with the Tlingit, they are known as the Giatkadeen, or the "People of all the Valley," meaning the lower valley through which the river flows; whereas the tribes on the upper river are known as the Giatwinikshilk and the Giatlakdamiksh, the "People of the Lizards" and the "People of the Pool." But if the Nass River is attractive because of its scenery, it is much more so on account of its productiveness.

For centuries the olachan fishing on the tidal waters of the river has attracted the Indians of the tribes from all quarters. From the interior, hundreds of miles distant, by the trail the Indians thronged thither carrying their effects on sleighs drawn by their dogs or by themselves, as they generally started early in the year while the snow was deep to reach the river in time for the fish, which usually arrive about the middle of the month of March. They brought with them also furs, the proceeds of their hunting expeditions, with which to pay the tribes resident on the river for the right to fish, and also for the use of their nets and for shelter in their fishing lodges during the season.

These furs were principally marmot and rabbit skins, generally sewn together to form rugs for bedcovers or robes. Martin, mink, and bear skins were also tendered and accepted. But not infrequently when pressed by famine, which was not unusual amongst the inland tribes, they handed over their young children in barter for food. These were in turn passed to the Haidas as part payment for their canoes, which were so necessary to the Indians in their hunting and fishing. I found a number of these enslaved amongst the Haidas, who had been sold in exchange for food when young. They had grown up in slavery, and knew nothing of their own people or of their own tongue. Under the teachings of Christianity the Haidas granted them their freedom. Some of them returned to their own

THE NASS FISHERY

people, but the majority preferred to remain where they had been brought up under the improved conditions. One fine young fellow, who had been thus sold as an infant, I succeeded in restoring to his mother and sisters in a Kitikshean camp in the interior. But they only gazed at him, and then his old mother exclaimed, "Naht! naht! naht!" bowing her head with each exclamation. They had nothing in common, and the knowledge that they had sold him did not tend to endear them to one another, so he soon deserted them again.

Before the coming of the white men if a delay occurred in the arrival of the fish in the river many of the Indians, especially of the older and weaker, died from scarcity of food. The coast Indians also from far up in Alaska and from the south came in large fleets of canoes to catch the olachan or to barter for the oil which is extracted from it, and upon which its chief value to the Indians belongs. For just as the Eskimo must have their whale blubber and seal oil, so these Indians find a suitable substitute in the olachan grease. Their dried salmon and halibut are eaten with this grease. The herring spawn and seaweed when boiled are mixed with a portion; and even the berries, crab-apples, and cranberries are mixed freely with the olachan grease when cooked and stored away for winter use. The olachan, because of its richness in oil, was formerly known as the "candle fish," as when partly dried the Indians used it as a torch by night. As already stated, the first shoal of fish arrive about the middle of March. I have witnessed them followed into the mouth of the river by hundreds of seals, porpoises, sea-lions, and fin-back whales, feasting both on the olachans and upon one another. So eager were they in the pursuit that the largest mammals almost grounded in the shallows, and when they discovered their position they struggled, fought, and bellowed in such a manner that they might have been heard for over two miles distant. None of our hunters would

THE NASS FISHERY

venture out in their canoes to attack them, so fierce was the fray.

The question has repeatedly been discussed by the Indians and others, how any of the fish survive to reach the spawning grounds, when their enemies are so numerous. The explanation is, we believe, that the shoals are not formed in the open ocean but rather in the mouths of the rivers, to which the fish make their way as the season approaches. Here they appear to swim around for a day or two till the shoal is formed, when they move onward to the spawning grounds. Prior to the arrival of the fish the river is a scene of desolation, especially if still frozen over. Not a sign of life can be seen, from the river to the mountain tops, but a continuous covering of snow. But with the arrival of the fish the scene changes. First there are the Indians in their boats or canoes, or with their dogs, hauling their sleighs along the ice to their various camps. Then the sea-gulls begin to arrive, first in flights of hundreds or more, but soon to increase to thousands and myriads, until they appear as snowflakes filling the air. They are usually accompanied by numbers of the white-headed eagle, which wings a higher flight, and circles round and round whilst the sea-gulls feast.

The Indians prefer to fish on the ice, as it is so much easier, and because they can use their dogs and sleighs to advantage. Each party or household proceeds to saw openings in the ice, which is usually from two to four feet in thickness. Two openings are necessary for each net, one about twenty feet in length by about one foot in breadth, through which the net is let down. This opening has a pole driven down at either end on which the mouth of the net is hung by rings made from withes of red cedar. These rings are pushed down by another pole with a crook on the end until the net rests on the bottom, when the mouth is kept open by a fixture for this purpose. As the net is long and purse-shaped, narrowing from the mouth, another

THE NASS FISHERY

opening is made in the ice at right angles from the first, about four feet by eight. Through this the narrow end of the net is hauled up with a stick shaped for this purpose, and as the smaller end of the purse of the net is open, but tied when let down, when drawn up the end is untied, and the fish thrown out on the ice or into the boat or canoe as the conditions may be. Should the ice have broken up and cleared out before the fishing opens, then all the work is done in their boats and canoes. Sometimes the fishermen are much troubled with drift ice, which comes down the river in great sheets, often carrying off their fishing-gear before they can ship it in their boats. Much of the fishing is done at night, as they must put down their nets with every falling tide; then hundreds of lanterns are seen flitting and flashing to and fro, which with the shouting and hammering produces quite a busy scene. During the day men and women and even the children are engaged with dogs and sleighs conveying the fish to the shore, where they are heaped up in square or oblong bins three or four feet in depth. Each household will thus have from five to ten tons of fish, and more, from which to extract the oil or grease after they have salted sufficient for future use, and also a quantity to be sun-dried or smoked. Formerly the grease was extracted from the fish by stones made red hot in large fires. These heated stones were cast into large boxes filled with fish and water, and the process was repeated until the grease floated freely on the surface, when it was skimmed off into chests made of red cedar. Now, however, the fish is boiled in large vats with sheet-iron bottoms. These are fixed on small fireplaces built of stone and mud, and the grease can be extracted with less labour and fuel and in a shorter time.

If only the Indians would extract the grease by boiling the fish while fresh, the grease would be as white and pure as lard, but instead of doing this they permit the fish to lie in the bins until they are putrid. This causes the oil

THE NASS FISHERY

to be rancid and discoloured, and unfit for wholesome food. It is sold in this state on the coast at two and a half dollars per tin of five gallons, but brings a much higher price in the interior. If manufactured from the fish when fresh, it would bring a higher figure.

Though the Indian fishermen land thousands of tons of this fish, yet the sea-gulls catch and consume a greater quantity. The Indians rather challenged this statement when I made it, but I convinced them of the truth of it in a practical manner. I called upon them to ascertain for themselves about how many fish a sea-gull devoured in a day. It was found that those sea-gulls which were shot at noon had swallowed six fish on an average, consequently it may be assumed that each bird would catch and consume as many more in the afternoon of each day. This would equal twelve fish on an average to each sea-gull, and on weighing this number of fresh fish it was found that they weighed just one pound. At this rate one hundred thousand sea-gulls would consume the same number of pounds of fish, or just fifty tons per day. This would equal fifteen hundred tons in a month of thirty days as April, when the fishing is in full operation. And if the sea-gulls make away with such a quantity, what shall we say of the seals with their greater capacity and opportunity, being in the same element? When the fresh fish become scarce, the Indians feast on both seals and sea-gulls, which are then in good condition, though savouring a little of the common dietary.

But this is not the only benefit derived by the Indian fisherman from the sea-gulls. I was not a little surprised, when I first encamped amongst them, to find many of them possessed of comfortable feather-beds and pillows. These I found were made from the feathers of the sea-gulls which they had killed for food, and from which they thus reap a double benefit. The sea-gulls move down to the ocean every evening, returning in the early morning to their feasting

THE NASS FISHERY

grounds. The Indians have a tradition that the birds moved away to a distant mountain to boil the fish which they had caught during the day, and to extract the grease. For several hours before dark every evening a long unbroken line, sometimes widening out to a quarter or even half a mile, may be seen winging their flight seaward, and even when too dark to discern them, they may still be heard calling and encouraging their companions in their seaward flight. It was no doubt principally in reference to this fishing that the Tlingit Indians named the river the Nass or Food Depot. For in addition to the olachan the Nass River abounds with salmon, several runs of different species resorting to it annually for spawning.

It can scarcely be wondered at that this fishing was a *casus belli* amongst the tribes during the past, when food was scarce and might was right. The Alaskan tribes, the Haidas, and the Tsimsheans all in turn fought to obtain the control of the fishing. But the Nishkas, occupying as they did the upper reaches of the river, were enabled to hold it against all intruders, whilst permitting the Tsimsheans, whom they recognised as their fellow-tribesmen, being of the same language, to retain their own fishing-camp on the lower waters of the river. The other tribes are content now to barter with the Tsimsheans and Nishkas for the fish-grease which they extract, and quite a market has been established by the outside demand for this much-esteemed article of food amongst the Indians of the north-west coast. The olachan is found also in other rivers of the British Columbian coast, but inferior in quantity and quality to those of the Nass.

In the history of mission work on the north-west coast it was early found that a camp where such numbers of Indians assembled offered special inducements and opportunities to the fisher of men. But the journeys to and from the fishery were not without danger, especially when they had to be made by canoes undermanned and overladen.

THE NASS FISHERY

And as the Mission had no place of residence then at any of the fishing encampments, the missionary had to rough it by living and sleeping in the fishing lodges, which were rough shelters constructed for the occasion of bark and split boards. In these the smoke was blinding, blown as it was by the wind in all directions, and when at length the inmates were compelled to seek respite and fresh air, the intense cold with the strong winds without, together with the dazzling whiteness of the snow, proved so trying to the eyes that it resulted often in a severe attack of ophthalmia. I found thus by experience that it was owing to these conditions that so many of the Indians were suffering from diseases of the eyes. Unable sometimes to clear away the frozen snow and ice, we erected our shelters on it, and in a day or two our fire had subsided two or three feet, leaving us seated around it on the icy hearth above. In such conditions the Indian dogs were to be envied, as they managed to find a cosy corner on a level with the fire. On these occasions I have often taken the precaution of folding up my bread and other provisions in such wraps as I could spare, and place all under my pillow, only to discover in the morning that they were frozen so hard as to defy cutting or consumption. I could but join with my Indian friends in their bursts of laughter at my disappointment and discomfiture. But it was good both for teacher and taught, as mutual trials excited mutual sympathy. And with the aid of my medicine-chest I was always enabled to alleviate their ailments, and was hailed as welcome at every camp I visited.

Suffering from an attack of acute ophthalmia on one occasion, I was glad to avail myself of an opportunity to escape to our Mission at the mouth of the river to seek relief. It was blowing a gale and the river was full of drift ice, which rendered it dangerous for canoe travelling. But the Indians with whom I was about to embark had received a message informing them of the death of a friend, and stating that his body awaited interment. The circum-

INDIAN WOMEN

Engaged in stringing olachan fish on sticks for drying in the sun. They are protected by a rough awning from the cold wind. The background shows the River Nass—the head-quarters of the olachan fishery.

OLACHAN CURING

Those in the tanks are waiting to have their oil extracted. Those on the racks are drying in the sun. The olachan is sometimes known as the candle fish, on account of its oily nature.

THE NASS FISHERY

stances appeared to warrant their adventure. With shortened sail we flew over the waves, all on the look-out for the ice, as we realised that to strike a block of ice when travelling at such speed would smash our frail craft, which was not even ribbed.

We had not proceeded many miles when we saw ahead of us an immense ice-floe blocking up the entire passage, which was several miles in width. As the cold was intense we shrunk from attempting to make the shore, which was also blocked with drift ice. All eyes were directed to seeking out an opening in the ice-floe, and at length it was resolved to try a point where the ice appeared to offer a passage. We pulled down our sail and every man grasped his paddle. We forced our way into the opening until we found the ice was closing in upon us, forced by the strong south-easter against the rising tide. Gradually the ice forced our canoe upwards until it was almost capsized. The ice was so broken up that no one could find a footing. So excited and terrified were they, that one woman permitted her baby to lie unheeded in the bottom of the canoe. When almost upset I inquired if they had an axe on board. Fortunately they had. I directed one of them to take it, and, standing in the bow, to break all the ice around it as small as possible. As he did so, I directed the others to push the canoe forward with all their strength. Gradually the canoe not only righted itself, but we were enabled to make some progress, and after a long struggle we succeeded in reaching open water on the sheltered side of the ice-floe. Not a word had been spoken during the crisis, but now every voice was heard in mutual congratulations. But as to my own feelings, physically, I seemed to have none. In my efforts I had forgotten my hands, which were completely numbed, and my fingers partly frost-bitten. Instantly urged by the Indians, I plunged my hands into the icy waters and then rubbed them with snow. This process restored circulation but the pain was intense. It saved my fingers, however, as I only lost the skin. The Indians of the encampment to which we were bound denounced our action in having embarked in such a gale, declaring that it was a wonder that we had succeeded in effecting a landing. A rest of some days restored my sight, and I was enabled to return to my labours.

CHAPTER V

STRIFE AND PEACE

"Cross against corslet ; Love against hatred,
Peace cry for war cry ; Patience is powerful :
He that o'ercometh hath power o'er the nation."
                LONGFELLOW ("The Nun of Nidaros").

IN one of my early visits up the Nass River, after a service held in one of the large lodges at Gitwinikshilk, I took a walk around the camp. The medicine men were carrying on their dark séances in a lodge near, from which men with painted faces and bands of cedar bark bound round their heads were passing in and out. They were initiating some young braves into the mysteries of their craft.

As I turned away from the scene, I was attracted by the sight of a broken-down grave fence almost concealed with the heavy undergrowth. As such a mode of burial was not customary amongst the heathen Indians, I forced my way through the bushes, and found the lonely grave had been marked with a wooden slab cut in the form of a tombstone. It was overgrown with moss and fungi. This I scraped off, and found inscribed underneath the name of the first convert to Christianity among the Nishkas. This was the tomb of the young man mentioned by Mr. Doolan in his journal, included in a preceding chapter, as the son of a chief who had placed himself under instruction with him, despite much opposition, and who, he hoped, would have been baptized the following spring as the first-fruits of the Nass for Christ. He was so baptized, and

STRIFE AND PEACE

proved faithful. But he caught cold, returning to his own village, on the ice, in the early spring, and this resulted in fever. During his illness the medicine men persisted in performing their incantations over him, but he protested against their action, and continued faithful unto death. He had been baptized by the Christian name of "Samuel," which was joined to his own Nishka name of "Takomash." This was the name I was enabled to decipher on the tomb: "Samuel Takomash, the first convert to Christianity from the tribes of the Nass River."

The remainder of the inscription was illegible. As I stood there by that tomb, I realised that the same blessed power and influence which had won Takomash for Christ and the truth, could also win these benighted Indians whom I saw and heard so engrossed in their heathen practices around me. And, with the Divine help, I inwardly determined to labour to this end.

Takomash's tomb has long since been lost to view, as a fire (which occurred in 1895) swept that village out of existence during my absence on a visit to England. Only a few totem poles escaped to mark the site where the village had stood from the time of the lava eruption. But Takomash was but the first-fruits of an abundant harvest which should yet be reaped and garnered into the fold of Christ. His brother was brought to the Mission station several years afterwards in a dying condition, suffering from typhoid fever. His aged mother accompanied him.

After a hard struggle with the disease, we were rewarded by his complete recovery. He was grateful for the care bestowed upon him, and the lessons he had learned on his sick-bed were not forgotten. Both he and his mother were baptized, and afterwards several other relations. His uncle, a hard-hearted heathen chief, refused to listen to the call of the gospel. At the olachan fishery one day, I succeeded in finding him alone, and got him in close quarters on the bank of the bay. We sat down on a

STRIFE AND PEACE

log together, and I put the question to him, "Agwelakah, how much longer are you going to remain in heathenism? Your nephew was the first to become a Christian, and he showed you the way. Why don't you follow it?"

"Oh, I am not a bad man," he replied. "Look at my hands; they are not dyed in blood—as some men's hands are. And I have Takomash's Bible in my box yet; I did not destroy it."

"Ah!" I replied, "that will only condemn you—if you have the light and do not walk in it, but hide it."

He continued to follow the old heathen customs until one day, when away on a hunting expedition, he was seized with a severe illness. Then, with the fear of death before him, he sent a messenger with all speed to inform our missionary, the Rev. J. B. M'Cullagh, that he was dying. A relief party was despatched to bring him back, and then it was that he surrendered. He recovered, but remained faithful to his trust unto death. The message of his nephew and his Bible was no longer a mere memory, but became to him a bright beacon, guiding him on in the way to the life eternal.

It was not so with another sub-chief of the same tribe. His son had long been a Christian, and at length the father decided to follow his son's example. Just then the sad news reached him that his son had been drowned when bathing in a distant river: he had been seized with cramp, and sank. When the old man heard the sad tidings, he said: "I was long in the darkness, when at length I saw a light. That light was being held out to me by my son. It became brighter and brighter so that it attracted me. I arose and was moving towards it when suddenly it went out, and now I have no light to guide me." I reminded him of the True Light which would never be eclipsed or extinguished. It had illuminated and attracted his son, and would also enlighten him.

One of the first of the Nishka chiefs to embrace Chris-

STRIFE AND PEACE

tianity was Kinzadak. He is referred to in the extracts given from the Rev. R. Doolan's journal in a preceding chapter, as a chief who was "doing all in his power to undermine the work." In this brief reference to Kinzadak he was giving a whisky feast to which, with some of his tribe, he was engaged in dragging along those who were unwilling to enter. I first met him in his house up the river, when he entertained my brother missionary and myself. He was then seeking after the light. He had been an adventurer as a young man, and led an expedition as far as the Takou Indians at the head of the inlet of this name in Alaska. Whilst there the Takous, eager to impress their guests with a sense of their wealth and power, bound some fourteen of their slaves and, having procured a young forked tree, placed it in position on the beach and then laid the slaves, who were bound, with their necks on the lower branch. The young men of the tribe then performed the death dance around them, accompanied by the noise of their drums and songs. Then, at a given signal, a number of them sprang on the upper branch, bringing it down by their united weight on the necks of the slaves, whose cries and struggles were drowned by the chant and drums. This was continued till their cries were hushed in death.

Shortly after, when all were engaged in a feast in front of the camp, suddenly one of the slaves who had been placed nearest to the extremity of the branch and had only been rendered insensible for a time, started to his feet and, uttering a wild whoop which awakened the echoes all around, rushed off into the forest. For a few moments all were paralysed with astonishment, as he appeared rather as a spectre than a being of flesh and blood. Then, having recovered from their surprise, the entire band of young men who had acted as the executioners gave utterance to one united whoop and rushed off in pursuit of the fugitive. After a long chase a chorus of howls, resembling that of a pack of wolves, announced his recapture. Soon they

STRIFE AND PEACE

emerged from the forest, and marching the unfortunate captive to the place from which he had fled, he was again laid on the branch, on which a number of them jumped and quickly crushed out his life. As slaves were the most valuable property possessed by the Indians, this was done to convince those whom they were entertaining of their wealth.

Kinzadak and his men were indignant at the manner in which they had been received, and on their return down the inlet they ransacked a village belonging to the Takous, carrying off much booty. This became a *casus belli* between the Takous and the Nishkas for a number of years, in which they avoided meeting one another. But as soon as Christianity triumphed amongst the latter, they issued an invitation to the Takous intimating their desire to restore the property they had carried away. In response to this invitation, the Takous sent their head chief, accompanied by a number of the leading men of the tribe. They arrived on the Nass in a large canoe, and a great amount of property was contributed and made over to them, and a general peace made and confirmed.

The following is a true copy of the letter sent by the Nishka chiefs to the chiefs of the Takou :

"Nass River,
British Columbia,
Aug. 19*th,* 1897.

"*From the Nishka Chiefs to the Chiefs of the Takou Tribes.*

" Our Friends, Taktotem, Gatlani, Yaktahuk, Neishloosh, and Anetlash.

" We, the Chiefs of the Nishka tribes living here on this river, desire to make friendship with you our friends. Many snows and suns have passed since the quarrel which took place between us and you. We are anxious to make it up now and to be friends. We are no longer in the

STRIFE AND PEACE

darkness as our fathers were, but the light has come and we desire to make peace. We want to see your faces, and grasp your hands. We want to spread our food before you that we may all eat together. We wish to scatter the swansdown over you, the sign of peace, and to make your hearts glad. We desire to return the property which was taken from you at that time. The eyes of many who were engaged in that quarrel have long been closed. We want you to come next spring time, when the ice has broken up on the rivers and the snow is melting on the mountains. We will welcome you; we are your Friends.

    (Signed) " Chief KAGWATLANE.
           ,, ALBUT GWAKSHO.
           ,, GEORGE KINZADAK.
           ,, PAUL KLAITAK.
           ,, A. W. MOUNTAIN."

To this overture of peace the Takous responded by sending a deputation headed by Anetlas, a fine-looking and intelligent chief. He and his retinue were well received and honoured at every encampment on the lower river. The swansdown was duly and freely scattered over them in the dance of peace, and they were feasted and fêted, as long as they remained. Anetlas wore a large medal on his breast, presented him by the first Governor of Alaska.

On his departure a letter, of which the following is a copy, was sent by him to his brother chiefs and their people.

  " *From the Nishka Chiefs and People,*

  " To their friends, the Chiefs and people of Takou.

  " We are glad that Anetlas has come. We welcome him as your Chief and representative. He came to us as the messenger of peace. We have long been anxious to make peace, because we have changed from the old ways. We have put away the spear and the gun and we have scattered

STRIFE AND PEACE

the swansdown. We desire to walk in the way of the Great Spirit. That way is the way of peace. The Great Spirit is our Father and your Father. We are all brothers, because we are all his children. And therefore we wish to love all our brethren. And now we open the way to our river to you. We will always welcome you our friends, when you come, and you have opened the way that we may visit you. Anetlas came in time to hear Kinzadak's last words. He came in time to grasp Kinzadak's hand. Kinzadak gave Anetlas his word of peace for you. We all join our words to his. We send you an offering of peace. We have written a list for you of the property we are sending you. Anetlas, your Chief and our brother, accepts our gifts for himself, and for you. They are as the blossoms on the tree of peace. The fruits will follow to us and to you. We invite you our brothers, to gather the fruits of peace with us, and we send you our united greeting.

    (Signed)   "ALBERT GWAKSHO, Chief.
                     F. A. TKAKQUOKAKSH, Chief.
                     KAGWATLANE, Chief.
                     KLAITAK, Chief.
                     ALLU-LIGOYAWS, Chief."

It was true as stated in their letter. Kinzadak just lived to assist in ratifying the treaty of peace. On the eve of Whitsunday, he sent for me and intimated his earnest desire for the administration to him of the Holy Communion. I informed him that there would be an administration of the Sacrament on the following morning, being Whitsunday, and that I should administer it to him also after the service.

"I am tired," he replied, "I desire to arise and go to my Father in heaven; I shall not be here to-morrow. I desire to partake of the Sign now."

Accordingly, I invited a faithful old Christian, a veteran in Christ's Army, to be present, and his own family, and

STRIFE AND PEACE

we had a solemn and joyful service. A Nishka hymn was sung. He shook me warmly by the hand and wished me "Good night." The following morning, after a quiet night, just as the sun was gilding all the snow-capped mountain-tops around with his golden beams, the old chief turned over on his side and, breathing a silent prayer, he fell asleep. Thus, on the morn of the birthday of the Church,[1] Kinzadak entered into the rest that remaineth for the people of God.

First, we see him as a heathen chief, in his paint and feathers, urging his people to his whisky feast, and opposing the efforts of the missionary. Next, we see him on the war-path, and then we see him as a peacemaker, sending a message of peace to Takou. And then, as his end on earth drew near, earnestly begging to be permitted to obey the Saviour's great command, "Do this in remembrance of Me." Kinzadak's great carved totem pole still stands at Ankidā, where it was erected by him and his tribe after he succeeded to the chieftainship.

A great potlatch was made on that occasion, to which all the Indian chiefs and people of the other crests were invited. It was in order to draw away the early converts from the vicinity of these liquor feasts and heathen practices, that the headquarters of the Mission was moved to Kincolith, twenty miles further down, and just at the mouth of the Nass. There were other advantages gained by this move. The present station is never frozen in during the winter, being situate on tidal water, whilst in the summer it is free from mosquitoes; whereas all the villages where the Mission was first established are frozen in for at least five months every winter, and in the summer the mosquitoes are in myriads, making life a misery. Shortly after the movement of the Mission to Kincolith, at a great carousal held at Ankidā, the site vacated, a quarrel arose between the Nishkas and the Tsimsheans in which a number on both sides were shot. The Christian Indians did not wholly

[1] Whitsunday.

STRIFE AND PEACE

escape. It was during the spring olachan fishing, and a canoe manned by adherents of the Mission, three men and a boy, had gone down the river, and, during their absence, the quarrel had arisen. A Tsimshean canoe had gone out intent on retaliation, and met this canoe of Nishkas returning to the fishery, all unconscious of what had occurred. They passed them within speaking distance in order to reconnoitre, and, as they passed them, inquired, "Did you see a whisky schooner down the coast?" They replied in the negative and continued on their way.

But just after they had passed them, some thirty or forty yards, the Tsimsheans fired a volley into them, killing two and wounding the steersman. The latter, though wounded, directed the boy, who was his nephew, to hide under his legs in the stern of the canoe.

"As I lay there," said he, when relating the account to me, "I could hear my uncle's blood gurgling out from his wounds. A second volley killed him outright, and splintered the canoe close to me." The murdering party then approached and, taking the canoe in tow, paddled for the shore. Beaching the canoe, they proceeded to pull the bodies out of it, and, dragging them ashore, left them amongst the trees.

"Whilst thus engaged, one of them discovered me," said the lad, "and held me up before the others."

"Hold him up while I shoot him," shouted the leader, as he stood with his gun presented at the bow of the canoe.

The man who held him was endeavouring to do so, when a third intervened.

"Hold on," he cried, "till I ask him a question. What is your uncle's name?" he inquired. The boy replied, giving him the name of his father's brother.

"I thought so," he replied. Then, seizing him, he cried to the others, "You must not shoot him, he belongs to my crest; whoever shoots him must shoot me first." The others were angry, urging that he should be shot, as,

STRIFE AND PEACE

if not, he would inform on them. But his defender persisted in his defence. He was conveyed to the Tsimshean camp. The following day it was decided to send the lad up to his friends by a neutral canoe owned by a Tongas Indian who was married to a Tsimshean woman. But the Tsimsheans had secretly instructed this man to do away with the boy on the way up the river. Accordingly, this man embarked with his wife, taking the lad with them. When sufficiently away from the camp, he informed his wife of the engagement he had made to kill the boy, and called upon her to sit clear of him so that he might shoot him. Instead of doing so, she seized the lad, and protecting him with her own body, declared that before she would permit him to injure the lad, he must first shoot her. Seeing his wife so determined, and fearing to persist further, he desisted, and so the lad was safely landed at the Nishka camp. Thus, twice he had narrowly escaped death, but on both occasions a protector had arisen, when least expected. He was spared to grow up, and married a young woman who had been trained in the Mission house. He is an active and leading member of the local branch of the Church Army, and a regular communicant. The bodies of the men thus murdered were recovered by a party from the Mission, and were interred on a rocky bluff just below the Mission station.

When the Tsimsheans at Fort Simpson heard of the quarrel, a party of them at once started on the war-path for the Nass, fully armed for the fray. They boldly touched at the Mission station on their way up, probably to learn, if possible, how the war was proceeding. The Rev. R. Tomlinson, who was then in charge, having first directed his people, the adherents of the Mission, to remain in their houses, walked down to the canoes, and, having ascertained their intention, informed them of the attack on the members of the Mission, and called upon them to surrender their guns, or prepare to bear the penalty. They were so taken by surprise that they permitted their weapons to be seized,

STRIFE AND PEACE

and consented to return again to their camp. They probably surmised that the missionary had a party prepared to support his demand, and the news of the death of the three men, which they feared might be charged on them, decided their action.

It was deemed necessary by the Government to send up a vessel of war, H.M.S. *Sparrowhawk*, with Governor Seymour on board, in order to make peace between the contending tribes and settle the dispute. It was on the return voyage of the *Sparrowhawk* that Governor Seymour died suddenly on board, his last official act being to ratify and confirm the peace thus made between the warring tribesmen.

In 1877, the Canadian Methodist Missionary Society established a Mission on the Nass near to the village where the Rev. R. A. Doolan had commenced the Church Missionary Society's Mission thirteen years previously. It would have been more in accord with the true spirit of Mission work had they occupied the upper river, where but little had yet been done. Here, there were two large villages, the Giatwinikshilk and the Giatlakdamiksh, both of which were eager to have a Mission established amongst them. A native teacher had been stationed at the upper village, which was the most populous of the two, and frequent visits had been made by our missionaries. In the Mission hospital at Kincolith, the Rev. R. Tomlinson, as a medical missionary, had treated several of this tribe, including an aged chief. Consequently, they always welcomed his visits and mine. Acting on the same principle as had been adopted in the establishment both of Metlakahtla and Kincolith, Mr. Tomlinson first inaugurated the Christian village of Aiyansh, less than two miles below the heathen encampment, and encouraged the first converts who came out of heathenism to establish themselves there. After Mr. Tomlinson's departure in 1878, to open the Mission in the interior, as the work on the river was under my superintendence, I visited the upper villages, and conducted services in the

STRIFE AND PEACE

head chief's house at Giatlakdamiksh occasionally, and also at Giatwinikshilk and Aiyansh.

To the little community gathered out of heathenism at the latter place, I gave a Church Missionary Society's banner, of which they were proud, and also a supply of school-books, and material for the native teacher stationed there. On my first visit I preached to them, assembled in the house of the first convert, from St. Luke xii. 32. They had not heard this message previously, and I have not forgotten the joy and satisfaction with which they received the Word. It proved specially appropriate, as they had just been experiencing much petty persecution from their heathen friends because of their separation from them. But deliverance and advancement were at hand.

In 1883, Mr. J. B. and Mrs. M'Cullagh arrived to take charge of the Upper Nass Mission. Mr. M'Cullagh established his headquarters at Aiyansh, and at once applied himself to acquire the language. Whilst thus engaged he formed his plans for the prosecution of the work of the Mission, and was soon labouring to evangelize and civilize the heathen tribes around. But he was not long in finding out the difficulties which beset his efforts, for the Upper Nass had always been a stronghold of heathenism. By persevering effort, he succeeded in winning their confidence. His labours have been rewarded with much success, as the model Mission settlement at Aiyansh indicates. Here he has built up a congregation of between two and three hundred Christians, drawn not only from the encampments in the vicinity, but also from the Giat-winlkōl tribe away in the interior.

And now all the Indians on the Upper Nass have surrendered to the call of the Gospel, and the villages which were heathen on his arrival are all now Christian. By his translational work, the Rev. J. B. M'Cullagh has done much to enlarge and inform the minds of his Indian converts, many of whom can both read and write in their own tongue.

STRIFE AND PEACE

But the great ambition of all the tribes is to know the English language; the Chinook jargon, which was formerly their only medium of inter-communication, is falling into disuse, whilst English is being freely used, both orally and by letter. They realise that a knowledge of English will open up to them a boundless field of information, both sacred and secular, and will also tend to unite them yet closer as Christians.

CHAPTER VI

THE HAIDAS OF QUEEN CHARLOTTE ISLANDS

"The last link in the golden chain."
—Oakley.

WHILST thus engaged in acquiring the language of the Tsimsheans and afterwards in itinerating and evangelising amongst them, I became deeply interested in the Haida tribes which inhabit the Queen Charlotte Islands and also the Prince of Wales Island on the south-eastern coast of Alaska. This interest was intensified by the stories related to me by the Tsimsheans, who manned my canoe in my journeys along the coast, of the depredations and deeds of blood wrought by these fierce islanders at the various encampments which we visited, and up the rivers and inlets of the mainland in the past. It reminded me of the records of the deeds of the Vikings and sea rovers in Northern Europe before the light of the Sun of righteousness had arisen upon them. So fearful were those Indians who accompanied me, that they often hastened to reduce the camp fire when darkness set in, lest it might attract an attacking party towards our camp during the night. In addition to this, Admiral Prevost had informed me that when as captain of H.M.S. *Satellite* he made his first voyage up the coast, he was surprised on landing at Fort Rupert, to the north of Vancouver Island, to see the heads and decapitated bodies of Indians scattered along the shore in front of the camp, and being washed up by the waves of the rising tide. On inquiry he was informed

CANOE-MAKING

Finishing touches being put to the bow of a large canoe, which is turned upside down for the purpose. These canoes were carved from a single cedar trunk and hence are called dug-outs.

HAIDA HOUSE

This house possesses no totems, but is ornamented with figures and surmounted by a shield. Strips of halibut may be seen drying on the rack outside. Behind it stands the forest.

THE HAIDAS

that a fleet of Haidas on their way south had attacked the camp and, having slain those who resisted, had carried off a number of captives to enslave them.

But even this was not the limit of the courage and ambition of these adventurers. On another occasion they threatened to attack Victoria, and Sir James Douglas, who was then Governor of the Colony, had to order the marines around from the vessel of war lying at Esquimault, in order to drive them back to their camp outside the city limits and thus preserve the peace. When Fort Simpson was established by the Hudson Bay Company in 1834, the Tsimshean tribes, attracted by the advantages afforded for trading there, removed from their old encampments at Metlakahtla and on the Skeena River and established themselves around the fort. To this point also the Haidas come every year to exchange their furs, principally the sea-otter and fur-seal skins, for guns, ammunition, and blankets. But few such visits passed off without a fight, as the Tsimsheans were jealous to see the Haidas possessing themselves of the white man's weapons, and they regarded them as intruders. They were able to open fire on the Haidas from the shelter of their lodges, whereas the Haidas were exposed in launching and embarking in their canoes. Nothing daunted, however, they returned the firing with effect, and were enabled to embark with their cargoes and push off to sea, only to return in greater force when least expected, to take summary revenge on their foes.

In the month of June 1874, for the first time, I witnessed a Haida fleet approaching the shores of the mainland from the ocean, and it left an impression on my mind not yet effaced. It consisted of some forty large canoes, each with two snow-white sails spread, one on either side of each canoe, which caused them to appear like immense birds or butterflies, with white wings outspread, flying shorewards. Before a fresh westerly breeze they glided swiftly onward over the rolling waves, which appeared to chase each other in sport as they reflected the gleams of the summer's sun. These were the northern Haidas, who were famed for their fine war canoes. They have always been the canoe builders of the northern coast. As they neared the shore the sails were furled, and as soon as the canoes touched the beach the young men sprang out, and amid a babel of voices hastened to carry up their freight and effects above the high-water mark. These then were the fierce Haidas whose name had been the terror of all the surrounding tribes. And truly their appearance tended to justify the report. Many of the men were of fine physique, being six feet in stature; whilst those whose faces were not painted were much fairer in complexion than the Indians of the mainland. Some of their women wore nose-rings, and not a few of them were adorned also with anklets, whilst all the women wore silver bracelets, those of rank having several pairs, all carved with the peculiar devices of their respective crests. In their language there was no similarity whatever to the Tsimshean, with which I was now familiar, and which sounded softer and more musical than the Haida.

Amongst the women I found one, a half-breed, whose mother was a Tsimshean and the sister of a chief then resident at Fort Simpson. This woman was the wife of a fine young Haida chief named Seegay, and as she understood both the Tsimshean and Haida tongues, I was enabled through her to open conversation with her husband. For this purpose I invited them frequently to the Mission-house. After several such visits I was enabled to inspire them with confidence, and to draw them out of the reserve so characteristic of the Indian.

I found Seegay's wife as ignorant as he was himself of the simplest truths of the Gospel, as whilst her tribe and people had, many of them, been led to embrace Christianity, she had remained in the darkness of heathenism through her union with the Haidas. It may appear strange that

QUEEN CHARLOTTE ISLANDS

such a union could be possible between the members of tribes so hostile to each other. But for some reason the Tsimshean chief, who was this woman's uncle, had always remained neutral in the conflicts between the Haidas and Tsimsheans, and from this position he had more than once been enabled to make peace between them.

The following year (1875) this Haida fleet again visited the mainland, as also several other lesser fleets of Haidas from Skidegate and the encampments to the south of the Queen Charlotte Islands. As Seegay and his wife accompanied them, I was enabled to renew my acquaintance with them, and again endeavoured to teach them the way of Life and Salvation. On this occasion, as Seegay's mind opened to the importance of the truth, he inquired why we had taken no step to send some one to teach his fellow-tribesmen, the Haidas, as we had done for the Tsimsheans? I realised the force of this inquiry, but the Haidas were not the only tribes then "unvisited, unblest." All along the coast, north and south, and up the rivers, the tribes were in darkness. Only amongst the Tsimsheans and Nishkas had our missions been established.

The Canadian Methodist Missionary Society had made the mistake of opening their first Mission on the northwest coast in 1874 amongst the Tsimsheans instead of pushing out into the regions beyond. Thus there were two missionary societies labouring among the Indians of one language, whilst those of four other different languages were without a missionary. They defended their action by asserting that the Church Missionary Society's missionary had abandoned Fort Simpson when he removed the headquarters of the Mission to Metlakahtla in 1862. But though he had thus removed the Mission, he had not abandoned the Indians at Fort Simpson, but kept up regular services there by the native evangelists, his object being to draw the Indians from the heathen camp and establish them as Christians in the new camp, away from heathen influences, and under improved sanitary laws and rules of civilisation. Shortly after my arrival in the Mission, and when I had paid several visits to Fort Simpson, I concluded that it would be impossible to draw all the Indians from that encampment, and therefore proposed that I should take up my residence there. To this our fellow-missionary strongly objected, asserting that I would thus frustrate his object, and prevent the Indians from joining the new station, where he was erecting a church capable of accommodating twelve hundred worshippers.

The following year (1874) the Methodist Mission was established there, and I at once determined to endeavour to "launch out into the deep" of the darkness around. It was just at this crisis that the call of the Haidas of Queen Charlotte Islands came to me through the question of this young chief, Seegay. I had been commissioned by the committee of the Church Missionary Society to take spiritual charge of the Metlakahtla Mission so soon as I had acquired a knowledge of the language, as Mr. Duncan had intimated his intention to leave the work there in my care, and to proceed to the islands or Fort Rupert to open a new Mission.

Now, however, that I had overcome the difficulties of the language, my colleague intimated his inability to leave; consequently the way was open. I wrote to the committee, strongly advocating the claims of the Haidas, and requesting permission to proceed to the islands.

At first the committee hesitated, as they feared the time I had spent in acquiring the Tsimshean language would be lost, but they shortly after approved of the proposal, and commended my action. I received a most encouraging letter from the Hon. Secretary, the late Rev. Henry Wright, which removed every obstacle. Shortly afterwards the Haida fleet arrived again on the shores of the mainland, but my friend was not amongst them. I received, however, an urgent message from him, inform-

QUEEN CHARLOTTE ISLANDS

ing me that he was very ill, and was most anxious to see me. He had been capsized from his canoe, with several of his tribe, in a sudden squall off the Rose Spit, a most dangerous point to the north-east of the Queen Charlotte Islands. He had been too long in the cold waters before being rescued, and chill had resulted in fever, followed by consumption. His name "Seegay" is the Haida term for "the ocean." And truly he was a son of the sea. He had no fear of its storms or waves, and was one of the most adventurous hunters among the Haidas. In search of the sea-otter or of the fur-seal, he would sail off to the west, until the land was lost to sight, and there with his two companions, when overtaken by night, would fall asleep in his canoe, "rocked in the cradle of the deep," then away again with the first gleam of daylight, to renew the quest. Nor would he steer his canoe homewards until he had secured a goodly number of valuable skins to reward his efforts.

He had early been inured to the dangers of the ocean. When but a lad, he was returning on one occasion with his uncle, the old chief Weah, in a large canoe from the Alaskan coast to the shores of the Queen Charlotte Islands with a number of others. The wind was fair, with a rough sea. With two sails well filled they sped onwards, and, lulled by the motion and the music of the waves, one after another gave way to slumber. Even the old chief slumbered at the helm. Seegay was the only one on the watch. As the canoe, which was well laden, rose and fell with the waves, suddenly falling from a high wave into the trough of the sea, she split from stem to stern, and all were precipitated into the deep. They soon all disappeared except young Seegay, who seized an empty gun box, to which he clung with one hand, whilst with the other he seized the old chief as he rose to the surface, and upheld him there. Another canoe, which was making the same passage and following in their wake, and had witnessed the sudden disappearance of the sails, bore down quickly on the spot, just in time to rescue the lad and his uncle. The shock and exposure proved too much for the old chief, and he died before they reached the shore.

Seegay alone survived. He passed through many similar experiences afterwards, but this last exposure had proved too much for him. It occurred early in the season whilst the waters were intensely cold, and he with those wrecked with him were unable to stand when they reached the shore, and with difficulty dragged themselves up the beach, to escape from the rising tide. His wife had also sent me an earnest entreaty to come and see him, as she believed he would not live much longer. Though unprepared, and unable as yet to enter upon the work for which I had thus volunteered, I could not set aside this appeal. It sounded as the cry of old, " Come over and help us."

On Tuesday, 6th June 1876, I embarked in a Haida-built canoe, with a Tsimshean crew, to make my first journey of some 100 miles to Massett, the principal Haida encampment, situate on the north of Graham Island, which is the most northerly of the Queen Charlotte Islands. My steersman was an old fur-seal hunter, inured to the dangers of the ocean, my bowman a young hunter, the son-in-law of the former, and a skilful canoe sailor, whilst the remainder were lads of some eighteen years, well trained in the use of the paddle, but unaccustomed to the open ocean.

We reached the outermost island off the coast of the mainland on the evening of the first day, and found there a number of fur-seal hunters encamped. They had been unable to put out to sea on the morning of that day, the wind being unfavourable. They were glad to see us, and I conducted a service for them and my crew in the evening. They had shot but few seals, owing to the bad weather. The fur-seal is generally found in schools or shoals, in the months of May and June, in the open waters at a distance

QUEEN CHARLOTTE ISLANDS

from the land. The hunters, when the sea is not too rough, hoist sail and glide over the ocean, often sleeping in their canoes; until at length they fall in with the object of their search, which in such cases are generally found sleeping on the water.

There are usually three Indians to each canoe, the steersman, the sailsman, and the marksman, which last is seated towards the bow. For this post the best shot is always selected. It is no easy task to shoot the seal when the sea is rough, as both the hunter and his object are being tossed up and down, now on the crest of the wave, and the next moment in the trough of the sea. It requires a steady nerve and good sight, with judgment, to fire instantly when the seal rises to the point of vantage. But in order to make sure of their aim, the hunters were in the habit of ramming a heavy charge into their guns. Four or five bullets were commonly used with a proportionate charge of powder to ensure success. These guns were the old long-barrelled Hudson Bay Company's flint-locks, which took the place of the bow and arrow, the spear and the harpoon, the Indian's original weapons. A few years afterwards the flint-locks were displaced by a similar weapon, but with the percussion cap. This also has long since disappeared, and now every Indian hunter is armed with the modern repeating-rifle.

It may be considered advantageous to the Indian hunter to be thus armed, but they assert that they were far more successful in the past when armed with bow and spear. But then the channels and inlets abounded wi h the sea-otter and the fur-seal, whereas now they are only to be found far from the shores in the open ocean, a nd in very limited numbers. In the narrative of Captain Meares' voyage along the coast in 1788 and 1789, it is recorded that the sea-otter were plentiful, and were purchased from the Indians along the coast in lots of from twenty to forty skins for a few beads or a few scraps of iron, or large nails.

THE HAIDAS OF

From that time onward there has been such a demand for them, that it may be concluded the Indian hunters have well-nigh annihilated them. My old Snider rifle, which I generally carried with me in my early canoe journeys, and which often provided myself and crew with provisions, when otherwise we might have suffered from want, was quite an object of attraction to those Indian hunters. After a careful examination of the weapon, accompanied by many questions, at length the leading marksman cast it aside, exclaiming that he believed it was worthless, and would not bear comparison with their weapons. This man was named " Nugwats Kippow," or the " Father of the Wolf," and being a daring and successful hunter both on sea and on land, his opinions carried great weight with the others.

Shortly after I had conducted morning prayer with them and my crew, they went out to practise with their guns. For this purpose they affixed a white clam shell as a target on a tree at a distance of some 150 yards. After each of them had tried his skill and the shell remained untouched, they sighted me standing at some distance, and at once challenged me to a trial with my gun. I accepted the opportunity to justify my weapon, which had been so unjustly condemned, and, taking careful aim, shattered the clam-shell target at the first effort. They looked at one another, and the " Father of the Wolf " exclaimed, " Well, the chief evidently knows his own gun," and, casting his own from him on the sand, retreated slowly into the hunting lodge. Trivial though this incident was, yet it gained for me an influence with these Indian hunters which I was enabled to turn to good effect afterwards. The " Father of the Wolf " became one of my most faithful friends, and died some years afterwards, rejoicing to the end in the faith of the Gospel. The report of my skill as a marksman spread to another camp, on an adjacent island, and in the evening I had all the hunters present at the service which I conducted in the open air, whilst the waves

QUEEN CHARLOTTE ISLANDS

of the rising tide, breaking in foam and spray on the rocks around, made wild music' which blended with our songs of praise.

It might be supposed from reading the first page of chapter xix. of Mr. Crosby's book that the Haidas had made application to the Church Missionary Society for a missionary, but instead they were strongly opposed to receiving any missionary. Without waiting for any invitation I visited Massett in June 1876, to see Seegay, who was dying. My experiences then are recorded in the following chapter. On the 1st November with my wife and family we took up our residence at Massett. The following year I visited Skidegate and Gold Harbour, and conducted the first services there. We then placed a native teacher at Skidegate, Edward Mathers, who remained and conducted services until the Methodist Missionary Society sent a white teacher. Gedanst (Amos Russ) came to Massett in 1877, and took to wife Agnes, the youthful widow of Chief Steilta, who had just died.

CHAPTER VII

LAUNCHING OUT INTO THE DEEP

> "Though the shore we hope to land on
> Only by report is known,
> Yet we freely all abandon
> Led by that report alone,
> And with Jesus
> Through the trackless deep move on."
> —Kelly.

THE following morning, Wednesday, 8th June, I was aroused from a sound slumber at about three o'clock A.M., before it was quite light. My Indian crew was already on the alert, and informed me that the wind was blowing freshly off shore and was favourable and likely to increase. After a hasty meal I commended myself and crew to the care and guidance of our Heavenly Father, and soon we were standing off with a "full sheet and a flowing sea." As the wind increased the sea arose and threatened to engulf our frail bark in its yawning depths. In six hours we had lost all sight of land, and even the mountain tops had disappeared. None of us were able to retain our seats on the thwarts, nor would it have been well to have done so, as they are only sewn to the sides of the canoe with thongs of cedar withes, and might easily have given way under the increased strain. In addition she rode better with the ballast low down, consequently all save the steersman had to remain huddled up in the bottom of the canoe. An occasional wave broke over us, which kept us all on the alert, and soon all four of our young sailors were seized with that dread ailment *mal de mer*. I,

LAUNCHING OUT INTO THE DEEP

together with my steersman and bowman, remained unaffected, for which I felt thankful, as it required all our efforts to keep our frail craft afloat. With shortened sail, and a bucket in hand to bail out the water washed into the canoe by the waves, our bowman laboured incessantly; whilst I had to assist the steersman with a paddle to keep the canoe up to the waves, and thus we appeared almost to fly onward. Early in the afternoon we caught sight of the mountains of Graham Island, the most northerly of the Queen Charlotte group, and shortly afterwards, away to the north, we descried the snow-clad peaks of the mountains of Prince of Wales Island in Alaska, and our hearts were gladdened by the sight. The wind gradually slackened as we approached the lee of the land, and just as we were congratulating ourselves on our success we sighted a dark ridge or wall of water rushing up rapidly towards us from the south. Apprehensive of being swamped or capsized, we furled sail, and, grasping our paddles, headed our canoe around to meet the approaching danger. It proved to be but the turn of the incoming tide, which rushes shoreward from the ocean at this point with great force. Continuing our journey we soon found ourselves off Rose Spit, which is a long and dangerous sand bar extending for several miles seaward from the north-eastern point of Graham Island, the largest of the Queen Charlotte group. This great sand-spit, which has always been regarded by the Haidas as the abode of some powerful "Nok-nok" or spirit of evil, has evidently been formed by the tides and storms from the west and south meeting here, and thus continually adding to the bank of sand. Two vessels chartered and freighted by the Hudson Bay Company were successively stranded and wrecked on this dangerous shoal. It was here, too, that Seegay, the young chief whom I was now on my way to visit, had been capsized in his canoe, and though he succeeded in reaching the shore, yet he had been so long struggling in the surf, that it had resulted in the severe

LAUNCHING OUT INTO THE DEEP

illness which now threatened his life. We effected a landing on the islands at about 4.30 P.M., and having been cramped up in the canoe for thirteen hours, we were glad indeed to be able to stretch our limbs on the island shore. I realised the importance of my visit, being the first messenger of the Gospel to the Haidas, and whilst my crew were engaged in lighting a fire and preparing some food, I seized the opportunity to enter the forest, and there in faith I bowed and entrusted the work on which we were about to enter to the Divine guidance and blessing. This was my first visit to the Queen Charlotte Islands by canoe. I made the passage seventeen times by canoe, and on three of these voyages we were well-nigh lost.

The northern shore of the islands from the north-east point to the mouth of Massett inlet is almost wholly free from rocks, and is fringed with a beautiful sandy beach, which extends, in an almost unbroken line, a distance of nearly thirty miles. Having partaken of some refreshment, we re-embarked and reached Massett, our destination, at about 7.30 P.M. On first sighting the encampment it reminded me of a harbour, where a great many vessels lay at anchor, with only their masts appearing in view. On coming nearer these mast-like posts were found to be the large totem poles, carved from top to base with grotesque figures, representing the crests of those who erected them. There are four leading crests found among all the Indians on the north-west coast, including the Haidas, Tsimsheans, Nishkas, Kitikshans, Klingit, and other tribes. These are the eagle, the bear, the wolf, and the finback whale. With each of these, other animals, birds, fishes, and emblems are grouped and associated. Thus, with the eagle the beaver is joined; with the wolf the heron is associated; with the bear, the sun, the rainbow, and the owl are connected; whilst with the finback whale, the frog and the raven are represented. These four crests are known by special terms in the various languages of the tribes.

LAUNCHING OUT INTO THE DEEP

Amongst the Haidas, the bear and the eagle clans were the most numerous.

This crestal system may be designated as a kind of Indian freemasonry. It is even more comprehensive in its influence and power, as by it the chieftainships are divided and allotted, marriages are arranged and controlled, and distribution of property decided. Indeed the entire social life of the Indians is controlled and regulated by this system. We landed in front of the large lodge of the leading chief Weah, who was the head of the bear clan at Massett. This numbered amongst its members the majority of the Massett tribe. The entrance to this lodge was a small oval doorway cut through the base of a large totem pole, which compelled those entering to bend in order to pass through it. On entering we found ourselves on a tier or gallery of some five or six feet in width, which formed the uppermost of several similar platforms rising one above the other from the ground floor below, and running all round the house. A stairway led down from this upper platform to the basement or floor. This was the plan on which all the Haida houses were built, the object being defence in case of attack. The small oval doorway cut through the base of the totem prevented a surprise or rush of an enemy, whilst when bullets were flying and crashing through the walls from without, those within remained in safety in the excavated space on the ground floor, in the centre of which was the fireplace.

The Indians on the west coast of Vancouver Island built their dwellings on exactly the same plan, and Captain Meares, on his first voyage to the coast in 1788, describes his visit to the house of Wicananish thus: " On entering the house we were absolutely astonished at the vast area it enclosed. It contained a large square, boarded up close on all sides to the height of twenty feet, with planks of an uncommon breadth and length. Three enormous trees, rudely carved and painted, formed the rafters, which were

LAUNCHING OUT INTO THE DEEP

supported at the ends and in the middle by gigantic images carved out of huge blocks of timber. . . . The trees that supported the roof were of a size which would render the mast of a first-rate man-of-war diminutive on a comparison with them; indeed our curiosity as well as our astonishment was on its utmost stretch, when we considered the strength which must be necessary to raise these enormous beams to their present elevation; and how such strength could be found by a people wholly unacquainted with mechanic powers. The door by which we entered this extraordinary fabric was the mouth of one of these huge images, which, large as it may be supposed, was not disproportioned to the other features of this monstrous visage. We ascended by a few steps on the outside, and after passing this extraordinary kind of portal descended down the chin into the house, where we found new matter for astonishment in the number of men, women, and children who composed the family of the chief, which consisted of at least eight hundred persons." The foregoing description of a chief's house at Nootka, on the west coast of Vancouver Island, as detailed by one of the first navigators who visited this coast in 1788, exactly describes the dwellings of the Haida chiefs a century later.

Around the fire a number of Haidas were seated, many of whom, both men and women, had their faces painted in red or black, whilst some were besmeared with both colours. The chief sat in a peculiarly shaped seat carved out of one piece of wood, a section of a tree, and placed on the first tier or platform, whilst around the fire a number of his slaves were engaged in preparing food. Large numbers of the Haidas pressed in to see us, and to learn the object of our visit, and as the chief understood sufficient of the Tsimshean tongue I was enabled to inform him of my mission to his dying nephew, Seegay. Him I found very low, and both he and his wife were indeed pleased to see me. He was evidently far gone in rapid consumption.

LAUNCHING OUT INTO THE DEEP

The bright sunken eyes and hectic glow, with the incessant cough, indicated the disease. He was eager to learn more of the Great Chief above, "Shalana nung Itlagedas," and of the way to Him. This led me at once to the all-important subject: I was enabled to tell him of Him who has declared Himself to be "the Way, the Truth, and the Life." I spoke in Tsimshean, his wife's language, and as she proceeded to interpret for me she broke down and was unable to proceed. I closed the interview with prayer.

On returning to the chief's house I found a large number of Haidas assembled in their paint and feathers. They had been engaged in a medicine dance, and as my Tsimshean crew, who were Christians, were anxious to lie down to rest after their long day's travel, I conducted evening prayer for them. The Haidas looked on in amazement, and continued smoking and talking during our service. My crew lay down to rest on the lower floor around the fire, whilst to me a place of honour was given on the upper gallery to the rear of the great lodge. But I could not sleep. Was it the exciting experiences of the day which prevented my sleeping, or was it the strange odours from the carved and painted boxes around? In these I knew were stored dried fish, dried herring spawn, dried seaweed in cakes, and boiled crab apples preserved in olachan grease. Yet it was not from these that this heavy and oppressive atmosphere arose. At the first gleam of the welcome day I arose and surveyed my surroundings. I concluded that the offensive odour came from without, through the numerous openings between the split planks with which the walls were constructed. I went out to reconnoitre and found, to my astonishment, a great pile of the remains of the dead, some in grease boxes tied around with bark ropes, some in cedar bark mats which had fallen to pieces, revealing the contents; whilst skulls and bones were scattered around. I needed not to be reminded that I was in a heathen camp. Everything around, within and

LAUNCHING OUT INTO THE DEEP

without, was depressing. As I turned from the weird sight a hungry, wolfish-looking dog challenged me. I had evidently disturbed him in his horrid feast, so I fled, and, re-entering the house, I aroused my Tsimshean crew. I pointed out to them the ghastly sight, which surprised especially the young men. The older men had known that this was the Haida custom. They never interred their dead. The mainland tribes cremated their dead, but the Haidas simply removed the body to the rear of their lodges, or a few yards distant, excepting the remains of those of rank, which were generally encased, if a chief, in the base of a mortuary totem pole erected to his memory by his successor, and elaborately carved with the crest of the clan; or, if a person of lesser rank, the body was placed in a large box-like structure supported by two great posts from 10 to 15 feet above the ground, as shown in illustration. These were erected throughout each camp, and on the decay of the wood the remains were scattered around. I instructed my crew to remove my blankets and bedding to the lower floor, where, though troubled by numerous dogs, I rested better while in the camp. On passing around I found that all the houses were constructed on the same principle as that of the chief in which I was lodging. Many of them were excavated to a greater depth, allowing a gallery of five tiers from the level of the surface to the lower floor in the centre, on which the fireplace was situated. Many of the doorways were also similarly constructed to that which I have mentioned, and could easily be defended by one man.

On one occasion a large number of the Haidas of another tribe had been slaughtered on the threshold of the great lodge in which I was. They had been insulted or injured by the Massett Haidas, who, in order to make peace, had invited them to a feast. They determined to avail themselves of this opportunity to avenge themselves, and came to the feast with their weapons concealed under their

INTERIOR OF HAIDA CHIEF'S HOUSE

The house is about 40 feet square, forming one large room. The upper cubicles are on a level with the ground, which in front of them is excavated so that the fireplace in the centre is twelve feet below the surface. A ledge, for the use of slaves and dependents, is left half-way down.

LAUNCHING OUT INTO THE DEEP

garments. A report of their intention had been secretly conveyed to the chief who had invited them. Intent on their own plan of revenge, they little suspected the change of fare which had been provided for them. Within the narrow doorway were posted two powerful warriors, one on either side, each armed with a war club. The guests arrived in a long line, led by their chief, each prepared for deeds of blood. But as each entered with head bowed low through the low and narrow portal, one powerful blow from the concealed guard was sufficient, and as the body was dragged aside quickly by those in waiting, they raised a shout of welcome in chorus to disarm suspicion in those following. In this way the entire number was disposed of, and only two great heaps of corpses to right and left of the entrance remained to tell the tale. The concealed weapon which was found on each of them satisfied their slayers that their action was well merited.

In this same house, with the chief's permission, I invited the men of the tribe to assemble on the evening of the day after my arrival. I was anxious to announce to them my desire to open a Mission amongst them. Accordingly a large number of the men assembled, among whom were some of the leading medicine men. One of these, who was not only a medicine man but also a chief, I had met on the mainland. It was easy to recognise him. His long hair, which hung down to his hips when performing his incantations over the sick, or when engaged in the medicine dance, was now rolled round a pair of horns and fastened to the back of his head. This, with his wild, restless eyes and shaggy beard, reminded me of representations of the Evil One which I had seen in illustrations from the old masters. He was the leading medicine man, and I knew I should find in him a formidable opponent. Many present were in paint and feathers, and as the dim light of the fire flashed occasionally on them they presented a strange appearance. I opened with prayer that the entrance of

LAUNCHING OUT INTO THE DEEP

the Divine Word might give light, and that the door might be opened amongst these long-benighted tribes for the Gospel. I addressed them in the T'simshean, which was interpreted by one of them.

"Chiefs and friends," I began, "I am not quite a stranger to many of you. You have met me on the mainland, where I have also seen you. I have heard much of you from the T'simshean chiefs who have received the message of peace. They have heard the word of the Great Chief above who is the Father of all. They have scattered the swan and eagle's down over their foes and have left the war-path for ever. Your friend and fellow-tribesman Seegay is sick. He longed to know the word of the Great Chief before he dies. I heard his cry. It came to me across the waves, and I have come at his call. I have brought to him the good word of the Son of the Great Chief of Heaven. It has made his heart strong. He of whom I spoke to him is the Way of life. He only is the Truth. He is the Life for ever. He has come down from the Great Father to seek us. He has given us His word. He has sent me to you with His message. I am ready to obey. I desire to learn your tongue to make the message clear. I shall be ready to come when the first snow falls on the mountain tops, and the wild fowl are returning southward. When the fire canoe makes her last trip, I will come. These are my words to you, chiefs and wise men. I have spoken."

When I sat down there was silence for several minutes. Then there arose a low, murmuring consultation from all sides which gradually increased in volume, during which the chief was in close consultation with his leading advisers. At length the loud tap of a stick by one of these caused silence, and the chief arose to speak. "Your words are good," he replied. "They are wise words. We have heard of the white man's wisdom. We have heard that he possesses the secret of life. He has heard the words of the Chief above. We have seen the change made in the

LAUNCHING OUT INTO THE DEEP

Tsimsheans. But why did you not come before? Why did the iron people (white men) not send us the news when it was sent to the Tsimsheans? The smallpox which came upon us many years ago killed many of our people. It came first from the north land, from the iron people who came from the land where the sun sets (Russia, from whence it was brought to Alaska). Again it came not many years ago, when I was a young man. It came then from the land of the iron people where the sun rises (Canada and the United States). Our people are brave in warfare and never turn their backs on their foes, but this foe we could not see and we could not fight. Our medicine men are wise, but they could not drive away the evil spirit; and why? because it was the sickness of the iron people. It came from them. You have visited our camps, and you have seen many of the lodges empty. In them the camp fires once burned brightly, and around them the hunters and warriors told of their deeds in the past. Now the fires have gone out and the brave men have fallen before the iron man's sickness. You have come too late for them."

He paused, and again his advisers prompted him in low tones, after which he resumed: " And now another enemy has arisen. It is the spirit of the fire-water. Our people have learned how to make it, and it has turned friends to foes. This also has come from the land where the sun rises. It is the bad medicine of the ' Yetz haadā ' (iron people). It has weakened the hands of our hunters. They cannot shoot as their fathers did. Their eyes are not so clear. Our fathers' eyes were like the eagle's. The fire-water has dimmed our sight. It came from your people. If your people had the good news of the Great Chief, the Good Spirit, why did they not send it to us first and not these evil spirits? You have come too late." With these words he sat down.

It was a sad recital, and for the moment I felt much like a prisoner charged and convicted before his judges.

LAUNCHING OUT INTO THE DEEP

I knew every eye was upon me, and I was rather glad it was dark in the great lodge. Summoning up courage, I replied briefly: " I have heard your words, chief, and I am sad. But the Kalikoustla came to your people before I could come. See; I have not delayed so long. My hair is not yet white. I am not as old as you. I came to the Tsimsheans, but as soon as I heard of your need I came to you. When Seegay's cry reached me I came. I have not come too late for him. The word of the Great Chief above has made his heart strong. I have not come too late for you nor for your children. For this I am glad."

One of the sub-chiefs then replied: " Yes, you can lead our children in the new way, but we do not desire to abandon the customs of our forefathers. We cannot give up the old customs. The Scanawa (presiding spirit) of our medicine men is strong. Stronger than the words of the Great Chief above, so you will have no power to change them. It would not be good for you to try. The ' Yetz haadā' had better return to his own people." Thus the council meeting ended. I was hopeful. The opposition had not been so active as I had expected. If they permitted me to teach their children I knew I should be enabled through their children to influence them also. Now that the consultation had ended the Haidas gave full vent to their views, and groups of excited men were discussing the question in high tones and with vehement gestures both within and without the lodge. Amongst these the medicine men were the most excited, and from the fierce looks with which they regarded me, I knew that from them at least I must expect active and organised opposition, as they realised their craft was in danger.

CHAPTER VIII

ARRIVAL FROM THE QUEEN CHARLOTTE ISLANDS BY CANOE

> " The red cross of our banner
> Shall float o'er every land,
> And claim in faith's obedience
> Earth's darkest, wildest strand.
> O labourers claim,
> In His dear name,
> The utmost isles at His command."
> —CLARA THWAITES.

THE day following, Edenshew, an influential chief, arrived from Virago Sound, accompanied by a large number of his tribe in several war canoes. His own canoe was manned principally by his slaves. He and his men were received with honours, and a dance of peace was accorded them. There had been a quarrel between the two tribes, and Edenshew with his leading men had been invited, for the purpose of making peace. As their large canoes approached the shore the occupants chanted the brave deeds of the past, and were answered in a similar strain by the concourse on the shore. The chanting was accompanied by regular and graceful motions of the head and body and waving of the hands. The time was kept by a large drum formed like a chest, and made of red cedar wood, painted with grotesque figures, and covered with skin. This was beaten by a drummer seated in the bow of the leading canoe. Naked slaves with their bodies blackened, each bearing a large copper shield, now rushed into the water and cast the shields into the deep, in front

ARRIVAL FROM THE

of the canoes of the visitors. As these shields are made of native copper, and inscribed with their crestal signs, they are very highly valued amongst the Indians, consequently this was one of the highest marks of welcome and honour. Not that the copper shields were lost to the owners, as they were recovered afterwards on the ebb of the tide. On landing the visitors were preceded by a number of dancers, male and female, specially arrayed and with faces painted, who led the way to the lodge prepared for their reception. The central seat was given to the chief, and his leading men were seated around. A messenger now entered to announce the coming of his chief and party to welcome his guests. These at once entered, the chief preceding and followed by the sub-chiefs, and principal men in their dancing attire. The head-dress or shikid bore the crest of the tribe on the front inlaid with mother-of-pearl, and surmounted by a circlet or crown formed of the bristles of the sea-lion, standing closely together so as to form a receptacle. This was filled with swan or eagle's down, very fine and specially prepared. As the procession danced around in front of the guests chanting the song of peace, the chief bowed before each of his visitors, and as he did so a cloud of the swansdown descended in a shower over his guest. Passing on, this was repeated before each, and thus peace was made and sealed. This custom is recognised and followed by all the tribes of the north-west coast. The calumet or "pipe of peace" is never used as such, but the Ithtanoa or scattering of the swansdown is held sacred, and as equally binding on those who perform the ceremony, and those who receive it. By it the tomahawk is buried effectually, and through it the pipe of peace is passed around in social harmony and true friendship. I have frequently, in preaching to the heathen, been enabled to make an effective use of this custom as illustrating how the Great Chief above, when we were at enmity with Him, made peace with us by the gift of His

QUEEN CHARLOTTE ISLANDS

only Son, who sends down the blessing of peace through the Holy Ghost. This chief, Edenshew, who was thus received, was formerly the most powerful chief on the Queen Charlotte Islands. His name was known and feared by many of the tribes both north and south. When the American schooner, the *Susan Sturges,* was captured, pillaged, and burned by the northern Haidas, and her crew enslaved, Edenshew asserted that had he not been present the crew would all have been slaughtered. He informed me that the Haidas were about to shoot them when he interfered and took them under his protection. On the other hand, some members of the tribe informed me that it was by this chief's orders that the schooner was attacked and taken. It is probable that both statements are true. These white men who had formed the crew were divested of their own clothing, which was appropriated by their captors, and received blankets instead, and thus barefoot, and with but scant clothing, they were enslaved by the chiefs, to whom they became hewers of wood and drawers of water. They were thus retained as slaves, until redeemed by the Hudson's Bay Company, who paid over to the chiefs a number of bales of blankets for their release.

Chief Edenshew understood Tsimshean, and could speak it fluently, consequently when he invited me to visit his nephew, a young man also in the last stage of consumption, I made it conditional that he should interpret for me, as I desired to address his people. This he engaged to do, and on our arrival we found his friend very weak and low. I conducted a service, Edenshew interpreting for me, as he had promised, but I saw that he hesitated and failed to convey much of what I said to his people. I found that he was averse to my proposed Mission, as he had a number of slaves, and feared that it might lead to their obtaining freedom, and his consequent loss. He had heard that those of the Tsimshean chiefs who had embraced Chris-

ARRIVAL FROM THE

tianity had freed their slaves or had adopted them into their families.

When quite a young man, the ship *Vancouver*, whilst on a voyage to the north of the Queen Charlotte Islands with a cargo of general merchandise, was driven on Rose Spit Sands. Edenshew was then residing with his uncle, who was the chief of an encampment at Yehling, near to this dangerous point. On seeing the ship stranded, with the waves breaking over her, he at once pushed off with a large party of the tribe in their canoes to take possession of the vessel. They boarded the ship, and, despite the efforts of the captain and officers, commenced to plunder her. A hand-to-hand conflict ensued, in which the ship's crew would most certainly have been overpowered, had not the captain ordered the magazine to be fired. The boats had already been lowered, and the next order was to take to them and push off from the ship. On seeing this hasty action, Edenshew apprehended danger. He and his men made a rush for their canoes, and paddled off, leaving their heaps of plunder on the deck. They were not a moment too soon, as they had just got clear of the vessel when she blew up with a tremendous explosion, scattering the wreckage far and wide on the waves around. The boats' crews were all armed, but, fearing to touch on the islands, they stood off for the mainland and Fort Simpson, some sixty miles distant, whilst the Haidas paddled back to their shores. The prompt action of the captain prevented the pillage of his vessel, and probably saved the lives of many of his men, who would have been overpowered and slain had they persisted in defending the vessel. Edenshew could never dismiss this act from his mind, as many years afterwards, when he met the first officer of the ship, who had in the meantime been promoted to the position of a chief factor in the Hudson's Bay Company, he declined to reply to his salutation, whilst most friendly disposed towards me.

Several years afterwards, when on a trading expedition

QUEEN CHARLOTTE ISLANDS

to the mainland, one of the officers of the Hudson's Bay Company showed Edenshew a piece of gold ore, and informed him that if he could bring him a quantity similar to the sample he would reward him with such a number of bales of blankets as would enable him to give the greatest "potlatch" ever given by any Haida chief, and thus yet further elevate his chieftainship. Edenshew took away the piece of ore, promising to inquire amongst his people concerning it. Shortly after his return, he went on a visit southwards to Skidegate and vicinity, where he had many friends of his own crest. Here he was royally entertained, and, whilst seated with his friends around the camp-fire, he exhibited the sample of gold ore, and inquired if any of them knew of any rock like it. It was passed round the circle for examination, when one of the women exclaimed that she knew where rock similar to it could be found, and that she thought she had a piece of it in her possession. She immediately proceeded to search her treasures, and produced a large piece, evidently richer in gold than the specimen. She agreed to accompany the chief on the following morning, and point out the rock to him from which she had obtained it. Accordingly, next morning Edenshew, having provided himself with the necessary tools, embarked in a small canoe, accompanied only by his wife and child, together with the old woman, his guide. The Eldorado was a rock overhanging the sea. Leaving the child, a little boy of some three or four years, in the canoe, the chief proceeded to chip off the golden ore, which his wife gathered into a Haida sack-shaped basket until it was almost filled. This she carried down, and emptied into the canoe. Returning with the basket, she continued collecting the ore as Edenshew chipped it off until the basket was again filled. It was now agreed that he had procured a sufficient quantity, and together they returned to the canoe, but what was their surprise to find that but a few pieces remained of the first basketful. The child, left alone in the canoe, had amused himself by throwing overboard piece by piece during their absence. Edenshew himself informed me afterwards, he was so enraged, that he would have thrown his child overboard also, had not his wife restrained him. As it was late in the evening, they returned with what they had.

On his next visit to the mainland, he brought the ore to Fort Simpson, where he received quite a cargo of blankets and other property as his reward. He consented, also, to act as guide to point out the treasure. A schooner was specially fitted out in Victoria, and a number of miners engaged for the expedition. Edenshew accompanied them on their arrival, and guided them to the spot. A large amount in gold ore was taken from the rock, but they failed to trace it farther from the shore. This place, not far from Skidegate, has been known since as "Gold Harbour."

That child, whose life would most probably have been sacrificed had it not been for his mother's intercession and protection, was spared that he might become the possessor of greater treasures than gold. Under his influence, also, Edenshew was yet to be led to discover the true riches which neither the world nor death could deprive him of. He was well rewarded for acting as pilot to the schooner which conveyed the mining party to the gold deposit, and this, together with the bales of blankets which he received on his first gold delivery, enabled him to give another great "potlatch," to which the members of all the other crests were invited from far and near. Thus his great gold discovery elevated him both in the estimation of Whites and Indians, and the promise made him by the Hudson's Bay Company was fulfilled.

I visited Seegay again for the last time, and commended both himself and his wife in prayer to God. He was trusting in the atonement and righteousness of the Lord Jesus Christ for salvation. Thus, for the Haidas, the darkness

QUEEN CHARLOTTE ISLANDS

of ages was beginning to pass away, and the true "light" of the Sun of Righteousness, which illuminates even the "Valley of the Shadow of Death," was shining. Our return journey was arduous and trying. Passing through Dixon's Entrance, we were overtaken by a squall which nearly tore our sail to pieces and threatened to swamp us. My steersman lost his cap, which was carried off by the wind. Off Rose Spit a large sea lion harassed us by following the canoe, and coming up now on one side and again on the other. My crew feared it might upset us, and, although we were sailing very fast, yet we could not outdistance it, so, acting on their advice, I seized my rifle, and, as it again emerged very close to the canoe, shot it through the head.

Towards evening the wind abated, and continued to do so until it was useless to keep up sail any longer. In Indian parlance, the western wind was "falling asleep." I felt as though I could have slept also, but, as we could just see the land ahead, we grasped our paddles, and pulled steadily through the night. When morning broke, we were still many miles from the outer islands off the coast, but, true to the Haida watchword, "Il haada seagai gu un shanzudie gum lāngung" (people should not rest on the ocean), we stimulated each other to fresh efforts by words and example, with an occasional burst of song. At length, after sunrise, we reached the first island, and, crippled from twenty-four hours in the canoe, with some difficulty we walked up the beach and, having lit a fire, proceeded to prepare a little food. Having appeased our hunger, we lay down to rest. Hardly had we done so when a favourable wind arose, which, in our exhausted condition, was not to be neglected. So, hastily re-embarking, we entered Metlakahtla Harbour at seven o'clock A.M. The steamer *Grappler* lay at anchor, and, as we passed her, Captain William Moore hailed us. Looking over the taffrail, he cried, "And where do you hail from so early, in that dugout?"

"We have just come from the Queen Charlotte Islands," I replied; "we left Massett yesterday morning, and we have been labouring all night to reach the shore."

"And have you really travelled from Queen Charlotte Islands in that craft?" he inquired. "I would not take all my steamer is worth, to venture on such a journey by canoe."

"Well, Captain," I replied, "we cannot all travel by steamer as you can." The good captain retreated without further reply, and we proceeded to land. That same steamer, which was formerly a gunboat in H.M. Navy, was afterwards destroyed by fire when on a voyage up the coast under the command of another captain, and some seventy lives were lost. Thus was accomplished my first visit to the Haidas. It was the first visit of a missionary to the Queen Charlotte Islands. One of the objects I had in view was to ascertain the best point at which to establish the Mission. From a geographical point of view, Skidegate might have appeared the most advantageous, being situated almost in the centre of the islands. But the tribes to the south of the islands had suffered severely from their periodical visits to Victoria and the cities on the Sound. They had imported drink and disease from these centres. The northern Haidas were more vigorous and healthy, with a larger proportion of women and children. I recognised in these the hope of the Haida race. From this as a centre, I hoped to be able to evangelise the tribes both north and south. For the Haidas were not confined to the Queen Charlotte Islands only. Across the waters of Dixon's Entrance, on the shores of the Prince of Wales Island in south-eastern Alaska, several encampments of Haidas were to be found.

These tribes speak the same dialect, and were originally one people. Many of them are related to families on the Queen Charlotte Islands, and there is continual intercourse between them. They were formerly encamped at Sisk and

QUEEN CHARLOTTE ISLANDS

North Island, where the remains of their great lodges and totems were still standing when I visited them. North Island is known amongst the Haidas as " Kaise Quiay," or the " Island of Kaise "; and the Haidas on Prince of Wales Island are yet known as the " Kaise haada," or " the people of Kaise." Consequently Massett, the place I had now selected for the headquarters of the Mission, was most central for all the Haidas, both of Queen Charlotte Islands and Alaska. For evangelistic and missionary enterprise must not be checked or limited by political or national boundaries. The great commission is, " Go ye into all the world, and preach the Gospel to every creature." In obedience to this command, we were now about to add another link to the great chain of Missions which, stretching from shore to shore of continents and islands, encircles the world with a girdle of light.

CHAPTER IX

OVERCOMING DIFFICULTIES

"If well thou hast begun, go on fore right,
It is the end that crowns us, not the fight."
— HERRICK.

IT is not known whether the Haidas of the Queen Charlotte Islands, or the tribes on the coast of the mainland, first saw the whites. Vancouver sailed up the coast before touching at the Queen Charlotte Islands. Captain Meares on his first visit crossed the Pacific from Calcutta, where he fitted out for the expedition, and reached Cook's Inlet, where he wintered and lost twenty-five of his crew, including the ship's surgeon, from scurvy. He experienced much trouble from the Indians, against whom they had to keep up a strict guard. In his third visit he sailed along by the Aleutian Islands, and thence southwards, bartering for sea-otter skins, wherever he touched. It was the chief of the Tlingit Indians, Kinnanook, who pointed out to Captain Meares the situation of the Queen Charlotte Islands, and intimated to him by signs that great numbers of sea-otter skins and robes were to be had there. Meares first sighted the most northerly island of the Queen Charlotte group on the 21st of August 1788, just eighty-eight years prior to my first visit and the establishment of the Mission. This was the island, now named Graham Island, on which I established the Massett Mission. These islands were first discovered by Captains Laurie and Guise in 1786. The following year, Captain Dixon of the *Queen Charlotte* touched there, and

OVERCOMING DIFFICULTIES

named the islands after King George the Third's Queen, after whom his ship was also named. "Dixon's Entrance," the strait separating Queen Charlotte Islands from Prince of Wales Island in Alaska, was named after the Commander. Many amusing incidents are related by the Indians of the mistakes and misunderstandings which occurred on the first advent of the white man. When the first ship was sighted off the north of the Queen Charlotte Islands, the Haida medicine men declared it was the Kali-Koustla, or the spirit of the smallpox, which had come back again. They had suffered so severely from the first visitation of that dreadful scourge, that they at once associated this strange phenomenon with it. Consequently the vessel lay at anchor unvisited for several days. At length a chief, named Coneyea, braver than the rest, determined to solve the mystery, so, calling for volunteers to man his large war canoe, he prepared to visit the "Un-nana" or evil spirit. His challenge was speedily accepted, and soon he was on his way to the ship. On drawing near they were astonished to see men moving about on board. These beckoned them onwards, and soon they were alongside. They were invited on board, and were lost in astonishment to find so much ironwork, even the ropes they described as being made of iron. From the impression thus received on their first contact with the whites, the Haidas have ever since designated us as the "Yatz haada," or the "Iron people." And surely, if the term was appropriate then, it is much more appropriate now, since the old wooden walls have given place to the steel-built vessels of war and merchandise.

Coneyea and his men had come out armed with their bows and spears, and the officers on board, seeing this, were desirous to exhibit their fire-arms. Taking up a loaded gun, one of them fired at a seal, which had come up not far from the ship, and shot it. Though greatly startled, yet these Haida warriors endeavoured to conceal

OVERCOMING DIFFICULTIES

their surprise. Another seal appearing within easy range, a loaded gun was handed to one of the Haidas, and he was motioned to fire. Unwilling to be considered as dismayed, and anxious to outdo his fellow-tribesmen, he seized the weapon, placed the butt of the musket against his nose, and, thus taking aim, fired. The rebound of the weapon was so strong that it almost knocked him down, and the blood gushed forth from his nose in a stream. He made a rush forward as though to seek revenge, but an exclamation from his friends, apprising him that he had killed the seal, abated his indignation, and, wiping away the blood, which he now regarded as an honour rather than as a disgrace, he handed back the gun with an expression of satisfaction and pride. And the proud distinction thus won, he retained, as none of his friends were willing to repeat the experiment. Before leaving the ship, Coneyea, who had not concealed his astonishment and admiration at all he saw, was presented by the captain with a new axe-head.

On his return to camp, he presented this to his wife, who was a great chieftainess, and a special box was made and carved for its safe keeping. This axe-head, as an ornament of inestimable value, was worn by the chieftainess at every great feast or entertainment as a jewel, suspended on her breast, and her fame spread far and wide as the fortunate possessor of such an ornament, which appeared to them as a veritable Kohinoor.

The Skidegate tribes had their mistakes also. The captain of the first ship, probably seeing their need of soap, presented them with a quantity of this useful article. Never having seen it before, they concluded it was part of the food of the Iron people, and the following day all were invited to the lodge of the happy possessor to partake of the treat. Fortunately the ship had weighed anchor early that morning, otherwise the indignant natives would most probably have resented their supposed injury.

A HAIDA INDIAN
Showing the characteristic figures used in tattooing.

A HAIDA CHIEFTAINESS
Clad in a blanket, and wearing nose-ring and labret. A gaudy silk handkerchief serves as a bonnet.

OVERCOMING DIFFICULTIES

As the Hudson Bay Company's steamer, the *Otter*, was about to make her last voyage of the year, and proposed calling at the north of the Queen Charlotte Islands, I resolved to endeavour to cross by her, and open the Mission without further delay. Accordingly, we left Metlakahtla, and proceeded to Fort Simpson by canoe on the 30th of October 1876. A number of Tsimshean Indians accompanied us in their own canoes. Here we embarked on the morning of November 1st, and, after a good run of about one hundred miles, anchored off Massett at nightfall. The captain, who was also a chief factor of the Company, and knew the character of the Indians better than any other person on the coast from his long experience in dealing with them, begged me not to risk my life, and that of my wife and two children, by attempting to remain there during the winter. He had been compelled to put up his netting to prevent them from boarding his vessel, more than once. Finding I had determined on remaining, he then requested me to permit my wife to return with the children to the mainland. To this I consented, provided she was willing to do so, as unfortunately we had no house to reside in. I had brought a few boards and a tent, hoping to be able to induce one of the chiefs to permit us to have a corner in one of their large lodges. My wife declined the good captain's proposal, stating she had come prepared to remain with me. " Well," he replied, " I shall not be surprised to find you have all been murdered when I return again next year."

It was not a very encouraging prospect, but we realised that He who sent us was with us, and would keep us. With the last canoe of Haidas leaving the steamer, we went ashore, after having said " Good-bye " to these last representatives of civilisation aboard. It was quite dark when we landed, and we knew not where to go. I had determined to visit the chief Weah, in whose large house we had lodged on my first visit, and whilst on our way thither I received

OVERCOMING DIFFICULTIES

a message from an old white man, the only one on the Islands, who was living with an Indian woman, and under her protection, stating that he could afford us shelter for the night. Thus was our way opened up, and we were indeed grateful for the invitation.

The circumstances under which this man came to the Islands were peculiar. An enterprising American, anxious to open trade with the Haidas for their fur seal and sea otter skins, arrived there on a sloop with a cargo of goods. Having secured the protection and support of one of the chiefs by a number of gifts, he succeeded in erecting a strong block-house. Here he landed and stored his goods. He had brought with him also a quantity of liquor and fire-arms and a small brass cannon. The latter would seem to be the necessary accompaniment of the former. The cannon he kept loaded, and placed in a position commanding the approach to the door. Yet all his precautions proved inefficient. One dark night the Haidas surrounded the house and proceeded to fire into it, so that, in order to save his life, having first barricaded the entrance, he escaped through an opening in the rear under cover of the darkness and fled to Skidegate, a distance of over a hundred miles, where he hired a canoe and crew of Indians to convey him to Fort Simpson.

Here he offered what remained of his house and stock to the Hudson Bay Company, who were desirous to establish a post on the Islands. They gave him a small sum for it, but their difficulty was to find a man to take charge. At length a man was found whose Indian wife, a Tsimshean woman, was known to the Haidas, and who guaranteed his safety should she accompany him. Her promise had been fulfilled, as she informed me that she had on several occasions saved him from the hands of the Haidas when they would have killed him.

Her association with this man had not enlightened her, but had rather retarded her from Christian influence and

OVERCOMING DIFFICULTIES

rooted her in heathenism, for, whilst many of her tribe had embraced Christianity, she yet remained a heathen. Strange to state, this white man with whom she was living was no better. He had travelled across the American continent about the time of the great Mormon massacre; had owned all the land on which Sacramento now stands, and had kept a liquor saloon there during the Californian gold excitement. There he had amassed fortunes, and had squandered them again, and at length had drifted up the coast to prospect for gold in Alaska. Now that he had settled down among the Indians, he had become as one of them, attending their "potlatches," receiving and carrying away what was given him, and, when his wife or daughter was ill, he called in the medicine sorcerers, and paid them for performing their incantations over the patient.

The morning following our arrival, I found a small log hut in which the skins of fur and hair seals had been stored and salted, but which was now empty. This I cleaned out, and in it erected a small stove which I had brought with me from the mainland, and here we were indeed glad to find shelter. It was only 10 by 12 feet, but I succeeded in partitioning off one end of it as a bedroom. The worst feature of our hut was its position, which I found was within a few yards of a broken-down dead-house which had been formed of bark. This was filled with dead bodies. In bark mats, in dirty blankets, and in old grease boxes the dead were heaped; and when the wind blew from that direction, our position became very trying. But this was not all. The Haidas, many of whom had never seen a white woman, crowded into our little shanty in their paint and feathers, and squatted down on the floor, so closely packed together that there was not room to move. Had it not been for the open door we must have been stifled, as the peculiar odour arising from their hunting and fishing garb was overwhelming.

OVERCOMING DIFFICULTIES

The only window—a half one at the end of the hut—was darkened by an array of faces besmeared with black and red paint, so that both light and air were scarce. Not knowing their language, I could not convey to them our desire, or, had I attempted to drive them out, I might have been ejected in turn, or subjected to even rougher treatment. I concluded, therefore, that what could not be helped must be endured. Day after day this continued, so that it was impossible to get near the stove or to prepare any food.

We had to be satisfied with two meals each day, viz. breakfast early in the morning, before our visitors began to assemble, and tea in the evening, after all had departed. Any article of wearing apparel within reach was freely made use of. Hats, coats, and boots were passed from one to another, each one trying them on, and inviting the opinions of the others as to their becomingness or otherwise. I now strengthened our partition, and affixed a door, which enabled us to hide away our clothing. I found several who understood a little of the Tsimshean language, and began to make use of them to obtain a few words of Haida. Remembering my success in acquiring the Tsimshean from the method I had used, I determined to adopt the same method for the Haida, and consequently succeeded in obtaining a translation of my key, which, it will be remembered, was "What is the Tsimshean name for this?" or "Gaulth sha wada Tsimshean qua?" This in the Haida is "Gushino Haadis adshi kiadagung-gung?" or "How do the Haidas cause this to be named?" Such of my visitors as could understand, I now kept busy whilst improving my own time, and the more indolent, not willing to be continually plied with my inquiries, soon took their departure, and thus I gained a double benefit.

I proceeded well in the compiling of my vocabularies, but in my endeavour to form sentences and phrases I met

OVERCOMING DIFFICULTIES

with a serious drawback. Having framed a sentence with the aid of one of them, I set it aside and awaited an opportunity to confirm or correct it with the aid of another Haida. But I was invariably met with the assertion that what I had written was incorrect. I was at length quite discouraged, and began to consider where the fault lay. I had noticed that on reading or repeating my sentence to any of them, their first inquiry always was, "Who helped you to know that?" and that on my informing them, the rendering was at once disputed. I determined therefore not to enlighten them for the future as to who had told me. I found the trouble arose from a desire on the part of each to be accounted more clever than others, and from this forward I made satisfactory progress.

It might be supposed that a knowledge of the Tsimshean, the language of the tribes of this name on the coast of the mainland, only a little over one hundred miles distant, would have been helpful in the acquirement of the Haida. It would have been so were there any similarity between the two languages. But there is no similarity whatever in either nomenclature, construction, or idea. One peculiarity of the Tsimshean is that it somewhat resembles the Latin in the person endings of the verbs, as for instance the verb "live," which is conjugated thus:

	Didolshu	= I live.
	Didolshun	= You live.
	Didolshtga	= He lives.
Pl.	*Dildolshim*	= We live.
	Dildolshashim	= Ye or you live.
	Dildolshtga	= They live.

The plural is sometimes rendered as *Dildolshimi,* &c. = We live, &c.

In two of the dialects of Tsimshean the third person

OVERCOMING DIFFICULTIES

plural is *Dildolchdet* = they live. In the Haida this verb is "Hinung-agung," and is thus conjugated:

	De henung-agung		= I live.
	Dung	,,	= You live.
	Il	,, ,,	= He lives.
Pl.	*Itil*	,, ,,	= We live.
	Dalung ,,	,,	= Ye or you live.
	Il	,, ,,	= They (many) live.
	Il	,, *awong*	= They (few) live.

Again, as to the difference in idea or conception of the same objects, the Tsimshean term for sunbeam, "Ashee Giamk," signifies the foot or limb of the sun; whilst the Haida term for the same, "Juie hunglth dagwuts," is literally the eyelash of the sun. In the Tsimshean the idea is that the sun is as a great body, the limbs of which extend to the earth; whilst the Haida conception is that the sun is a great eye, of which the rays are the eyelashes. In the Haida the term for our word "echo" is "hants kil" or the "spirit voice"; whilst in Tsimshean it is "gwul aght," or the reverberations of the lips. That the Haida is the more difficult of the two languages is evident from the fact that, whereas I have known several Haidas who understood and could speak the Tsimshean, yet I have never found any Tsimsheans who could speak the Haida, except several who had been captured by the Haidas and retained for many years in slavery. Indeed the Haida term for the Tsimsheans is "Kil-las haada," or "the people of the good language," which is significant.

Whilst thus acquiring the language, I resolved to endeavour to make some little effort in evangelising from house to house, and making use of the Chinook and the Tsimshean. The Chinook is the trading jargon of the coast, and is known by some of the inland tribes also. It was introduced by the Hudson's Bay Company's officers, and would appear to have had its origin from intercourse

OVERCOMING DIFFICULTIES

with the tribe called the Chinoock, amongst whom the Company established the first trading post, Fort Oregon, from which the State in which this fort stood probably derives its name. An interesting incident is recorded in connection with this fort, which illustrates the method by which much of the Chinook was formed. One of the officers of the Company named Clarke lived outside the fort, and on the officer of the watch opening the gate in the morning he generally greeted him with the salutation of " Well, Clarke, how are you ? " The Indians, waiting around to enter for trade, hearing this salutation frequently, concluded that it was the general greeting for all, and so on entering would address the first white man with the words, " Clak how ya ? " This is now generally used as the equivalent for " How are you ? " However well the Chinook may be adapted for trading purposes, it is but a poor medium for communicating religious instruction. But the importance of the missionary message compelled me to have recourse to the use of it whilst acquiring the Haida, so, having provided myself with large scriptural cartoons, I began at one end of the camp, and conducted a short service in one lodge each evening. As there were several families in each lodge, I generally found a sufficient number of hearers. Placing my illustration in a prominent position, I commenced by singing a verse or two of a hymn in either English or Tsimshean, which before long I was enabled to render in Haida. This was followed by a prayer, after which I delivered the message, assisted by the use of the illustration. I had strange congregations in those days. Sometimes on the arrival of other tribes a large number of stalwart Haidas would saunter in from the dance or potlatch, all gorgeous in paint and feathers, with bear skins or blankets wrapped round them, and would squat down on the floor. Lighting their pipes, they would discuss me and my action in loud tones, with an occasional burst of laughter. It was but a repetition

OVERCOMING DIFFICULTIES

of the criticism to which the first great missionary to the Gentiles was subjected when his more cultured hearers exclaimed, "What will this babbler say?" And if I was not clearly understood, I realised at least that I was preparing them for the reception of the message which would yet change these savage sea rovers into civilised Christian citizens, yea, and impart to them a claim to citizenship in the "city which hath foundations, whose builder and maker is God."

CHAPTER X

SICKNESS AND TRIAL

"I had much seed to sow, said one ; I planned
To fill broad furrows, and to watch it spring,
And water it with care. But now the hand
Of Him to Whom I sought great sheaves to bring
Is laid upon His labourer, and I wait
Weak, helpless, useless, at His palace gate."
—Frances R. Havergal.

IT was about this time that I began to realise the necessity for a building in which to conduct regular services. There was an old dance-house standing in a central position in the camp, which was constructed in the regular Haida style, having a pit or amphitheatre in the centre, surrounded by three tiers, rising one above the other until level with the ground on which the outer walls stood. As this building had fallen into disuse, and had become dilapidated, I was enabled to purchase it for a small sum, including the site. I succeeded in inducing a number of young men to assist me in preparing this structure, by paying them in kind, which they preferred to money payments. Powder and shot, tobacco and matches, hard ship biscuits and rice, also blankets—these articles could always command labour, being just such things as they required in their hunting expeditions. All the northern Haidas are skilful canoe-makers, consequently they are familiar with the use of the "hadha." This is a native adze made by themselves from any piece of iron or steel, which they temper, shape, and sharpen, and then lash it to a wooden handle. A similar weapon was used by them in fighting, and was really their tomahawk. Prior to the introduction of iron and

SICKNESS AND TRIAL

steel amongst them, their adzes, hammers, and axes were all of stone, which were in use up to a comparatively recent date.

I had the thick split cedar planking taken down piece by piece, and adzed on the inner side and edges, thus making them like newly prepared boards, and at the same time fitting them more closely. In doing this they had their adzes injured and blunted repeatedly by coming into contact with numerous bullets imbedded in the plank, the evidences of the frequent attacks made on the inmates in the past. I had yet another difficulty to contend with. Several large carved poles stood in front of the building, of which one stood on either side of the door. These were beginning to decay near the base, and my workmen did not improve them while passing in and out, so that the decaying forms of the dead encased in them could now be seen. As these were the remains of chiefs and others of high rank, I could not remove them with impunity. In order to avoid the necessity of passing in and out through them, I had a door opened towards the rear of the building for my own convenience, and I congratulated myself on the improved arrangement.

But my congratulations were premature. For not many days afterwards, after a stormy night, when opening my door the following morning, I was startled at receiving a smart lash as though from a whip on the side of my face. Looking up to see the cause, I perceived that the wind had blown the side out of a mortuary chest which was supported by two great posts, and in this receptacle lay the skeleton of a woman, the long black hair of which was being blown to and fro by the wind as it hung down fully three feet from the scalp. I was startled by this unexpected discovery, and speedily beat a retreat in order to avoid a repetition of the punishment which the unknown was unconsciously inflicting upon me. I called two slaves, and giving them a bark mat, secretly instructed them to dig a grave not far from the spot at midnight, and then to

SICKNESS AND TRIAL

remove the remains from the elevated platform it occupied and inter it. They at first hesitated, fearing that whoever claimed relationship might shoot them if discovered, but by my promising them employment they consented. Thus my doorway was again rendered accessible to me as before.

While completing the renovation of the old dance-house with a view to public services for religious instruction, my plans were well-nigh upset by the action of one of my workmen. This man, who was the member of a family which bore the character of being amongst the fiercest of the tribe, was anxious for a supply of tobacco. I accordingly handed him an order on the storekeeper to supply him with the same.

On reaching the blockhouse which served as a store he found it closed. He proceeded to the shanty occupied by the storekeeper and presented my paper. The storekeeper declined to return to the store to supply him, and the Haida, becoming angry, rushed out uttering threats, and banged the door with such force that it almost gave way. This act so infuriated the storekeeper, who was also a man of a violent passion, that he seized a stick and rushed out after him. Fortunately I had only just returned to my hut, and saw the two closing in a deadly struggle. The white man endeavoured to strike again and again, but the Haida avoided his blows with cat-like agility, and, drawing his hunting-knife from his belt, was watching his opportunity to use it upon his opponent when I rushed in between them. Being fresh and eager I succeeded in separating them, and hearing the angry shouts, my wife came to my help. With her aid we induced the storekeeper to return to his shanty, whilst the Haida stood like a tiger at bay staring after him and muttering " Memaloose, Memaloose," which is the Chinook for " Kill, Kill." He permitted me to lead him to my hut, where I endeavoured to calm him, and at the same time to warn him that should anything happen to the storekeeper he would be held responsible, as I had witnessed what had occurred and had

SICKNESS AND TRIAL

heard his significant threat. I afterwards succeeded in reconciling them, and the storekeeper confessed that he had permitted his temper to overcome him. Had I not been near, he would probably have lost his life in the fray, as other Haidas were rushing to aid their tribesman.

It was at this time that we began to experience the effects of the tainted atmosphere in which we were living. Our eldest child was seized with fever, which turned out to be an attack of typhoid. Anxious to prevent the overcrowding to which we had been subjected, I constructed a half door and hung it in position. This I fastened with a bolt so low down that it could not be opened from without. This simple contrivance debarred the usual inrush of visitors.

As they crowded around to endeavour to obtain admission, I pointed them to the sick child and explained as best I could the position, which appeared to satisfy them. Notwithstanding all our efforts the symptoms grew worse, until we began to fear the worst. As the crisis approached we stood by him at midnight, and believing him to be dying, we commended him in prayer to our Heavenly Father. His breathing had ceased and no pulse could be felt, when suddenly a perspiration began to break out on his forehead, and with a sigh almost inaudible the breathing slowly, and at first imperceptibly, returned. He had passed the crisis, and from that time he gradually recovered.

Before he was convalescent, however, I was stricken down myself with the same dread disease. As my symptoms increased, fearing that I should become delirious, I instructed my wife as to the future treatment. It was well I had done so, as shortly afterwards I became insensible to my surroundings. While in this state a band of medicine men, who had learned of my illness, came and demanded admission. It was a critical moment. My wife knew that should they succeed in effecting an entrance all hope of recovery would be ended. They asserted that my illness was caused by one of the evil spirits which had caused the

SICKNESS AND TRIAL

death of so many of the Haidas, and that they alone possessed the power to expel it. The leading medicine man, with his long hair rolled around a pair of horns, had his medicine rattle and charms in a bag which he generally carried when on his visits to the sick. His associates were also similarly arrayed and prepared.

Finding that my wife would not admit them, they attempted to force open the door, but I had expected just such attempts, and had consequently constructed the door strongly to resist such attacks. When they stretched over to endeavour to withdraw the bolt she pushed them off repeatedly. At length, uttering threats and denunciations of death against us, they withdrew, and my life was saved. For had they succeeded in their attempts to enter they would have danced around and over me, accompanying their wild cries with their rattles, until I had succumbed. Or even had I survived such treatment and recovered, my influence would have been lost, as they would have proclaimed throughout the camps that they had saved the white man's life by casting out the demon of his disease.

In a few days the crisis came, just as it had in the case of our child, and accompanied by the same symptoms. The delirium passed away and the fever gradually subsided, leaving me weak and low. How I longed for an egg or a little milk, but neither could be had. When in this state my friend the storekeeper ventured to look in on me. He kept away through fear, because he believed the word of the medicine men, who had proclaimed my approaching end throughout the camp, and in consequence he informed my wife that my death was certain. But notwithstanding medicine men and false friends I could cry out in faith, " I shall not die, but live and declare the works of the Lord," as now I realised I should recover.

In response to my appeal for a little fresh meat, he engaged to kill a pig provided I should take half of it, which I gladly consented to do under the circumstances.

SICKNESS AND TRIAL

The following day he sent it over, and pleased at the prospect of a little fresh meat I seized my walking-stick and determined to take my first walk after my illness. The snow lay lightly on the ground, and I had just reached the confines of the encampment when I witnessed a sight from which I fled. The three remaining swine had dragged a corpse from its rude covering, and were engaged in devouring the remains. I returned to the hut, where I found dinner prepared. I was invited to partake of the longed-for dish, but I turned from it with loathing. When pressed for the reason of my refusal I was compelled to disclose the secret. The pork was quickly removed, and a passing Haida was presented with the entire supply, cooked and uncooked. No doubt he invited his friends to partake of the treat. But in such case I fear the old proverb that " ignorance is bliss " would not apply, as they must have known that these unclean animals were cannibals of the most degraded type.

A few days after this event a large fleet of Haidas arrived from several other encampments to attend a great " potlatch." As they came by special invitation a great reception had been prepared for them. As their large canoes approached the shore, each propelled by from twelve to twenty rowers arranged in equal numbers on either side of the canoes, a skilful display of paddling was given. Now they made the stroke as one man, without causing the slightest sound or raising a ripple on the water, indicating the stealthy manner in which they approached their foes in a night attack; then at a given signal, with a loud war whoop they dashed their paddles deep into the water, causing the foam to fly, whilst the canoes were almost lifted by the stroke as they made a united dash upon their supposed enemy. Instantly this was changed to a pæan of triumph, whilst they kept in perfect time to the chant with their paddles; and lastly, they swept shorewards, imitating the flight of the weary eagle by two strokes and

SICKNESS AND TRIAL

a rest between, alternated with three strokes and a pause. This exhibition was ended by every two oarsmen crossing their paddles in mid-air over the centre of their canoes as they touched the shore.

The chiefs and leading men occupied the seats between the rowers, whilst the women and children, with their provisions and bedding, were accommodated on the bottom of the canoes, thus ballasting their light craft. Several of the leading canoes had small cannon mounted on the bows. From these a salute was fired on nearing the shore; but the concussion was too strong for one of the canoes, as it caused it to split almost from bow to stern, and would have proved serious had they not been so close to land. The occupants remained quite composed although the water was rushing in, and they succeeded in beaching the canoe just as she was sinking. But as the chanting and dancing were well sustained by the occupants of the other canoes this accident passed almost unperceived by the others.

Many of the dancers wore head-dresses and wooden masks of various patterns, but in every case the mask or head-dress indicates the crest to which the wearer belongs. Thus the masks and head-dresses worn by the members of the eagle crest bear a resemblance to the eagle either by the likeness of the nose to the eagle's hook-shaped beak, or by the white eagle feathers surmounting the mask. The members of the finback-whale crest wear masks surmounted by a large fin; whilst the wolf, the bear, and the frog are all well represented by the members of the crests of which these are the signs.

It is not a little significant, however, to find how very closely the use of the ermine skin by the Indians of all the tribes on the north-west coast approaches the use of it in the state dresses of royalty and nobility in England. The higher the rank of an Indian chief, the greater the number of ermine skins he was entitled to wear attached to his *shikeed,* or dancing dress, and hanging from it down

SICKNESS AND TRIAL

his back, in rows of three to six in width. The Master of the Robes in the English court is careful that neither duke, earl, or knight may adorn himself with more ermine skins than is permitted by court etiquette. And, as it cannot be said that the Indians have adopted the custom from the whites, and we hesitate to admit that the whites have acquired it from the Indians, we can only recognise in it the similarity of human nature, and admit that here, indeed, the extremes meet in the tastes and adornments of the highest civilisation and the gay trappings of the untutored Indian chief.

A great feast had been prepared for the visitors in the houses of the leading chiefs, and to this they led, preceded by the dancers. On entering, great fires of logs, piled several feet in height, diffused a glow of heat around, and the blaze was intensified by slaves pouring seal-oil and olachan grease in large quantities upon the fires. The visitors having been seated according to rank, their entertainers entered arrayed in their dancing costume, of which the most attractive objects were the *dudjung*, or dancing head-dress, and the *shikeed*, or dancing robe. The crown-shaped receptacle on the top of each of the dancing head-dresses was well filled with the swan and eagle's down, and, as they danced in and around before their guests, they bowed before each, causing a shower of the down to fall on each guest, a most significant mark of both peace and honour. The dance was accompanied by the music of the chant and drum, whilst the words of the chant expressed their pleasure and the rank and record of their guests. When the *lthdanua*, or down, had thus been scattered, their feasting began.

It was not uncommon to place a small canoe filled with berries, preserved in grease and mixed with snow, before a number of their guests. The chief dishes were served up in wooden bowls and trenchers, skilfully carved, and inlaid with mother-of-pearl. Dried salmon and halibut with

AN INDIAN SUB-CHIEF IN FULL DRESS

Mantles such as this were woven by the Indians from the hair of the mountain goat, and were very costly. Ermine skins adorn the head-dress.

SICKNESS AND TRIAL

olachan grease followed, with boiled seaweed (dulse), also mixed with fish and grease, and, lastly, as dessert, a bitter-tasting berry (*hūgutlite*), beaten up with water until it became a mass of froth. This was eaten in a peculiar manner, with long, narrow wooden spoons (shaped like miniature oars or paddles), being pressed out of the mouth and quickly drawn in again in order to expel part of the air with which it is mixed. This is attended with an unusual sound, and in endeavouring to imitate and execute this native custom, the white man, if a guest, is seldom successful, and must be prepared to be greeted with salvos of laughter at his failure.

The first item in the programme of this great " potlatch " to which these visitors had been invited was the erection of a great totem or crest pole. Amongst all the tribes on the coast, none surpassed the Haidas in the construction and erection of these totems. In this, and in the designing and finishing of their large war canoes, the Haida Indians excelled all the coast tribes, whether in British Columbia or on the Alaskan coast. They had one natural advantage, in the very fine cedar trees which were to be found on their islands.

A tree, proportionate to the dimensions of the totem required, and free from large knots or blemishes, was first selected, roughly prepared, and conveyed to the camp. Then the chief of a crest differing from that of the chief for whom the totem was to be carved, was invited to enter upon the work. If he was not sufficiently skilful himself, he called one or more of the most skilful of his own crest to assist him in the undertaking. Having received instructions as to the various figures to be represented, their number and order, proceeding from base to top, the workmen commenced operations.

In the carving of a totem pole very often a legend or tradition in which the ancestors of the chief and his crest were the chief actors is selected, and thus the totem is but

SICKNESS AND TRIAL

an illustration of the legend. In some villages may be seen totems surmounted by figures resembling men wearing tall hats. This indicates that the owner's ancestor or ancestors first saw the white men who are here represented. Standing by a skilled carver on one occasion who had been engaged to carve a very elaborate totem, I was surprised at the apparently reckless manner in which he cut and hewed away with a large axe as though regardless of consequences. "Where is your plan?" I inquired. "Are you not afraid to spoil your tree?" "No," he replied; "the white man, when about to make anything, first traces it on paper, but the Indian has all his plans here," as he significantly pointed to his forehead.

Having cut out the outline roughly with the axe, he then proceeded to finer workmanship with an adze, and on my last visit I found him polishing off a perfect pattern with the dried skin of the dogfish, which is much more effective for this purpose than sand-paper. When it is remembered that formerly all such work as the preparation and carving of their totem poles, the construction of their well-proportioned canoes, and the building and decoration of their dwellings, were executed with stone tools, it will appear less surprising that they can accomplish such work now with the improved tools and implements which the white man has introduced. The chief or chiefs who are engaged to carve the totem or crest pole are not paid until the " potlatch " takes place. They are then rewarded, not according to their time and labour, but rather according to their rank and the amount of property at the disposal of the chief for distribution to those who have been invited.

But there were yet other customs amongst the Haidas connected with the " potlatch." One of these was tattooing. I had occasion to enter a lodge one morning shortly before a " potlatch " took place, and was not a little surprised to see all around the lodge men in every attitude undergoing this painful operation, some on the chest, some on the

SICKNESS AND TRIAL

back, and others on the arms, all being tattooed with the figures peculiar to their own crest, which in this instance was the eagle and the beaver, as they belonged to the eagle crest.

The operators were evidently quite expert in their work. Each of them had a number of thin strips of wood of various widths, in which needles were firmly fixed as teeth in a comb. Some of these sticks had but two or three needles, others more, according to the width of the pattern or device to be marked. The peculiar sound caused by such a number all pricking the skin of their subjects caused quite a nervous sensation in the bystander. Blood was flowing freely from many of them, and that it was rather a painful process was evidenced by their faces. Many were smoking, thus seeking to conceal their misery and console their feelings with the pipe. Others had their lips firmly compressed, but not one by either sign or sound indicated the painfulness of the process. That the subsequent suffering when inflammation had set in was severe I discovered by a number of them coming to me for some application to subdue the swelling and soothe the irritation. This was caused by the poisonous colours which had been rubbed in.

Not a few of the Haidas had their faces tattooed when I first went amongst them, and these reminded me strongly of the Maories of New Zealand, but the few of these who now remain are ashamed of the disfigurement, especially on embracing Christianity. When the "potlatch" took place these men who had been thus tattooed were rewarded by receiving blankets or other property proportionate to the honour which they had thus rendered to the chief. But yet worse practices were sometimes resorted to in the erection of the totem at a great "potlatch." It was not uncommon formerly, when the opening had been dug out in which the totem was to be erected, to bind one or more slaves, either male or female, and cast them alive into the opening. Then, amidst shouting and clamour which drowned

SICKNESS AND TRIAL

the cries of the victims, the great totem was hoisted up into position by hundreds of helpers and the opening around it filled in with stones and earth firmly beaten down.

On one occasion a young woman, a slave, fled to our mission over one hundred miles in order to escape such a terrible fate. The night before the day fixed for her destruction she succeeded in launching a small canoe unaided and unperceived, and fled. The punishments and privations which she had passed through had prostrated her, and although we used every means to restore her to health she succumbed to her injuries three weeks after her arrival. There was hope in her death, as we had with the assistance of another freed slave endeavoured to lead her to a saving knowledge of the Truth. With the introduction of the teachings of Christianity and the advance of civilisation the "potlatch" has been denuded of all its worst associations.

When the day for the great event has arrived all the property is brought forth and exhibited in heaps within and without the lodge. The guests are then arranged around according to the rank, their first or inner row being formed of the leading chiefs. Behind them sit the sub-chiefs or those of the second rank. Next appear the "haade" or free men. These are the counsellors to the chiefs. The next rows are arranged according to the social position in the tribe. On the outside are assembled the slaves. The presiding chief then delivers an introductory speech, recounting the rank and deeds of his ancestors and his own exploits and position amongst them. Not infrequently this opportunity is used to resent an insult either actual or supposed, or to inflict one. The chief's assistants, being sub-chiefs of his own crest, then call out the name of each recipient and the amount and description of property given.

Often large numbers of slaves were first given away, then copper shields, furs, blankets either in bale or numbered, guns, rifles, canoes, and latterly, as currency has become more common amongst them, both gold and silver is dis-

SICKNESS AND TRIAL

tributed; also whole pieces of print, white calico, and flannel. These latter are generally torn up in pieces and strips, and given away to the rank and file, as also blankets, &c. At one of the latest "potlatches," where I was permitted to enter and conduct a short service, I observed near to where I stood a wash-basin nearly full of silver, in one-dollar and half-dollar pieces, for the "potlatch." Much has been said and written, both for and against this custom, principally by outsiders who are unacquainted with the social life of the Indians. Having resided amongst them for three decades, and learned their languages, Tsimshean, Haida and Nishka, I can testify from knowledge and experience that the "potlatch" of to-day is not what it was in the past. The same may be said of the heathenism of the present as compared with that of a quarter of a century ago. Both have been reformed by the influence of Christianity. The tearing and devouring of dogs and human flesh was then almost a nightly practice in every heathen camp. Now it is unknown. Slavery has been abolished. Sorcery is ashamed to declare itself, and the medicine man has been denuded of all his terrors.

Notwithstanding, the "potlatch" is a hindrance to the advancement of the Indian. The tribe or band which follows it cannot become thrifty or prosperous. It is a barrier to industry. Note the number of weeks lost to the Indians when they assemble for the "potlatch." During this time they are almost constantly engaged in gambling. How are they clothed? For the most part they have only a dirty blanket thrown around them, and their habits are filthy, very seldom attempting to wash themselves or clothing. The heathen "potlatch" is incompatible with Christianity and civilisation. It tends to demoralise and degrade its followers, and it has been proved that the civilised and industrious Indian earns and expends five times more than the devotee who wastes his life in the practice of the "potlatch."

CHAPTER XI

IN PERILS BY WATERS

" He who 'mid the raging billows
Walked upon the sea,
Still can hush our wildest tempest
As on Galilee."

TOWARDS the end of March there was a stir in the camp. The canoe builders, who had been working on their canoes ever since the close of the great "potlatch," had finished their work, and all along the shore in front of the camp their canoes lay ready for launching. Some of them were large, some of medium size, and some small, ranging from fifty feet in length and six and a half feet beam, down to half this size and less. The largest were for ocean travelling and freight, and resembled the old war canoes; whilst those of medium size were used for hunting the fur seal and sea otter. All were perfect in outline and beautiful in construction. The late Admiral Prevost once remarked to me, when looking at a large Haida canoe, that it was as perfect in outline as an "Atlantic greyhound," which is the term commonly used to describe the large and fast steamers now running between Europe and America. And yet the Haidas were able before the advent of the white men to turn out their canoes as perfectly with their stone tools as they do now with steel.

During my stay on the islands a large war canoe was found in the forest almost completed, with the stone adzes, hammers, and chisels as left in it. It was concluded by

IN PERILS BY WATERS

the Haidas who found it that it was being constructed when the first great smallpox epidemic visited the islands, and all the workmen had perished. The stumps of some trees may still be pointed out which bear the unmistakable marks of having been cut down with the stone axe of the past.

In their canoes then, thus prepared, the Haidas were about to cross to the shores of the mainland. Their object was not, like that of the past, to kill and plunder and enslave, but rather to visit the great olachan fishery on the Naas River and procure a supply of the oil extracted from this little fish.

As my wife was suffering from a painful ailment, and I was anxious for a change on my own account as well as for our child after our recovery from typhoid, we determined to embark with them. Though our first winter had been a most trying time, yet we were not discouraged. We had succeeded, in the face of much opposition, especially from the medicine men, in establishing the Mission. I had gained an influence with several of the leading chiefs, two of whom had permitted me to conduct services in their lodges, which were the largest in the camp, and I had made considerable progress in acquiring a knowledge of the language. The fears of the captain of the steamer which had brought us over five months previously had proved unfounded, as instead of being murdered we were about to take our passage with the Haida fleet instead of waiting for his return. So, like the first great missionary, we were enabled " to thank God and take courage."

As the weather at this season of the year is usually rough and uncertain, consultations were held night and morning by the weather-wise among them, and at length, on the 29th of March, early in the morning some thirty large canoes started. The Haidas are as careful as courageous in their adventures on the ocean, and so meet with but few accidents in their canoe voyages. Before starting

IN PERILS BY WATERS

on a voyage they exchange their children and other relatives with one another for the occasion. This binds them together in a common interest, and unites them in the hour of danger when overtaken by a storm.

We started with a favourable wind, and had travelled through Dixon's Entrance to the north of the islands for some thirty miles, when suddenly we saw the leading canoes turning and heading for the shore near the north-eastern point of the islands known as "Rose Point" or "Rose Spit." All the fleet followed the leadership of those in front, and made for the shore also. On landing explanations were demanded by those who were anxious to proceed as to why the leaders had changed their course? Edenshew, the chief whose canoe had first turned, explained that he had seen a small cloud moving rapidly from the northeast, which had decided his action; and as they all knew that Edenshew was no mean authority in such matters, further explanations were unnecessary.

We had embarked with chief Weah in his large canoe. He was himself both steersman and captain. He no longer regarded me with suspicion. I had attended his aged mother, who could not have been far short of one hundred years old when she died. Her hair was as white as wool with age, a most unusual feature in an Indian. At her own request her friends had prepared a box-shaped coffin for her body long before she died, and this was placed alongside where she lay. I had acquired sufficient knowledge of the language to enable me to point her to Him who is "the Way, the Truth, and the Life." After this, notwithstanding the opposition of the medicine men, he had permitted me to conduct an occasional service in his great lodge. Probably, it had dawned upon him that after all I had not come too late, as he had asserted at my first visit. On this occasion he was accompanied by his two nieces, and the husband of the eldest, also two of his slaves, and our party, making a total of ten.

INDIAN WEAPONS

The upper horizontal club was carved by a Haida from a whale's jaw-bone. That beneath it is made by a Nishka Indian from an elk's horn. Clubs and double-headed daggers are on each side; between them are scalp caps and bead-work shields.

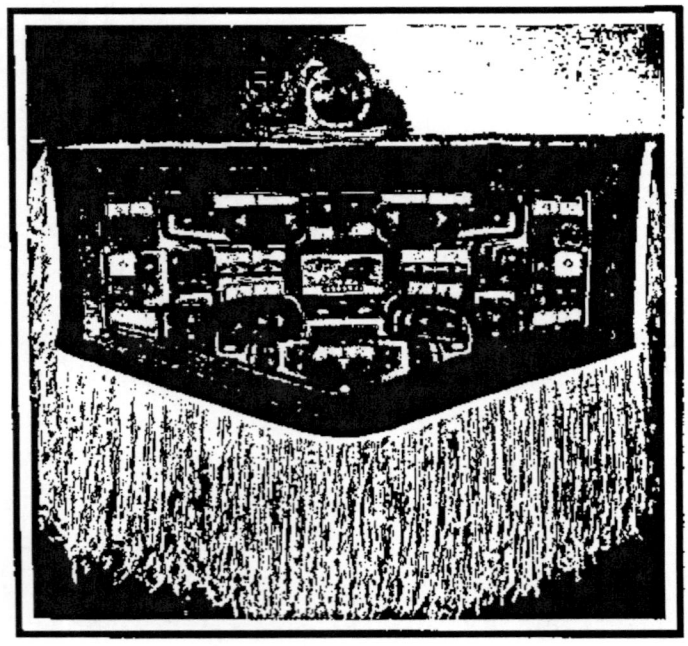

INDIAN CHIEF'S DRESS

The mantle was used only when dancing on state occasions. Above the mantle is seen a chief's head-dress, used at the same time.

IN PERILS BY WATERS

All was now bustle and excitement along the beach; discharging their freight, hauling up their canoes, erecting sails for shelter, and gathering wood for camp-fires, engaged the energy of all. After which, when all had settled down in groups around large fires, the cooking and preparation of the evening meal was proceeded with. We feasted on the flesh of the fur seal which some of the tribe had shot during the day. It is not so oily as the ordinary hair seal, and is therefore more palatable.

We had had a rather rough passage, and the children's caps had been carried off by the wind, as well as some loose articles, so that we were not sorry to land. I conducted a short service on the shore before all turned in for the night. It was a novel experience for the Haidas. The following morning the wind was fair but strong, which caused a heavy surf, and rendered embarkation difficult. One canoe, in endeavouring to get off, was smashed to pieces; the occupants with difficulty were rescued, but all their goods and effects were lost. They were left standing on the shore in dire distress, and nothing remained for them but to walk back again thirty miles to the nearest camp.

I saw that our canoe was likely to meet a similar fate, so, calling on two slaves and Macaie to assist me, we rushed into the surf, two of us on either side of the canoe, and held on to it, the incoming waves, as they rolled shoreward, lifting us with the canoe, but as the waves receded we were enabled to steady the subsidence of the canoe on the beach. Hastily embarking our party and effects, we watched our opportunity, and pushed out on the crest of a wave as it receded, and thus escaped the fate of our fellow voyagers. I was wet up to the waist, and, being unable to divest myself of my wet clothing, I wrapped a rug around me, and, seizing a paddle, I pulled vigorously in order to prevent a chill, as I had not quite recovered from the effects of the fever. But as the water had been intensely cold, I

IN PERILS BY WATERS

was seized with a severe cramp which lasted for about half an hour.

We continued to paddle for fourteen hours, when a good breeze sprang up, which increased to half a gale, and caused us to ship some water owing to the waves which broke over us, and this kept one of the slaves busy bailing it out. We reached the outer islands long past midnight, all weary, exhausted, and wet. Fortunately the children had fallen asleep, which rendered them unconscious of their misery. Owing to the heavy sea which had been running during the afternoon, all were so dizzy that we had to crawl up from the canoe on all fours. We kindled a fire, and I hastened to prepare some hot tea, but before it was ready all were sound asleep.

The following morning being Saturday, we re-embarked and, with a fine day and a favouring breeze, reached Fort Simpson at about 6 p.m., having been out just three days in making the passage. Finding no surgical aid available at Fort Simpson, I was compelled to perform a small operation, under which my wife fell away in a faint, but instant relief was afforded, and a good night's rest gained. Mr. and Mrs. Morrison, who were then in charge at the Fort, showed us every kindness, and under the care of this lady my wife rapidly regained strength and spirits.

The following day being Sunday, I conducted a Tsimshean service by special request in the Methodist Church, as the resident missionary was absent. A large number of my Haidas were present. This was the first occasion on which the Tsimsheans were addressed in their new church by a white missionary speaking to them in their own tongue, as their own missionary had not yet acquired their language sufficiently to speak without an interpreter. In the afternoon I conducted an open-air service for the Haidas on the shore in front of the Fort, a large number of Tsimsheans being also present. Here, on the very spot where they had formerly met in deadly strife in the con-

IN PERILS BY WATERS

flicts in the past, they were now united in learning the message of Him whose advent was first announced with " peace on earth and good will to men." On the following day we embarked for Metlakahtla, where we received a hearty welcome, though all were surprised at our having made the passage by canoe so early in the year.

Thus our first winter among the Haidas had been completed, and we had proved the promise of His presence, " Lo, I am with you all the days." In much weakness we had raised the banner of the Cross amongst the Haidas. We realised that the seed sown in weakness would yet be raised in power, and in this faith I at once commenced to make preparations to return as soon as possible, and erect a Mission-house on the islands. The remembrance of what we had endured in the " hut " during the preceding winter was a sufficient stimulus to rouse me to action.

But first I resolved to visit the Indians gathered at the olachan fishery on the lower Nass River, whither the Haidas had also gone. Here I renewed my acquaintance with the Tsimsheans, among whom I had laboured for several years. Here also I had the pleasure of meeting a brother missionary, the Rev. R. Tomlinson, and his wife, who had proved herself a faithful missionary and helpmeet to her husband in the Nishka Mission.

As we had no Mission-house then at the fishery, I spent my time amongst them, visiting from camp to camp, conducting services, and prescribing medicine for the sick. On my return to Metlakahtla, I engaged a Tsimshean Indian who could square timber and otherwise assist me in the erection of the proposed Mission-house' on the islands. As the Stikeen gold excitement was just then arising, we found that the steamer was on her way to Wrangle at the mouth of the Stikeen River with a large number of miners anxious to reach the new Eldorado in time to avail themselves of the favourable season.

Wrangle had been a large encampment of the Tlingit

IN PERILS BY WATERS

Indians, of which Kinnanook was the chief; but the arrival of a large number of miners and of those of doubtful character who generally follow such a rush, had not tended to benefit the tribe. Like the chiefs of many of the coast tribes, Kinnanook derived much profit from the inland Indians on the upper reaches of the river. These were not permitted to come down to the coast to trade their furs, but the chiefs near the mouth of the river of which Kinnanook was the head, supplied them with such articles as they most needed, and took their furs in exchange. From this the coast chiefs reaped a large revenue, as the furs from the interior are always superior to the furs obtained on the coast, and secure higher prices.

This is especially true of the marten, the mink, and the silver fox. The advent of the miners, and consequent opening up of the country, had effectually changed all this, as stores for the supply of the miners had been started on the upper river, and here the Indian hunters received a fair market value for their furs; and consequently their income had improved whilst that of the coast tribes had proportionately diminished. In addition, the introduction of strong drink, with all its attendant evils, had degraded many of the tribe, so that they were but little better than the Indians I had seen in the vicinity of the large white centres.

The United States Government had also stationed a garrison at this point, as also at Tongass and Sitka, and these, though preserving law and order along the Alaskan coast, had not tended to improve the moral condition of the Indians.

Finding that our steamer had to wait some hours for a party of miners expected from the interior, we decided to conduct a service. This was held in the head chief's house, and we were encouraged to see the Commandant of the garrison present, accompanied by one of his officers. They evinced much interest in the efforts to evangelise

IN PERILS BY WATERS

and elevate the Indian tribes. Afterwards, together with a Methodist missionary who was a fellow-passenger on the same steamer, we held an English service for the miners in a building known as the "Dance House." It was well filled by a most attentive audience, and at the close quite a number of those brave pioneers pressed forward to say good-bye. Several of them expressed their thanks, stating it might be their last opportunity, as they were going to an unknown region, and probably some of them would succumb to sickness and exposure there.

The Presbyterian Church of the United States not long after this established a Mission here, which was, I believe, the first Mission begun by the Churches of the United States in Alaska. The Alaskan coast tribes from Taku and Chilkat had begged for teachers some years previously during their trading visits to our Mission at Metlakahtla, and we had forwarded their petition, and pointed out their need in a letter to the American Board of Missions. This letter was signed by Messrs. Duncan, Tomlinson, and myself, as we were the only missionaries then labouring on the North-West coast.

As yet the Churches of the United States had not realised their responsibility and opportunity regarding Alaska. Now all the Churches of the States are labouring together in the work of evangelisation, and the United States Government has assisted their efforts in the work of education, and a large central Industrial Boarding School for Indian children has long been established at Sitka, and a similar institution had been established at Wrangle for girls, under Mrs. McFarlane, who was the first superintendent. It was a very necessary step in order to rescue them from the temptations with which the new order of things now surround them.

This institution was ably conducted by the lady missionaries, who did a good work in it, but after some years it was destroyed by fire. The names of Dr. Sheldon

IN PERILS BY WATERS

Jackson, Mrs. McFarlane, and the Rev. S. H. Young and D. F. McFarlane, with other courageous and self-denying labourers, deserve to be recorded as the pioneers of missionary work in Alaska. In connection with the Protestant Episcopal Church of the States, the labours of Bishop Rowe and his missionary staff are well known.

On my return to Massett, my first object was to select a suitable site for our proposed Mission-house. Reluctantly I was compelled to pass over the best sites, owing to the remains of the dead which were to be found scattered over the cleared land around the camp. We selected a site on a raised plateau on the edge of the forest behind the village, and succeeded in inducing a number of the young men to assist us in clearing it.

But the Haidas were not familiar with regular work, and we had to be content with an occasional spurt. I succeeded, however, in persuading some of them to procure me a raft of cedar logs, and, having provided myself with a whip saw, I constructed a saw-pit, and taught them how to saw every log just down the centre, having first hewn off two sides. In building I erected these, all being made equal in length, with the sawn sides turned inwards, thus giving me a smooth surface on the interior. By first placing the wall-plate in position, each upright was spiked to this, and thus my walls stood firm.

I was unfortunate, however, in my sawyers, as one after another they were seized with hæmorrhage, caused probably by the continual up and down motion of the arms acting upon the lungs. The medicine men were not slow in making use of this to my disadvantage, by assuring them that it was owing to my sorcery, as I was endeavouring to kill them.

With the aid of my Tsimshean, who was a good workman and a faithful Christian, I encouraged them to resume work. I had some difficulty in persuading them to rest on Sunday. Hitherto every day had been alike to them,

IN PERILS BY WATERS

and as my Dance House had now been transformed and prepared for our services, I was anxious to assemble as many as I could for instruction. Accordingly I had a flagstaff erected, and, having provided myself with two flags, one small and one large, I publicly announced that the smaller ensign would be displayed on the Saturday, whilst the large flag would be hauled up on the day of rest.

From this, Saturday became known as "Sunday ga hwitzoo," or "little Sunday," whilst the Sunday proper became known as "Shantlan shanzotang" or "the rest day." It is interesting to note in this connection that the Tsimsheans had learned to designate Sunday as "hali kanootk" or "the dress day" prior to the advent of the missionary; but under Christian teaching Sunday is known by a term similar in meaning to the Haida, viz. "hali squait-ka-sha," or "the day of rest." In the same way the Tsimsheans had acquired from the employees of the Hudson's Bay Company the idea that Christmas was the great dress day, or "Welaixim hali-kanootk," and from the Tsimsheans the Haidas had learned of this. Consequently my congregation at the first Christmas service on Queen Charlotte Islands was the most singular I have ever ministered to.

As the Dance House had been fully prepared for service, I sent out messengers to announce the service, and informed them of the occasion. I had induced two fine young chiefs, who had evinced their desire to help me, to act as stewards or sidesmen, and to preserve order.

As the Haidas began to crowd in, I was surprised at the strange garments in which many of them were clothed. A sub-chief entered arrayed in a dressing-gown with a large old-style pattern on it, reminding one of the garbs worn by the victims of the Inquisition when proceeding to an *auto da fè*. He was followed by his wife, with a bright counterpane fastened around her by a girdle of rope. Next my attention was attracted by musical sounds approaching,

IN PERILS BY WATERS

and a young lad, the son of a leading chief, entered in a harlequin's dress of many colours, trimmed around with many small bells, which jingled and tinkled with his every movement, and which attracted the attention of all. The next most striking figure was that of an old chief, gaunt and of great stature, dressed in an admiral's uniform, which was much too small for him. The sleeves of the coat only extended below his elbows, whilst the epaulettes stood out from his neck somewhat like a horse collar, and the trousers only reached a little below his knees. On the back of his head a tall beaver hat was fastened, to prevent it from falling off, as it was also too small. He evidently considered himself a most important personage, as he waited till one of the attendants approached and conducted him to a seat.

All shapes and colours of garbs were in evidence, especially naval and military uniforms of English and United States patterns. I was reminded rather of a fancy dress ball than of a congregation gathered for a religious service. But the most striking figure was yet to come. The building was crowded, and I had just stood up to commence the service, when the door was thrown open, and a leading medicine man appeared, arrayed in a white surplice. His long hair, significant of his craft, was rolled around a pair of horns, which extended out from either side of his head at the back, giving him a demoniacal appearance. He advanced steadily, without looking to either side, and made his way towards the platform on which I stood. Suddenly it flashed upon me that he considered it his right to occupy a place beside me, because of his robe of office. To my great relief, however, he stopped short, and took his seat just beside the platform.

With some difficulty I collected my thoughts, and proceeded with the service, which was indeed unique, whether as regarded the building, the congregation, or the occasion. They had obtained these dresses and uniforms by barter

IN PERILS BY WATERS

with the southern tribes during their annual expeditions to the south. The surplice which the medicine man appeared in had probably been stolen, and then sold to the Indians. But these showed that they were beginning to realise the necessity of something more suitable in which to array themselves than a bearskin or a blanket. And I never saw these again. Before the next Christmas came round, the Haidas had become more enlightened in regard at least to dress.

One of their objections to the reception of the truths of Christianity was that it had impoverished the Indians who had abandoned the "potlatch" and the old heathen customs, and had accepted it. "Formerly," I was told, "the Tsimshean lodges were well furnished with boxes all filled with blankets and other property, but now their chests are empty. Our chests are well filled now, but, if we become Christians, we too shall be poor." "Yes," I replied, "but the Tsimsheans have all good clothing now, both for Sundays and dress days, and also for working in, and their houses are more comfortable and better furnished. This is better than heaping up blankets for the 'potlatch.' And after a 'potlatch' you are really poor, for you have given away all you had."

This lesson was learned, if not then, yet afterwards. For the Haidas as heathen were the most cleanly in their habits of any tribes on the coast. And as Christians they are yet in the van.

CHAPTER XII

A CANOE CATASTROPHE

"So on I go not knowing, I would not if I might;
I'd rather walk in the dark with God,
Than go alone in the light.
I'd rather walk by faith with Him
Than go alone by sight."
—M. G. BRAINARD.

OUR Mission-house was fast approaching completion when one day I was surprised to hear a cry of "Yetz haada!" "Yetz haada!"—"A white man!" "A white man!" Proceeding towards the shore, I saw a white man disembark from a canoe which had just arrived. I found he was a chief factor of the Hudson's Bay Company. He was on a tour of inspection, and on arrival at Fort Simpson had heard that I had crossed several times to the Queen Charlotte Islands by canoe, and, being anxious to visit the post there, he decided to make the passage in the same way. Accordingly he engaged a canoe and a crew of six Tsimshean Indians, one of whom, a chief named Shashak, was the owner of the canoe and captain.

As he informed me that he intended remaining about a fortnight on the islands, I arranged to accompany him on his return to the mainland, together with the Tsimshean whom I had brought over. He was very much gratified at this arrangement, as he had found it difficult to communicate with his captain and crew, not knowing anything of their language, whilst they knew nothing of Chinook, which is the trading jargon of the Company with the Indians. He was present at the Haida services on the

A CANOE CATASTROPHE

Sunday, and was much surprised at the large congregation of Haidas, and the order and attention manifested. But my arrangement to accompany him on his return to the mainland was frustrated in a remarkable manner. Whilst seated at breakfast early one morning, suddenly a violent gale burst in from the south-east. The first gust shook our shanty, and carried away the chimney of our stove. I called to my assistant to follow me, and rushed away to have the rafters, which had been just erected, braced and secured. But on reaching the ridge which afforded a view of our new building, a yet stronger gust came which almost lifted me off the ground, and instantly I saw the first pair of rafters giving way and falling against the next pair, which in turn gave way in like manner, bearing down the next, and with the increasing momentum of the weight and wind the whole fourteen pair of rafters fell with a crash which threatened the destruction of the entire building. The Haidas came rushing up in large numbers, and with them came my white friend and his Tsimshean crew. A large shoal of dogfish had been stranded on the shore during the preceding night, and the Haidas had been engaged in gathering them in heaps when the gale struck, and they had been attracted by the noise of the falling building.

I came down from where I had been inspecting the damage, and informed my friend that I had abandoned all hope of embarking with him, as I could not now leave the structure until the damage had been repaired. He was greatly disappointed, and trusted my Haida workmen might by themselves re-erect the fallen rafters. But this was not the only injury, as in their fall they had strained the entire framework and forced the lower walls out of-plumb. So that I could not alter my decision. I little thought then that life or death depended on it. But so it proved.

Early on the morning of the following Friday, he embarked with his crew of six Tsimsheans. But they

A CANOE CATASTROPHE

never reached their destination. When about thirty-five miles from Massett, the wind increased and veered round to the south, raising a rough sea, and being anxious to sail close to the wind in order to reach Dundas Island, they hoisted a second sail on their canoe. This proved too great a strain for the craft, and a strong gust of wind striking it at the same moment with a heavy sea, the upper part of the canoe was wrenched from the lower, and all the occupants were left struggling in the waves.

I had called on him the evening before he embarked, and endeavoured to dissuade him from starting, as I apprehended boisterous weather. My little aneroid, which had often proved useful to me in my voyages, had been steadily falling, and a bank of fog hung over the valley behind the camp. This to the Haidas was always a sign of bad weather.

But yet another cause had induced me to visit the dwelling in which my friend and his crew were encamped. He had been anxious to witness a Haida dance, as he informed the officer in charge of the post that, judging from the influence I was gaining amongst them, there would be but little hope of again witnessing such a performance in the future. I regretted his action, for I knew all the baneful practices of heathenism with which such a dance was associated. A few responded, but these were paid, and amongst those who declined to be present were his entire crew, with only one exception.

Admiring their consistency, I invited my Tsimshean workman to accompany me, and together we conducted an evening service of prayer and praise. Before we had concluded, our friends returned from the dance, and beat a hasty retreat when they found how we were engaged. Probably none of them surmised that it would be their last opportunity for such a service again on earth. But may we not believe they were but tuning their hearts to join in the spiritual praises of the inner sanctuary.

A CANOE CATASTROPHE

The only survivor informed me afterwards that when tossed about on the waves, lashed to a piece of broken canoe, the memories of that prayer meeting encouraged him to struggle on, and he never abandoned hope.

It appeared, from this man's account of the wreck, that after the canoe had broken up they all clung to it, and succeeded in lashing the pieces together with the sail ropes. Some of them were enabled to climb up on the broken canoe and paddle a little, whilst the others (including the Hudson's Bay Company's officer and the chief) clung to the wreck with only their hands and shoulders out of the water.

Our white friend, Mr. Williams, realising that they were face to face with death, nobly rose to the occasion, and called upon his crew to join him in song. And there amid the storm they raised the song of praise which has been so often used on similar occasions:

> " Jesus, lover of my soul,
>   Let me to Thy bosom fly,
> While the nearer waters roll,
>   While the tempest still is high ;
> Hide me, O my Saviour, hide,
>   Till the storm of life is past;
> Safe into the haven guide,
>   O, receive my soul at last."

The Indians knew this old familiar hymn, as it was among the earliest translated. He then took off his hat, and, casting it upon the water, called upon the Indians to join him in prayer. And whilst he prayed in English, they responded in their own tongue, the Tsimshean; after which he cried "Good - bye, boys," and, relinquishing his hold upon the wreck, floated for a few moments and then disappeared. Shortly after, the chief, whose canoe it was, fell off exhausted with the waves which were washing over them, thus leaving five of them hanging on to the broken canoe.

As the evening drew on, and the shades of night began

A CANOE CATASTROPHE

to gather, one of them became demented, and, notwithstanding the efforts of the others to prevent him, drew his hunting-knife from his belt and severed the ropes which held the wreck together. The canoe thereupon fell asunder, three of the natives clinging to one part (one of whom was the Indian who had thus divided them), whilst the survivor, with another, drifted away upon the other section of the broken canoe. For a short time each party could see the other now and again as they rose on the crest of a wave, and then they were lost to sight, to meet no more in this life.

We shall record the story of the survivor in his own words: "My companion then began to talk at random, and to pray to the sea-gulls which sometimes flew around us, crying to them to save him. And although we were far from land (only the mountains of Prince of Wales Island, in Alaska, showing, as we were tossed up on the waves), yet I had always a presentiment that I would be saved. Some words that you spoke in the address you gave us the evening before we embarked remained in my memory and encouraged me to hope. I had lashed myself to the wreck shortly after we had parted from our friends, and it was well I did so, as, when night fell, I lost consciousness.

"Early in the morning I was aroused to consciousness again by the warmth of the sun, and found myself still lashed to the piece of the wreck which had been drifted on a point of rock to the south of Prince of Wales Island. I was in a stupor, and thought it was a dream. But as I looked at my surroundings, and found that I was lashed to the piece of broken canoe, my memory returned with all the terrible experiences of the preceding day, and I realised that I was saved.

"Just then I was aroused from my reverie by a wave of the rising tide washing over my feet, and I felt that the sea might yet overtake and engulf me. My first effort

A CANOE CATASTROPHE

was to detach myself from the portion of the wreck, but I found that my body was so sore and my hands and feet so numb that I could not move them. But I struggled resolutely, and at length succeeded in cutting the lashings which bound me, and then inch by inch I crawled up the rocks, barely keeping in advance of the rising tide, until I reached the high-water mark, where I knew I was safe. Here I found the skin and bones of a deer which had been devoured by the wolves, and I seized a bone and endeavoured to break it on the rocks in order to suck the marrow, but I failed from weakness and exhaustion.

"I then gnawed the skin, and continued to do so until I fell asleep with the exertion. I must have slept twenty-four hours, for when I awoke it was morning again, and I was so refreshed with the rest that I was enabled to creep along the shore and seek for roots. These I ate, but my thirst was so intense that I felt I should die unless I found water. I found a little rain water in the hollow of a rock above the tide-mark, which, though rendered brackish by the spray, yet quenched my thirst. Soon I was enabled to stand and walk a little, though with pain. My first thought was to know how to move away from this barren and lonely shore, and I determined to construct a raft with driftwood, of which there was an abundance in the bays and fissures amongst the rocks. But whilst engaged in cutting some green withes and branches with which to lash my raft together, I stumbled against a small canoe which was hidden away in the undergrowth. It had been left there by the fur seal hunters, and I knelt down and thanked God for it, as I felt it was left specially for me."

Such was the story of his escape from the death which befell all his friends and fellow-voyagers. He succeeded in launching his canoe and provisioned himself with shell-fish, and by coasting along in calm spells he reached an encampment from which all the Indians were absent. He succeeded in entering one of the houses by removing a board in the

A CANOE CATASTROPHE

wall, but failed to find any food. Continuing his journey, he at length reached a village of the Tlingit Indians. A number of them came down and looked at the strange arrival with astonishment. And well they might. Almost naked, with his face and arms skinned from the friction with the broken canoe and the long immersion in the salt water, his own friends could not have known him. As their language was unknown to him, he inquired in the Chinook jargon if any of them had been to Port Simpson lately? They replied in the affirmative, and, probably suspecting the connection, informed him that the Tsimsheans were uneasy about six of their fellow-tribesmen who had accompanied a white man in a voyage to the Queen Charlotte Islands, but had not returned, though long overdue. He then informed them in a few words of the loss of the entire party except himself, and begged them to convey him to Port Simpson, where they should be well rewarded by his tribe.

They carried him up to their camp, and prepared food for him. Whilst partaking of it he fainted away, and on reviving he found a medicine man with his rattle and enchantments practising over him. He beckoned to him to cease, and informed them he had no faith in the heathen customs as he was a Christian, but repeated his request to be conveyed to his tribe. They acceded to his request, and, strange to relate, he was brought to Port Simpson at the same hour that I arrived at Metlakahtla, having passed over the same route which they had attempted: 117 miles in fifteen hours. We had had a narrow escape, as in a rough sea, with a new and untried canoe, an alarm was raised that our frail craft had split in falling from a wave into the trough of the sea. Instantly all was commotion, and the sail was at once lowered and taken down, whilst signals for help were made to the nearest canoe.

On their arrival we transferred some of our freight to them, and examined our canoe for the damage. It had

HAIDA TOMB

The two side-posts are solid and fixed in the ground. The horizontal piece is hollow, and contains the square box into which the corpse has been tightly packed

HAIDA WAR CANOES

The top figure represents an old-style canoe; the lower, a more recent design. These canoes were sometimes 72 feet long, and carved out of a single cedar trunk.

A CANOE CATASTROPHE

been caused by the strain on a weak spot where three knots in the wood in a straight line rendered it liable to split under a strain of weather or in a heavy sea. We changed with our luggage to the other canoe, and continued our journey, making our destination in record time; only to find that our friends, who had left ten days in advance of us, had never arrived. I had given them letters to friends on the mainland, but they had not been delivered. The following morning, whilst making preparations to send off a party of Indians to make inquiry along the coast, a large canoe, fully manned, was seen approaching, and the manner in which they were paddling betokened that they carried important tidings. It was to inform me of the arrival of the survivor, and of his report of the loss of all who had accompanied him, and also to beg of me to return with them, as they feared their friend would not survive his lengthened exposure and hardships. They had learned of my arrival from a canoe which had left Massett with me, and as the rumour had spread that I had also been lost, there was much excitement.

I accompanied them to Fort Simpson, and found the survivor very weak and unable to speak above a whisper. His face, arms, and legs were skinned and bruised with his long exposure and struggle for life. I remained with him, and attended to him until he was out of danger. Thus, owing to the damage wrought by the sudden gale of that June morning, which at the time was regarded as a misfortune, we were prevented from embarking on a journey which would most probably have proved fatal to us, as it had to all the ill-fated occupants of the canoe with this striking exception. And it was indeed fortunate that his life was spared, as had all perished, the Tsimsheans would most surely have believed that they had perished at the hands of their old foes, the Haidas; and thus strife and bitterness would have arisen which might have caused the sacrifice of many lives.

CHAPTER XIII

RETURN TO QUEEN CHARLOTTE ISLANDS

" Once Thy servants toil'd in rowing,
  On the Galilean Sea,
Waves rose high, rough winds were blowing,
  How they longed, O Lord, for Thee :
Lord, still toil thy sons and daughters,
  On the world's dark troubled sea,
And 'mid roars of winds and waters,
  Still they look and long for Thee."

HAVING prepared such things as were necessary for the completion of the Mission-house, I seized the opportunity of the return of the Haida fleet to the islands to accompany them. There was but one canoe that I cared to travel by, which was that belonging to Chief Edenshew and his son Cowhoe, with several of his slaves as crew. All the others were old canoes, which the Haidas had taken in part exchange for the new canoes which they had brought over from the Islands for sale or barter. This they did regularly year by year. As they gradually abandoned their marauding and slave-hunting expeditions, they applied themselves principally to canoe building, when not engaged in the pursuit of the sea otter and fur seal. The fine red cedar trees which attain such immense proportions on the Queen Charlotte Islands afforded ample material for the development of their ability in the building and construction of the finest canoes in the world. It was this advantage and ability, united to their fierce and warlike disposition, which made them the pirates of the coast in the past. A whole fleet of new canoes are brought

QUEEN CHARLOTTE ISLANDS

over annually, and sold to the mainland Indians, one proviso demanded in the payment being an old canoe or derelict, in which to make the return voyage to the Islands. Having obtained the old canoes, they set themselves to repair and strengthen them, and then, filling them with cargoes of fish grease and other provisions, they make the return journey by coasting along the south-eastern shores of Alaska until Cape Muzon or Chacon is reached. Here they encamp, and await a favourable opportunity to sail across to the north of the Queen Charlotte Islands. On the Sunday before we started, as a large number of the Alaskan Indians had arrived from Chilcat and Taku, I conducted services for them and the Haidas in the Market-house. I spoke in Tsimshean, whilst two interpreters rendered my words, one in Thlingit and the other in Haida. Thus these three nationalities—Tsimshean, Haida, and Tlingit—so long separated and opposed to one another, were being drawn together by the glorious Gospel, the key-note of which from the beginning has been " Glory to God in the highest, and on earth peace, good will to men."

On reaching Fort Simpson we found a number of Haidas there ready to accompany us, and so on the following morning all embarked for the Alaskan shores. We reached Tongas, the most south-easterly Indian encampment in Alaska and close to Kannaganoot and Sitklan Islands, only separated from them by the narrow channel which the Alaskan Boundary Commission declined to make the dividing line at this point. Instead, it was ruled that the channel to the eastward of these islands was the proper outlet of Portland Canal, thus allotting these islands to Alaska. But Wales and Pearce Islands, which had formerly been regarded as Alaskan, and were so marked on Governor Trutch's maps of 1872, were by the same Commission secured to British Columbia. The Tlingit tribe of Indians at Tongas were formerly numerous, and their chief is mentioned in Captain Meares' *Voyages* as " Kinnanook," which is the same name by which his successor was known when I visited it. This tribe was the first to find out the way of manufacturing the " hootchino," or fire water. It had been acquired by them from a soldier who had been discharged, or who had deserted from the United States garrison which had been stationed for a short time near this point. Almost every Indian lodge in the camp possessed a still. This was generally made up of coal oil cans, the worm being long hollow tubes of kelp, a species of seaweed, joined together. In their drunken carousals recourse was generally had to their fire-arms to settle their disputes. This chief, Kinnanook, with two of his men, had been brought to us at Metlakahtla on one occasion severely wounded. He had received three bullets in his side, each of which had found a separate exit. For weeks he was unable to lie down, and could only rest and sleep by inclining forward on a form placed across his bed, which was on the floor. When at length he was so far restored as to be enabled to return to his tribe, he carried with him quite a number of pieces of shattered bone which had been extracted from his wounds. Being as yet a heathen, he feared that any medicine man or sorcerer obtaining a scrap of bone belonging to him could by witchcraft accomplish his destruction. In consequence of the care and kindness shown on that occasion, I was invited to his lodge, and hospitably entertained. His father, a venerable-looking old chief named Andah, was still living. His hair was as white as wool, which is but seldom seen among Indians. He was evidently well cared for by his daughter, whom I had known previously, as she had made an unhappy union with a Nishka chief, which caused her on one occasion to make an attempt on her own life. This old chief, her father, died some time after my visit. He had adopted the name of " Ebbits," from the captain of some ship whose acquaintance he had made and whom he admired. Before his death he had a great totem pole prepared and erected, and on a

QUEEN CHARLOTTE ISLANDS

tablet near this totem is inscribed, "To the memory of Ebbits, Head Chief of the Tongas, who died in 1880, aged 100 years." The Haidas who accompanied me numbered some thirty canoes, and they were all received and lodged in the camp. We arrived on the Saturday, and on the following day, being Sunday, I was enabled to conduct two services and a Sunday school at mid-day. Here again I had the Indians of three languages present. I preached in Tsimshean and in Chinook. Knowing the serious mistakes which some speakers have fallen into when using Chinook, I have always declined to use it except when unavoidable. It is related of the late Bishop of Columbia, Dr. Hills, that on his first visit to Nanaimo the Indians assembled to meet him, when he addressed them in English, which was translated to them in Chinook. "Children of the forest," he began, which was rendered, "Tenas tilicum mitlite kopa stick," or "Little men stationed among the sticks." After such an introduction, the Bishop must have been discouraged by the lack of interest manifested by the Indians in his address. It no doubt conveyed a very different impression to that intended by the good Bishop.

I was thankful at the close of the day that I had thus had an opportunity of proclaiming the message of salvation to the three nationalities—Tsimshean, Haida, and Tlingit—in a camp where heathenism had so long held undisputed sway. As I had learned from Chief Edenshew that the Haidas could not leave for a day or two, I determined to pay a flying visit to Metlakahtla to greet our good friend, Admiral Prevost, who had arrived on a visit after my departure. Finding that Edenshew and Cowhoe were both desirous to see the Admiral also, whom they had not met since the time when, as captain of H.M.S. *Virago*, he had threatened to shell their encampment for the destruction of the American schooner *Susan Sturges*, I invited them to accompany me. Accordingly, we embarked at midnight, and, favoured by a fair wind, we reached

Metlakahtla early the following morning, having run some thirty-five miles. We found the camp in holiday dress, with flags flying and Indians rejoicing at the visit of the Admiral. Together with my Haida friends, I joined in the welcome, which was warmly reciprocated by the Admiral. I introduced Chief Edenshew to him, and reminded him of the difficulty he had when, as captain of H.M.S. *Virago*, he visited this chief's camp on Virago Sound. Indeed, it was from this visit that the Sound had received its name. Edenshew and his tribe had been involved in the capture of the *Susan Sturges* and her crew, as well as in other raids. He could, at that time, boast of possessing a larger number of slaves than any other chief on the Islands. But now he no longer feared to face a naval officer, as he had learned not only to obey the law himself, but to lead his tribe to do the same. The Admiral was delighted to learn that the Haidas were abandoning the war-path and devoting themselves to follow the path of peace. We re-embarked early on the morning of the following day (Tuesday), and, favoured by a breeze from the southeast, which gradually increased to a squall, we reached Tongas at noon. As we approached the shore, we were surprised to find that of some thirty Haida canoes which we had left drawn up on the beach, not one was now to be seen. We at once apprehended mischief. Our fears were increased on seeing canoes of the Tongas who appeared outside their lodges with their faces blackened.

Instructing the Haida chiefs to remain in the canoe, prepared to put off at once, I walked up to the chief's house, and, entering, inquired the cause of the disappearance of the Haidas. I was informed that after I had left at midnight on the Sunday, one of their men had brought out some "hoochino," or "fire water," and had dealt it out to his Haida guests. He then offered to sell a quantity and found many purchasers. They continued drinking until almost all of them were intoxicated. In this state

QUEEN CHARLOTTE ISLANDS

a Haida entered the chief's house, he being absent at the time, and, seizing a seat, hurled it at the chief's old father. He might have killed him had the seat struck him on the head, but fortunately he was able to ward off the blow, but, in so doing, his arm and shoulder were badly bruised and lacerated. Had Kinnanook been in the camp at the time, he would have shot his father's assailant at sight. This would have caused the Haidas to have taken to their guns, and much loss of life would have ensued on both sides, as not many years previously the Haidas had made a raid on this camp, and after many had been killed on either side the Haidas had succeeded in capturing a number whom they carried off into slavery. Fortunately there were several of the Haidas who had refused the liquor and remained sober. One of these, a sub-chief, instantly seized and ejected the offender. Then, calling several of his friends to his aid, he brought a peace-offering of fifty trading blankets and a new gun, which he laid before the old chief. This done, they called on all who were sufficiently sober to aid in launching the canoes, and, hurriedly shipping their freight and effects, they cast in those who were unable to care for themselves, and put off to sea, so that before the dawn of the following day they had left the Tongas camp far behind. Thus the few who had remained sober had saved the situation, and wiped out the disgrace by the timely peace-offering thus made. Nevertheless, as I reminded those of them who had gathered around me to relate the grievance, the mischief had originated with themselves in introducing the liquor. The daughter of the injured chief agreed with me, and expressed her satisfaction that Kinnanook was away at the time, as, being of a hasty temper, he would at once have sought revenge for the insult and injury inflicted on his father in his own camp and dwelling.

Without further delay we re-embarked in search of the fleet, but did not come up with them for two days. When at length we sighted them they were emerging from the bays and shelters where they had encamped. The majority of them had their faces blackened, and were evidently prepared to fight had they been followed. As the weather was unsettled, we put into a small harbour near Cape Chacon, a point which has latterly become widely known as being the starting-place of the Alaskan boundary line. Here we remained weather bound for a fortnight. Day by day passed without any abatement of the frequent squalls from the south-west. At length our food supply having run out, we were compelled to gather shell-fish and crabs for our sustenance. The time was not lost, however; I found special opportunity whilst thus encamped with the Haidas, both in the acquirement of the language, and also in imparting instruction to them. As Chief Edenshew was a fluent Tsimshean speaker, he was able to assist me in this. Some of them learned to sing songs of praise during that period which I often heard afterwards when in camp.

At length, at daybreak one morning, there was a stir in the camp. I arose hurriedly, and found all busy launching canoes and embarking their freight. It was a fair morning, but on looking at my aneroid I found it had fallen during the night, and the dark clouds which were rising in the south-west betokened bad weather. It is a clear run of some forty miles across Dixon's Entrance from Cape Chacon to Massett. It was just 4.30 in the morning when we started, and with a beam wind for the first five hours we made good progress. We had just reached a point in mid-ocean, when a strong south-westerly squall burst upon us from the Pacific. It was accompanied by a driving rain, and in a short time every sail was lost to view. The sea arose, and great waves crested with foam threatened continually to swamp our frail craft. As the large boxes of fish grease broke loose from their fastenings, they were tossed about, until their lids were loosened and fell off. Then every wave that struck us caused the grease to splash forth over every-

QUEEN CHARLOTTE ISLANDS

thing. I was soaked with it from head to foot. When the storm broke, I had divested myself of all but my underclothing, and put on my life-belt, which I had provided myself with for long canoe journeys.

The Chief Edenshew, who was a good seaman and was steering, reminded me that it would only prolong my misery if we were capsized, as I could never reach the shore. I reminded him that none of the bodies of those lately lost had been found, whereas a life-belt would probably have floated anyone wearing it to the shore, whether dead or alive. This statement satisfied him, as he concluded that should we be wrecked my body would enable those finding it to realise their fate, as well as mine. Just then the chief's son, Cowhoe, arose in the canoe, and called upon us to assist him in casting the grease boxes, with what grease remained in them, overboard. A huge wave struck us at the time, and he was well nigh gone, but by clinging to the thwart he was saved. We were all opposed to casting the grease overboard, as it not only ballasted the canoe, but also the grease, as it was washed overboard smoothed the waves, and prevented them from breaking over us in full force. By bailing out the water with buckets as it washed into the canoe, and with but two feet of sail to the wind, we ploughed onwards. Every wave threatened to engulf us, and as we could only see a few yards ahead, we feared we might be running towards the dangerous shoal to the north-east of the islands named Rose Spit. It was about nine-thirty when the squall struck us, and at about one hour after noon it began to lift, and we found to our great relief that we were not far out of our course. We were also enabled to sight some of the other canoes which had outlived the squall, though they had lost in the property which they had been compelled to cast overboard. Large numbers of the Haidas came down to the beach to see us land, and with them came also my old friend the trader : " Whatever caused you to venture on the ocean in such weather as this ? " he

QUEEN CHARLOTTE ISLANDS

inquired. "Our provisions ran short," I informed him. "Well," said he, "you are a desperate man. You are determined to die in the water." "Squire," I replied, "how would you like to be encamped on the rocky shores of Alaska for days without any food but shell-fish?" I asked. "Not at all," he replied, "yet to be drowned is worse"; and, having thus declared himself, he turned and walked off grumbling about "desperate men" and "great dangers." But we realised that He who had calmed the angry waves of the Galilean sea had been with us, and His blessed assurance, "Be of good cheer, it is I, be not afraid," encouraged us when otherwise heart and strength were failing.

CHAPTER XIV

FIRST VISIT TO SKIDEGATE

> "Sow in the morn thy seed,
>   At eve hold not thy hand;
> To doubt and fear give thou no heed,
>   Broadcast it o'er the land.
> Thou knowest not which may thrive,
>   The late or early sown;
> Grace keeps the chosen germ alive,
>   When and wherever strown."
> —MONTGOMERY.

"Cast thy bread upon the waters: for thou shalt find it after many days."—*Ecclesiastes* xi. 1.

ASSOCIATION and companionship with many of the Haidas when travelling with them, both in storm and sunshine, had led to a measure of mutual confidence. Like most Indians, they were pleased to see that the white man could endure hardship just as well as they themselves could. I had travelled with them in their canoes, had shared in their dangers, had partaken of their peculiar dishes, and by so doing I had gained an influence of which the medicine men and their followers were jealous. Consequently I was not greatly surprised when secretly informed one night by a young chief that the medicine men were plotting to take my life. They had used all their enchantments, and had even succeeded in obtaining some articles of clothing belonging to me over which they had exhausted all their orgies in vain. And now they had summoned all the young men to drink of the salt water in order to ascertain if all were faithful to them. This man, in order to escape

FIRST VISIT TO SKIDEGATE

the penalty, had hidden in the forest, from which he had now ventured under cover of the darkness to apprise me of their designs. They discovered him, however, on the following day, and, having bound him hand and foot, he was carried down to the sea, and submerged again and again until almost drowned, in order to compel him to swallow a sufficient quantity of the salt water. It is believed and asserted by the necromancers that the salt water will kill and expel the evil spirit which is causing trouble in the camp, and should anyone shrink from the ordeal the accusation is sure to fall upon him. Hence the friends and relations of this young chief were the most eager to discover him, and compel him to undergo the test, in order to deliver him from the ban of the medicine men, which often resulted fatally to the accused.

This practice of drinking large quantities of salt water is not only followed to divert suspicion of guilt when trouble is abroad in the camp, but also when about to set out on a warlike expedition. In the war that occurred between the Northern Haidas and Tsimsheans some time prior to the establishment of Missions on the coast, the story is told that when the Haidas of Massett determined to attack the Tsimsheans in return for injuries inflicted upon some of their people by the latter, they banded together and began to drink sea water. After drinking this for six nights, they set out to war in ten canoes. When they reached the mainland, some stopped at Quado in Metlakahtla Inlet. Whilst concealed there, they attacked a number of canoes which were passing to Kshwahtlins and Kloiyah, two fishing stations near to the present site of Prince Rupert, and in one day these Haidas captured and destroyed seven canoes and killed about twenty-eight of the Tsimsheans. This was in revenge for the injuries inflicted by the Tsimsheans on them in the early summer, when they had visited Port Simpson to trade. Latterly I have seen the sea water drunk by the Haida hunters when about to embark in quest of the

FIRST VISIT TO SKIDEGATE

fur seal and sea otter. It was just at this time, when I was harassed and discouraged by the evil devices of the medicine men, that a little incident occurred which served to encourage me. The young chief Cowhoe came to me one day, bringing with him a little book. "Some years ago," he said, "when the fighting fire-ship came here to punish us for having seized the American schooner, and to set the crew whom we had enslaved free, the captain called me to him, and spoke kindly to me, though I did not know what he said, as he spoke in the white man's tongue. Then he brought me this book, which he wrote in before he handed it to me. I have kept it carefully in my box ever since, and now I have brought it to you so that you may tell me what it is, and what the words are which he has written in it."

I took the book, and found it was a copy of the New Testament as published by the "Naval and Military Bible Society," London. On the fly-leaf was written: "To the Indian Boy, Edenshew's son. I trust that the bread cast upon the waters will soon be found.—James C. Prevost, Captain, H.M.S. *Satellite*, 1859."

"How wonderful!" I exclaimed, as I looked from the book to its owner, and realised that the good captain's desire and prayer were being fulfilled. Not just as he would have had it, "soon," but just as it had been promised, "after many days." For eighteen years had passed away, and now at length the bread was being found indeed. "Why, this," I said, "is just the good news that I have been telling you and your people. This is the word of 'Sha-nung-Etlageda,' the word of the Chief Above!"

"Is it indeed?" he exclaimed. "Is it really so, and I never knew it. I was foolish then, I was but a small boy, and I had almost forgotten it. But your arrival, and your words seem to have reminded me of it. I must endeavour to learn to read it now."

I took it out of his hand again, and turned to a text I

FIRST VISIT TO SKIDEGATE

had just been teaching them. It was St. John's Gospel, the third chapter, and the sixteenth verse. This I read to him, first in English, and then in the Haida: " Alzeil Sha Nung Etlagedas hahada wautliwan il quoyada uan, alzeil Laou'l Keet an swanshung tlak Laou'l ishthian alzeil wautliwan kestho Laou'l yetang, kum l goowangshang waigen hininga et shwanung shang laou'l keyiyen." " And are these words really there?" he asked; "and I have had it so long, and yet did not know it, but now I shall learn to read it myself." And as he carried away his prize with a face beaming with satisfaction, I was reminded of another passage from the inspired word, " Thy words were found, and I did eat them, and Thy word was unto me the joy and rejoicing of my heart." From that time he became one of my most attentive and persevering pupils. Being a chief, and the son of a leading chief, his influence was powerful for good, especially among his own tribe and those of his crest. It was just at this time that an old chief came to me begging that I should go and see one of his slaves, who he feared was dying. He informed me that the medicine men had exerted all their powers over him, but had failed to afford him any relief. I informed him that I was willing to act if only he could send away the medicine men. I had decided to keep to this condition, as I found that, when I had prescribed medicines, if the patient recovered they claimed the credit, whereas if the symptoms increased or the patient died they accused me as the cause. I accompanied him to see the patient, and found his face and head swollen to such an extent that his features were unrecognisable. It was a case of facial erysipelas, and, as the fever and inflammation ran high, the rattling and whooping of the medicine men had worked him up to a high fever of nervous excitement. Indeed he was almost demented. I therefore repeated my decision, and the old chief who evidently feared to offend the medicine men, promised to do what he could. He came to me shortly after, and informed

FIRST VISIT TO SKIDEGATE

me that he had induced them by large payments of property to cease their treatment. I at once had his slave's long hair cut off, applied blisters behind the ears and to the scalp, had his feet and legs kept in mustard and hot water, and administered suitable medicines, and in twenty-four hours the symptoms began to abate. In a few days he had recovered. It was a clear victory, and the medicine men were furious. The impression made on the old chief was deep and lasting. He lost all faith in the powers of the medicine men, and both he and his slave Kowtz became catechumens. The following winter this chief fell sick and died, but not before he had called a number of his tribe, and declared before them all that he had given Kowtz his liberty. This he did at my suggestion. It caused some excitement amongst the slave-owners, who feared that such action would produce discontent amongst their slaves. Sometime after his chief's death, Kowtz, fearing that he might be enslaved again, procured a stone for erection in memory of his master, and on it was inscribed his dying words, in which he granted this man his freedom. This he regarded as the charter of his liberty. The old chief had himself by faith obtained true freedom in Christ, and had been baptized.

I now made arrangements for a visit to the south of the Islands, and engaged Chief Edenshew and his son Cowhoe, with a crew of his young men, to accompany me in a large canoe. The distance from Massett to Skidegate is about a hundred and twenty miles by water, as it is necessary to stand well out from the north-easterly point of the island. We were met by strong south-easterly gales, which compelled us to encamp for several days at Cape Ball, known to the Haidas as "Altlin's Kwun." On reaching Skidegate we were well received. A band of young men, numbering some twenty-five or more, met us on our arrival, and carried up our canoe and effects. We were hospitably entertained by the head chief, named "Kahala" or

FIRST VISIT TO SKIDEGATE

"Nang-sin-wass." The encampment is well situated on a crescent-shaped bay, with a smooth beach, the Indian lodges following the curve of the shore, whilst a high bluff behind the centre of the camp lends a picturesque appearance to the whole. As at Massett, in front of every dwelling several totem poles were erected, displaying the crestal signs of the owners. These were skilfully carved, and in many cases coloured. Here and there mortuary totems and structures stood, containing the remains of the great chiefs of the past. They had heard of the medicine man of the "Iron people," who had come to their islands to tell of the "Sha-nung-Etlageda," the great "Chief of the heavens," and so they crowded in to see me until there was not standing room. Those who could do so mounted on the roof, and peered down through the smoke hole. In the meantime food was being prepared, and, as soon as common curiosity had been gratified, a great fire was erected on the hearth, consisting of logs of four feet in length, over which frequent libations of fish grease were poured, until the flames issued above the roof, causing the spectators who had assembled there to descend in dangerous haste.

Cedar-bark mats were spread for us to the rear of the lodge in the centre, whilst the men composing our crew were seated on either side. Water, soap, and towels were first brought, and each of us invited to wash our hands. The first food offered us was dried salmon and olachan grease, of each of which a large portion was placed before Edenshew, Cowhoe, and myself. Each dish, before being served, was brought to the chief, our host, who tasted it, and signified his approval. The next dish was boiling dulse, a species of sea-weed, which, when gathered, is made up into square cakes about twelve inches by twelve and about one and a half inch in thickness, and dried in the sun. Before boiling, this is chopped fine, and it is also mixed with olachan grease before being served out. Large horn spoons were then handed round, those given to the chiefs

TOTEM POLES
The figure in the foreground is a mortuary totem surmounted with an eagle. Other totems are seen in the background.

INDIAN MEDICINE MEN
In full dress, prepared to begin their incantations. They belong to the Nishka Tribe, on the River Nass, B.C.

FIRST VISIT TO SKIDEGATE

being inlaid with abilone or mother-of-pearl. As a special mark of honour, I was given a large silver-plated tablespoon, which became so heated with the boiling sea-weed that I could not permit it to touch my lips. Accordingly I called upon them to change it for one of their horn spoons. This caused much hilarity amongst them to find that the " Yetzhahada " preferred a spoon of their manufacture to that made by his own countrymen.

After this dish we were served with dried halibut and grease, and then with boiled herring spawn. During this repast I had remarked two young men, stripped to the waist, beating up in tubs dried berries with water until it became a frothy substance, not unlike ice cream in appearance. This was served up last as dessert, and is eaten as described on a preceding page, but I was careful not to endeavour to imitate their manner of eating it, as my failure would have excited much mirth at my expense.

The meal concluded, I stood up, and having thanked them for their kind reception, I announced the object of my visit, and informed them that I proposed to conduct two services on the following day, being the " Shantlans Shanzotang " or rest day, and would proclaim to them the message from the " Great Chief above." We adopted the method used by the chief when calling his people to a feast in order to summon a congregation together for the first time. This was done by suspending a triangular bar of steel from a pole on the roof and beating it with an iron rod. I had a crowded congregation, dressed many of them in paint and feathers, and so intent were they in hearkening to the word that though a large canoe arrived during the service conveying an invitation from a tribe to the south, which they announced from the canoe with blowing horns and beating of drums, yet not one went out to witness their arrival. This was the first religious service held at Skidegate. In the afternoon I proceeded to a village in Gold Harbour, where I conducted a service also.

FIRST VISIT TO SKIDEGATE

On this occasion I first made the acquaintance of Chief Nansteens of the most southerly Haida village on the Queen Charlotte Islands. It was situated on a small islet off Cape St. James, the southern point of Prevost Island. This tribe was always noted as being the most successful sea-otter hunters of the Pacific. Being favourably situated for the pursuit of the otter, they not only succeeded in securing large numbers themselves, but also exacted toll from hunters coming from other tribes to hunt the sea otter in their vicinity. They were physically the finest looking of the Haida tribes, but they, like the sea otters which they hunted, have almost disappeared. The few who were left have become absorbed in the Skidegate tribes. They early found out the way to the white settlements and cities on the Sound, and from that time forward they deteriorated. Drink and disease proved their destruction. The last time I saw Chief Nansteens was on the deck of a steamer from Victoria standing beside a coffin which was covered with a Union Jack. He was evidently in deep sorrow. The coffin contained the remains of his wife, and but a few of his tribe accompanied him. The majority had returned to the islands by canoe. He was grateful for the few words of sympathy with which I addressed him. I had advised them against going away on such expeditions, but the attractions were too strong for them. He had been greatly attached to his wife, who was not only a chieftainess by rank, but adorned her position by a native grace and dignity seldom met with in uncivilised tribes. During my stay at Skidegate I was surprised at the youthful appearance of our hostess, the wife of Nangsinwass. I had supposed she was his daughter. On the opposite side of the great lodge an old woman and a young man scarcely out of his teens had their quarters. I had regarded this young man as the old woman's son, and referred to him as such when speaking to my friend Cowhoe. He burst into loud laughter, in which Chief

FIRST VISIT TO SKIDEGATE

Edenshew joined. Inquiring the cause of their amusement, I was informed that this youth and the old lady were man and wife. He was the chief's nephew, being his sister's son, and consequently the heir to the chieftainship. As a proof and assurance of this to the tribe, the chief had given his old wife to his nephew and had taken the young woman, whom I had supposed to be his daughter, to wife. This I found to be a recognised custom amongst the Haida tribes, to unite a young woman with an aged man, or an old woman with a youth, as in the above instance. They deem it necessary to unite wisdom and experience with youthfulness and vigour.

This was the first visit of a missionary to Skidegate and the southern villages. I promised to send them a teacher before leaving, and on my next visit to the mainland I was enabled to fulfil my promise by sending a young man, a Tsimshean native teacher, who had long been under Christian instruction at Metlakahtla. He erected a small Mission-house at Skidegate for his wife and family, who accompanied him, and did a good work whilst there. But the Haidas of Skidegate were anxious to have a white missionary, and for this reason a deputation of the leading men came to Metlakahtla. They were received by Mr. Duncan and myself. Chief Nangsinwass was the spokesman of the party. "You have gone to Massett," he said, "and made your residence there, whilst you have only sent us a Tsimshean to teach us. This is not as it should be, as Skidegate was formerly just as powerful as the North, and we should have a white teacher also." To this Mr. Duncan replied: "Chief," said he, "supposing I had found a supply of good food, and I called a slave and delivered him a quantity of it to convey to you, would you refuse to accept it because I had sent it by the hand of a slave?" "No!" replied the chief, "I should not refuse it, I should accept it." "Well," replied Mr. Duncan, "we have sent you the Gospel message of the rich provision the Great Chief above

FIRST VISIT TO SKIDEGATE

has made for you, by a Tsimshean, and if a white teacher was sent he would convey to you just the same message." "True," replied Nangsinwass, "the food is the same, but the white teacher is a better cook than the Indian, and could serve it out to us so that we would relish it and be eager to eat it. We were always the victors in our conflicts with the Tsimsheans in the past, so we cannot accept them as our teachers now." I was strongly in favour of acceding to their request, but my senior Duncan was not of the same mind, so the deputation proceeded to Fort Simpson and proffered their request to the Methodist missionary there. The result was that a white missionary was sent there by the Canadian Methodist Missionary Society and we were compelled to withdraw the native teacher. I have in my possession his journal showing the attendance at the services and the subjects of his addresses, and from it I concluded that he was by no means ignorant in the preparation and presentation of the food of the Divine message. Nevertheless, by this mistaken policy of seeking to supply the new Missions with native teachers, we lost Fort Simpson first and afterwards Skidegate. But by it the Master's quotation is confirmed, "Herein is that saying true, One soweth and another reapeth." We were overtaken by heavy weather on our return northwards, and I took the precaution of putting on my life-belt under my overcoat. When the storm struck, and the waves crested with foam were breaking over our frail bark, I quietly and quickly inflated my belt. Just then, as our canoe fell from the crest of a wave, the chief's son, who sat in the stern, was thrown right upon me in the middle of the canoe. With hands outstretched to save himself, he struck me fairly on my belt, which yielded freely to the pressure. He recoiled with terror and continued to gaze at me until reprimanded by his father for not holding on to his seat. He evidently believed that a white man's body was of a different substance to their own. He was not aware that I had on a life-belt.

FIRST VISIT TO SKIDEGATE

As there is but little shelter on the east of Graham Island in a gale, and there are many boulders lying off the coast, it is dangerous. But Edenshew knew it well, as he had been reared at Cape Ball and at Yehling, near Tow Hill, consequently he steered a safe course.

Shortly after my return to Massett I was called to see a young man who was suffering from an attack of brain fever. It had been brought on by plunging into the cold waters of the sea when overheated, in order to cool himself. The Haidas believe that all such ailments are caused by the " Stlique," or land otter, which all the Indians believe to be possessed with supernatural powers. I had his hair cut short and applied blisters freely, and instructed them also to procure ice and apply it to his head. I then prescribed suitable medicine, and was gratified to find the patient improving under my treatment. Just when he was progressing towards recovery the medicine men returned to camp. They had been attending a great " potlatch " in the vicinity of Virago Sound.

In the middle of the night, whilst engaged in treating a serious case of croup in my own family, I heard them in their wild orgies over my patient, whooping and rattling so that they could be heard all over the camp. They continued at intervals throughout the night, and when I entered in the morning the leading medicine man had just sunk down exhausted by the side of the sick man, who was now in a raging delirium. And little wonder, when one medicine man after another had been performing over him through the night, now singly and then in chorus with their rattles to drive out the demon of disease. The house was filled with the followers of the medicine men, who sometimes joined in the chorus with them. The sick man was being held down by two attendants, one on either side, and it was with difficulty they retained him on the floor. I stooped and felt his pulse, though I knew there could be no hope for him now under such treatment. It was bound-

FIRST VISIT TO SKIDEGATE

ing, and I shook my head to indicate my conclusion. Instantly the medicine men started to their feet and assumed a threatening attitude towards me as the leader exclaimed, " He will recover, as we have expelled the evil spirit, which your medicine could not do." I turned to the mother and inquired if her son was not improving under my treatment. " Did you not inform me that he had rested peacefully for the two nights preceding the arrival of the medicine men ? " She replied in the affirmative, though with fear. The leading medicine man, with his long hair falling down to his waist, scowled at her. I then addressed to all a few words in Haida. " Your forefathers followed this practice because they knew of no better way. But the light has come to you now, and it is time you abandoned it. The noise you have made over this sick man will kill him." Just then a chief arose to speak. " It is the first time I have seen the white man's medicine acting in opposition to ours," said he ; " my uncle was a medicine man (conjurer), my father was a medicine man, and I should have been one also, as I was initiated, but I succeeded to a chieftainship instead. If this man recovers I shall know that our medicine men are true and strong ; but if he dies then I shall know our way is false and the white man's words are true : hearken all to my words ! " I left as he ended his speech.

The sick man died on the following morning. During the day there were rumours of the anger of the medicine men and of their designs of revenge. At midnight a number of Haidas approached the house and demanded admittance. I hesitated for a few moments, and then realising that it was best to show no signs of fear, I threw open the door. The leading medicine man and the chief who had been with him when I visited the dying Indian led the party. They scowled at me in anger as they stood around me. I inquired why they had come at such a late hour. " You have shamed us before our people," the medicine man replied, " and we have come to demand satisfaction.

FIRST VISIT TO SKIDEGATE

We must have payment from you for this or we shall wash off our shame in your blood."

As each of them had a blanket around him, I could not see what they concealed, but I knew they were prepared to take vengeance on me. This was their object in coming so late. I closed the door, and locking it, requested them to be seated. My action disconcerted them, and looking at one another they reluctantly obeyed. "Did I not tell you truly," I asked them, "when I said the man would die? Is he not dead?" "Yes," they replied, "he is dead." I then reminded the chief of his promise, to which there were many witnesses. "You engaged before all, that if the man died you would no longer believe in your medicine men. And now that he is dead and that the medicine men have caused it, what are you here for? A chief should be true to his word," I added. The medicine men saw that the chief was wavering, and so repeated the demand for payment. I repeated what I had said, and I added, "The Great Chief of Heaven forbids you to continue your witchcraft over the sick." To this there was no response. At length the leading medicine man exclaimed, "Well, will you put the sign of the Chief of Heaven upon me and I shall be satisfied. It will give me new power with the people!"

I saw that it was but a repetition of the request of Simon Magus in another form. "Give me also this power, and I shall be a greater conjurer than before." Seizing a medicine bottle which stood near, I inquired, "Do you see this label on the bottle? This indicates what the bottle contains. What would you think of the man who sells me this medicine, if, when I ordered medicines from him, he sent me only empty bottles labelled as though they contained good medicines? Or, yet worse, if he sent me bottles containing poison, and put the label or sign of good and wholesome medicine on them? And yet this is what you ask me to do, to put the sign of the

FIRST VISIT TO SKIDEGATE

Great Chief above upon you when as yet you have not believed His Word, nor received His Spirit in your hearts. This would cause the Great Chief to be displeased both with you and with me." To this the chief assented. "You must give up your medicine craft and conjuring and learn God's way. I am ready to teach you, and when you accept and believe the Truth I shall be enabled to put His sign upon you."

It was the sign of baptism which he sought, as he had seen it administered, or perhaps had only heard of it from others. Their temper was subdued, and they took their departure. The medicine man returned again and again, and became a catechumen. As he was a chief also, he begged for some scriptural illustrations from which he might teach some of his people. He came to me several times in distress because the " Scahanawa " or evil spirit had troubled him and would not permit him to rest, endeavouring to tempt him to resume his conjuring over the sick. He promised him large amounts of property if he would but obey him, and threatened him with poverty if he disobeyed. I instructed him how to meet the tempter should he assail him again, and he went away satisfied. And who can deny that "the strong man armed" does make a struggle with the soul, endeavouring to cast off his yoke in a heathen camp where hitherto his authority has been undisputed?

Shortly after this he had his long hair cut off, and was baptized. The sign he had at first asked for, in ignorance, he now received in spiritual understanding and truth. I saw him afterwards, coming forward with a number of his fellow-tribesmen to receive the Holy Communion. He was no longer like the demoniac of Gadara, as I had so often seen him, but decently clad and in his right mind.

Being skilful in carving, he supported himself and his wife by his labour. He continued faithful unto death, and departed this life in the faith of Christ. He is not forgotten amongst the Haidas.

MEDICINE MAN'S RATTLE

The face is a conventional representation of the moon. The figure is hollow, and contains small stones. The whole is carved in wood.

INDIAN MASKS

The eyes and lower jaws are movable, and were cleverly manipulated by the wearer by means of strings.

FIRST VISIT TO SKIDEGATE

The gamblers now began to occasion us some trouble. Throughout the heathen tribes on the north-west coast and in the interior, I found gambling largely practised by the men. To outsiders the game appears much more complicated and difficult than any game of chance known to white men. It is carried on by means of short sticks of hard wood about four inches in length, polished and marked. There are about eighty sticks in a pack, each of which is known by a distinct name. Each pack of gambling sticks is kept in a leather pouch tied with a thong of the same material, and fastened by a piece of carved bone attached to the end of the thong. A chief's set of gambling sticks include a number inlaid with abilone shells. Some of them are carved to represent miniature totem poles. As the game is generally accompanied by beating with the sticks on a board, it becomes objectionable when carried on by a number of players. Quarrels are not unusual over the game, and fighting often ensues.

Some years since, whilst an exciting game was in progress, a fierce Indian who had lost heavily approached the man who had fleeced him, from behind as he sat playing, and pulling back his head, stabbed him to the heart. This murderer I knew very well, and on one occasion he informed me he had killed several others, but that he intended to repent and abandon his evil ways.

A young woman came to me one day crying and begging my aid. Her husband had gambled away all they had. "I have no clothing left me," she cried, " and now he has lost both our canoe and axe, so that we cannot procure firewood, and both blankets and pillows are gone." It was a hard case, but not too hard for the power of the Gospel. This man abandoned the custom, became a Christian, and is now, with his wife and family, respectable and industrious.

A Haida who was a noted gambler on the Alaskan coast visited Massett. I learned that a plot had been formed by the leading gamblers to induce him to play for high stakes

FIRST VISIT TO SKIDEGATE

so that they might break him. He was bringing over a canoe full of blankets and furs to pay off some debts contracted at his marriage. I sent for him on his arrival and warned him not to engage in gambling while in camp. He promised not to do so. But the passion for play overcame him, and trusting in his own ability to outdo them, he consented. The gambling was continued both by day and night until this champion had won from his opponents almost all their property. He locked his gains up in the lodge of a friend, and went up the inlet for a few days. During his absence the losers broke into the house, forced open the chests, and carried off the goods they had lost. Not content with this, they also appropriated some of his own effects. On the return of this man with his friend whose house had been broken into, finding what had occurred, they at once suspected the guilty parties. Guns were loaded, confederates called, and an attack was about to be made on the lodge in which the guilty parties resided. I sent a man whom I could depend on to call the offenders to me.

There were three of them, a father and his two sons. The former was famed as being fierce, and his face tattooed with strange devices seemed to confirm this. They came in response to my call, accompanied by my messenger. I informed them of the position and inquired if they were aware of their danger. They replied that they were prepared for an attack. I declared that they had caused the trouble throughout, as they had first induced their visitor to gamble with them, and then had broken into the house and stolen the property. They asserted that they had only taken their own goods, which was not stealing. I proved to them that they had according to their own rules forfeited all right to the property they had lost. I then called upon them to bring all the goods they had taken to me, and on their doing so I would make peace. This they refused to do, whereupon I quietly moved towards the door, which I locked and placed the key in my pocket. I then informed them that

FIRST VISIT TO SKIDEGATE

I would detain them until they consented to bring the goods to me, and that in doing so I had their safety in view rather than any other object. I called my friend aside and warned him to be on the alert in the event of attack, as I feared they might have weapons concealed. They too had a whispered consultation, at the close of which the father intimated his willingness to produce the disputed property. I requested that the young men should bring up the stuff whilst the father remained as a surety. My plan evidently baffled them, as they hesitated to act. Seeing I was determined, they consented, and set out for the goods, which were all carried in. I made an inventory of them in their presence and then sent for the injured party, as also three chiefs as witnesses. When the complainants found that I had the goods in my possession to be adjudicated upon as soon as convenient, I had but little difficulty in making peace between them, which was confirmed by the witnesses present.

From that time onward I took a stand against gambling, and made several raids upon parties of gamblers whom I discovered engaged at it in the open spaces in the encampments. I succeeded on these occasions in capturing several sets of gambling sticks which they abandoned as they fled at my approach. Those who persisted in following it had to betake themselves to the woods for their games. But their wives and families were the sufferers, as they were often left without fire or food, which caused trouble and sickness amongst them. And gradually the numbers of those who practised it decreased, until it no longer caused such strife and brawling as it had done previously throughout the camps. Thus despite many discouragements and occasional defeats I realised that the dawn was breaking, and trusted ere long to see the light from the Sun of Righteousness illuminating the hearts and lives of the islanders with His beams.

CHAPTER XV

THE CONFLICT DEEPENING

"Saviour, lo the isles are waiting,
  Stretched the hand and strained the sight,
For Thy Spirit's new creating,
  Love's pure flame, and wisdom's light.
Give the word, and of the preacher,
  Speed the foot, and touch the tongue,
Till on earth by every creature,
  Glory to Thy name be sung."   A. C. Coxe.

"Had I lived, I should have been first in the way of the Great Chief above."

STEILTA, the Head Chief of the Eagle Clan, now became seriously ill. He had been indisposed for some time previously, and as he was unable to attend our services, I conducted an evening service occasionally in his large lodge. He had a number of slaves, and these, together with his family, formed quite a congregation. In addition many of his tribe were always present. The figure of an eagle with wings outspread, carved in wood over the doorway in front of his lodge, indicated his crest, whilst his rank was represented by the number of elaborately carved totem poles standing in front of the dwelling. In the interior a large oval-shaped opening cut in the centre of the wooden floor was used as the fireplace. The hearth was always covered with white sand and shells from the beach, and the large fire of logs kept up by the slaves illuminated and heated the interior. Steilta was a fine-looking chief physically before he began to fail. Tall and well-built, with a fair skin and a black beard and moustache, he might have passed as a white man, had it not been for his Haida features. He was a true chief, and commanded the respect

THE CONFLICT DEEPENING

and obedience due to such. But as in the case of another great and worthy chieftain of Bible history of whom it is recorded, he was a great man and honourable, " but he was a leper," so in Steilta's case we must add that he had, like many others, too great a desire for the " fire-water." This they continued to manufacture from molasses procured from the Hudson's Bay Company's store, and from potatoes and berries. In answer to my inquiry as to the cause of his ailment he replied, " I fear the Hootchino has done it, I have been foolish to have drunk so much of it. The firewater has burned me deeply." His ailment increased, and then the medicine men gathered in,

> " As you have seen the ravens
> Gather round the dying deer,"

to increase the symptoms and hasten his end by their noisy fanaticism. I called to see him one morning, as I had heard the whooping and rattle of the medicine men at intervals through the night. I found the chief much worse. He was faint and exhausted from want of sleep and rest. His tormentors, the conjurers, were there in force, and were holding a consultation when I entered. They evidently resented my visit and scowled at me, whilst they muttered to one another in disapproval. Without noticing them, I approached the sick man and sat down. I felt his pulse and perceived he could not long survive the treatment he was being subjected to, and I told the medicine men so. They angrily asserted that he would not die, as they had succeeded in expelling the demon of the disease. The sick man had vomited a quantity of dark clotted blood, and this they declared was a sign that he should recover. Without noticing them further, I addressed myself to the dying chief and reminded him of what I had taught him. Raising his voice sufficiently for all to hear, he exclaimed, " Had I lived, I should have been first in the way of the Great Chief above."

" You may be first even now," I replied, " and His way will lead you to life eternal." And seizing the opportunity

THE CONFLICT DEEPENING

I bowed with him in prayer. He endeavoured to follow me, and responded to my petitions. The medicine men attempted to drown my voice, as they were annoyed at my interference. A number of his slaves were seated on the opposite side of the great hearth, and the chief himself, though dying, was not lying down, but supported in a sitting posture. He grasped my hand as though he would fain retain me, and I promised to send my wife to see him and make him some nourishment.

We decided it best that a little food should be made in the presence of all, otherwise the medicine men would accuse us of having poisoned him. Whilst my wife was there administering nourishment to him, she noticed one of the slaves, a young man, bound hand and foot with thongs of bark. Her attention was drawn to him by one of the attendants who kicked the poor wretch. He rolled over on his back almost in the fire, being unable to help himself. At the order of the chief's sister he was carried out by the other slaves and thrown in an outhouse behind, where he was confined. The medicine men had accused this slave of being the cause of his chief's illness. They had discovered that he was possessed of the evil spirit which was in the form of a mouse. If this could be expelled from him the chief would recover. Consequently this slave had been kept bound for three weeks, and had been tortured daily by burning him with torches of pitch pine to drive out the demon. Another slave had been instructed to shoot him should the chief die, and was stationed, prepared with his loaded gun, beside him for this purpose.

I determined at once to endeavour to save this man's life, and was on my way for this purpose when I met a messenger who informed me that Chief Steilta desired to see me before he died. We had not proceeded far before the report of the cannon announced his death to his tribe. Instantly the weird sounds of the death chant arose from the lodge, accompanied by cries and screams. As I entered, a scene

THE CONFLICT DEEPENING

of indescribable confusion was witnessed. The women were pulling handfuls of hair from their heads, and casting it on the fire. Others around the corpse were engaged in painting the face, preparatory to dressing and enthroning it, with all his property spread around. His aged father rushed to the fire and threw himself on it. Assisted by another chief I rescued him, but not before he had been badly burnt. Just then I saw the slave, with gun in hand, press through the crowd and pass out on his mission of death. I called two chiefs and requested them to prevent the deed. They were men I trusted in—Chiefs Weeha and Cowhoe. The former was chief of the bear crest. They at once rushed after him and were just in time. He had dragged his victim to the door of the shed in which he had been confined, for execution, and had just lifted his weapon to fire, when Cowhoe sprang upon him and wrested the gun from his grasp. They then cut the bark ropes and set the slave free, but he was unable to stand. The thongs of bark had cut to the bone on his legs and arms, and his back from hip to shoulder was literally roasted. I directed them to have him conveyed to the Mission-house, where my wife dressed his wounds and administered restoratives. Meanwhile I returned to the house of mourning, and taking a stand I awaited a pause in the death chant, when I exclaimed, "You all heard your chief's last words to me this morning, that had he lived he would have been first in the way of the Great Chief above. And did he not send for me again to convey to me his last word?" There was a murmur of assent. "For this reason," I added, "I do not wish to see him painted and set up, I want to show you a better way." The majority were opposed to my interference, but I appealed to the father of the deceased, with whom I was on friendly terms. He assented, and I sent several slaves for some boards with which I formed a raised platform. On this I had the body placed, which they had already dressed in the uniform of a naval officer. I sent to the Mission-house for a silk scarf

THE CONFLICT DEEPENING

which I had, and directed them how to place it on the corpse. This arrangement turned the tide of popular feeling in favour of my action as he lay, indeed,

"Like a warrior taking his rest."

The leading men now came forward and engaged that my arrangement would not be interfered with, but they stated the members of his crest (the Eagle) would seek to scatter the swansdown over the corpse when they returned to the camp. To this I offered no objection, as it would have been injudicious to have done so. I felt I had gained two points, first in rescuing the slave, and again in the laying out of the corpse. On entering the following day I found the corpse covered with the down which they had scattered over it as they performed the death dance around it. This was continued for several days, when I ventured to propose that they should permit the remains to be interred. I had selected a small island at the mouth of the inlet separated from the camp only by a slough, as a suitable burying-place in the event of my succeeding to induce them to bury their dead. The bodies of deceased conjurers had been placed there on the lower branches of the trees. They declined to permit the body to be buried there, but consented that it should be interred on a rising ground immediately behind the lodge from which it could be seen. I directed and assisted in the making of the coffin. The cannon was again fired as the remains were carried to the grave covered with an ensign, and I took a portion of the burial service over the grave. Another important advance had thus been effected, as though they could not agree to making use of the burial-ground on the island which I had selected, yet the fact that I had succeeded in having the remains of a chief interred according to the Christian rite, and in a becoming manner, would, I knew, act as an example. The medicine men were greatly incensed and aroused by my action. They had withdrawn at the death of the chief because they had asserted he would recover. They now

THE CONFLICT DEEPENING

circulated a report that my object was to cause the death of as many of the Haidas as I could, as the chiefs of the "Iron people" (whites) had agreed to pay me a large sum for every Haida whom I thus buried. This they declared was the reason which had led me to save the life of the slave who had bewitched the chief, and caused his death. For some time this report was believed, and my congregations fell away. At length a young chief, the same who had warned me previously, came by night and informed me of the necromancers' scheme to frustrate my efforts and overthrow my influence. Only a short time previously I had publicly warned them against the fire-water which they were making in large quantities. One sub-chief named "Kilslayoway," whilst intoxicated, had kicked and maltreated his wife, and caused her death, as also the death of her child. He was greatly attached to her, and when he recovered from his debauch and found what he had done, he became wild with grief, and had to be watched to prevent him from taking his own life. He came to me, and remained for hours with his face buried in his hands. I reminded the young chief of all this, and instructed him to go and tell all his friends that if the medicine men's story was true, how was it, then, that I opposed the fire-water, which would have caused the death of so many? The inquiry spread and revealed the fallacy of the medicine men's report, and again my services were well attended.

But rumours now ran through the camps that a chief named "Kinneelawash-Haung" was about to resort to force in order to obtain some slaves from the successor to the chief whose death had been recorded. Kinneelawash-Haung had been absent on an expedition when his uncle died. The late Steilta had taken over the slaves during the absence of the heir to the chieftainship. But when he returned Steilta refused to part with the slaves. At length he promised to return them at his next great "potlatch," and to make reparation. But before the preparations for this "potlatch"

THE CONFLICT DEEPENING

were completed Steilta fell sick and died, as above recorded. His successor refused to give up the slaves. In consequence of this Kinneelawash-Haung resolved to take them by force. For this purpose he summoned a number of the Haidas of Prince of Wales Island in Alaska to assist him. These were of his own crest. On their arrival he issued his challenge to the chief who held his slaves to fight.

The manner in which a challenge is given is this. The challenger has a tent erected in the near vicinity of the party challenged. From this he emerges occasionally, and, with loud shouts, heaps abuse on his opponents. All the failures, offences, and disgrace of their ancestors, and of themselves, with much more added, are cast in their teeth. While thus engaged, his party are all prepared and on the watch for the first sign of hostilities. An arrow or a shot from the accused precipitated the conflict. In the present instance the challenge had been given. All work was suspended in the camp. At this crisis my friend, the old white trader, appealed to me. He had closed his store, and feared the worst.

"They are about to fight," said he, " and we shall all be slain. Could you not endeavour to make peace?"

"I am quite willing," I replied, "if you will but accompany me."

"I could not help you; my presence would but irritate them," he answered. "You will do better alone. If you do not go we shall all be killed, and your wife and children will not escape. They generally avenge their quarrels on others when blood begins to flow."

I agreed to make an effort, and I recognised the truth of his statement that his presence would not help me, as I had only a short time previously rescued him from an onslaught of the Haidas. It occurred in this manner. His Tsimshean wife and daughters had come rushing to me, crying out that the Haidas were killing "Squire," which was the sobriquet by which he was known. I hastened to the rescue, guided by the outcry, and found him on his back, behind the counter,

THE CONFLICT DEEPENING

struggling with several Haidas, who were endeavouring to overcome him. One of them had a large knife, which he held in a threatening attitude over him. The store was filled with an excited crowd, and I at once ordered them off the trader, at the same time requesting him to be calm and to leave them to me. He was terribly excited, as he believed they were about to kill him. With some difficulty I persuaded him to accompany his wife and daughters, who led him off to his dwelling. I then ordered the offenders to the outside of the counter, and Chief Edenshew, who entered just then, assisted me to clear the building. On inquiry I found that a small balance of some eight dollars was owing to two hunters on their furs, for which the trader had given them a credit note. This they had lost, and as he had no entry of it on his books, he refused to pay unless they produced the note. Hence the assault. His temper had embroiled him in several serious quarrels of late, consequently I concluded it was best to act single-handed in the present serious crisis.

I proceeded first to those who held the slaves in dispute. The fires were all extinguished, and they were seated with faces blackened around their guns, which were all loaded and primed, ready for the fray. A guard was on the door to prevent a surprise. I was admitted, and took a seat in silence. No one spoke, and I remained silent for several minutes. At length I addressed them. "So you are about to fight," I said; "I am sorry, because I fear some of you will fall, even though you may gain the victory. If Steilta had lived this would not have happened. I know what his word was about the slaves. But I have not come to ask you to fulfil all his words. I want you to fulfil a part. I have only one desire, and that is for peace. Now, hearken, friends, to my words. I want you to consent to hand over to the other party fifty blankets, six guns, one box of dancing ornaments, and one slave. I do not ask you to answer me now. I am about to proceed to the others to make the same proposal. This is my word; consider it, and give me your reply when I return."

THE CONFLICT DEEPENING

I then left them to consult. My object in asking them to deliver the slave was this. She was a young woman who had been badly abused, and a young man, who was also a slave of the opposing party, had asked her in marriage and her owners would not consent. He then appealed to me to help him. I knew it was the only escape for the unfortunate creature, who was badly treated where she was. On reaching the summit of the hill on which the men of Kinneelawash-Haung were encamped, I found the large lodge well filled with men, all of whom were in good spirits. They, too, were all fully prepared. The women and children had all been sent away, and they had piled their guns and painted their faces. They were evidently determined to fight to a finish. They looked at me in surprise, and after a considerable pause I announced my message. I reminded them that though they seemed confident of victory, yet it was doubtful, and in any case some of them would die! My words were received with derisive laughter.

Then one of them replied: " Does the ' Yetzhahada ' think that we fear? We never yet found a foe we feared, whether on land or sea! We can die as our fathers have died before us, with our face towards the fight; but to submit now would be our shame." An aged man then arose towards the rear of the lodge and spoke: " My elder brothers and my younger brothers, the words the Ironman has spoken are good. I do not fear, for as you know I have been in many a fight. But age brings wisdom! Look at my head! My hair testifies to my age. Many sorrows have turned my hair to the colour of snow! To accept his offer will not bring shame. I am for peace." He sat down, and the chief arose to speak. " Well, brothers, speak out your heart's words now. If our friends who have come across the water to help us are willing to accept the property proposed, I am content. But I shall yet recover my slaves." There ensued a general discussion, during which I could learn some were eager to fight and

THE CONFLICT DEEPENING

others were for peace. The voices of the latter prevailed, and one of them was selected to convey to me their reply: "We see that you are for peace. You have not thus come for gain. And you hold the balance fair between us. If Steilta's party consents to your words, we are content; but if not, we shall fight." I promised to let them know at once, and hastened to ascertain the decision of the opposing party. To my great joy, I found they had accepted my proposal. The large dance-house which I had prepared stood between the contending parties. I had it thrown open, and sent messages to summon the neutral chiefs and leading men. They took their place in the pit or body of the building, whilst the leaders and chiefs of the opposing parties occupied the side galleries. When all were seated, Steilta's slaves entered, carrying the property demanded.

Fifty trade blankets valued at one dollar and a half each were placed in front of Kinneelawash-Haung and his men, also six rifles and a box of chief's dancing ornaments, and lastly the young woman named Oahla. She was evidently not averse to the change. To her it was a step towards liberty. The neutral chiefs then one after another made speeches, approving and confirming the peace; after which the two chiefs who had well-nigh met in deadly strife came forward, and I joined their hands. A feast was afterwards prepared by Chief Weah, to which both the chiefs and their followers were invited; and at this feast the eagle's-down was scattered freely over all, thus cementing the peace made. With a light heart I returned for rest and refreshment after an anxious day, and communicated the good news of another success for the truth and right. Squire, who was anxiously waiting to learn the results, was loud in his praises at the result of my effort, and I realised that I was gradually winning him and his wife and family out of the darkness of heathenism towards the true liberty wherewith Christ makes His people free.

CHAPTER XVI

MAKAI

"See the hills for harvest whiten,
All along each distant shore,
Seawards far the islands brighten,
Light of nations lead us o'er;
When we seek them,
Let thy Spirit go before."

C. F. ALEXANDER.

THERE was one man in the camp at Massett named Makai, who was really a Tlingit Indian of Alaska, but he had become a member of the Haida nation by taking a Haida wife. He was amongst the wildest and most reckless in the camp. When intoxicated he cared little whom he injured, and when I ventured to warn him he threatened to take summary vengeance on me for my interference. His wife's name was Kandiwass, whose mother's sister was a great chieftainess of the same name.

She, with a number of her tribe, was returning from a trading expedition, when, owing to a contrary wind, they were driven on the Alaskan coast, where a number of the Tlingit Indians were encamped. These invited the Haidas to a feast and then fell upon them and killed them in order to seize their property. But their evil purpose was defeated, as the five slaves who had been left in charge of the canoe, which was a large war canoe, sixty feet in length, suspecting foul play, put up their sails and ran out to sea, before the Tlingits could board them. But in their haste to escape from their enemies they ran on a rock and capsized, losing all the property and barely escaping with their lives. This

MAKAI

was the beginning of a long period of strife between the Haidas and the Tlingit tribes. Makai's uncle was one of the Tlingit warriors, and when the Haidas came to avenge the death of their friend, he was surrounded, together with a number of his men, in a large war canoe.

How the Tlingits fought on that occasion is best told by a Haida warrior who passed through the fray:

"As the Tlingit canoes approached their men stood in lines down the centres of the canoes back to back. This position was to keep the canoes steady, as well as to offer a bold front to the enemy, whilst a number of rowers paddled on either side. As they drew nearer they chanted a war song to which they beat time on their canoes.

"When near enough they fired a volley, and something, probably a splinter of the canoe, struck me on the head and I became unconscious. When I recovered I found several of our men had been shot. Some were lying in the canoe and several were hanging over the sides. Having fired their volley, they retreated in order to reload, and we followed. For to attack at close quarters was always the Haida plan of action. We ran our canoe up to them, and as we touched I sprang into their canoe. I was stabbed by the nearest warrior, but as his dagger struck me on the shoulder-blade the wound was not serious. I slew him and two others, and was about to attack a fourth when he motioned to me that he surrendered, so I seized him and cast him into our canoe. Another rushed at me, but I overpowered him, and he surrendered also. In our struggle he was wounded. He was one of the leading warriors amongst the Tlingit. Some of them, when hard pressed, jumped overboard and fought in the water. When the fight was over we found we had many severed heads and some slaves, and the other canoes had taken heads and slaves also, together with much property.[1]

[1] The coast Indians did not usually take the scalps of those whom they slew, as was the custom of the Indians of the interior. They

MAKAI

"On our return voyage from the Alaskan coast, where this battle was fought, we fell in with a number of sea otters, many of which were asleep on the water. Though weary and wounded with the fight and with our captives on board, we could not permit such an opportunity to slip. We succeeded in shooting several, whilst another canoe secured a number of skins also." Makai was amongst those captured on this occasion, and being young he became a member of the Haida tribe encamped at Massett, and because of his rank amongst the Tlingits a chief's daughter was given him to wife. But he had abandoned himself to every vice amongst the Haidas, and as I passed along the camp at night I could hear his voice, a shrill tenor, leading in the chorus of the medicine men, or his shouts in the feasts of fire-water. His wife, despite his threats, attended the services, and as her knowledge of the truth increased her anxiety for her husband increased also. Her uncle being a leading chief, the husband feared to injure her, for he would have fared badly. She wisely avoided him when intoxicated, and thus prevented any open rupture.

But one night in a frenzy of intoxication, whilst singing and dancing in his paint and adornments, he burst a blood-vessel and I was summoned to his aid. They were gradually gaining confidence in the white medicine man and his remedies, and losing faith in the rattle and incantations of their own necromancers. I was enabled to check the flow of blood by administering a powerful astringent, and as the hæmorrhage had tended to sober him, he was prepared to obey my directions for his treatment. He was very weak and low, but after a few weeks he was able to walk around again. He became a regular attendant at the services, and appeared deeply interested. But it was evident that consumption had seized him. As he became weaker he begged

---

severed the heads, which they carried back as trophies in their canoes. The scalps being so much lighter, the interior Indians took those, which they carried off in their belts.

to be baptized. I consented, as I realised from my intercourse with him he had accepted the truth, through faith. He could not walk to our place of assembly in the large dance-house, but our friend the trader had lent his large living-room for the purpose. He had dressed himself decently and becomingly for the occasion, and sent invitations to several chiefs and friends to be present. And there, seated in their midst, he was admitted to be a member of the infant church, now inaugurated and established on the Queen Charlotte Islands. After the administration of the sacrament rite he requested permission to address a few words to his friends, to which I gladly assented. "You know," he said, " my friends, chiefs, and brothers, how I have ever been a leader amongst you. In your fights and feasts I have never sought to conceal myself. None of you can accuse me of fear. I have always sought to be first and foremost. But whilst I was thus rushing on, it seemed as though I saw a deep, dark pit opening right in my way. And into that pit I would have fallen, but for the light. The bright light from above flashed upon me and showed me the danger, and the Word of the Great Father above warned me, and the same light that showed me the danger revealed to me also the cross and the sacrifice of the Saviour for me. And now, chiefs and brothers, who have followed with me in the dark path of danger, will you not follow with me in the way of the Great Chief above? It is the way of peace. These are my words to you." He could not proceed any further. It was affecting to see the interest with which these stalwart Haidas received his words.

It was his parting charge to them. A few days afterwards I received a message from him at midnight expressing an earnest desire to see me. As I entered the lodge in which he lay he was told I had come, when he turned round, and looking up at me, extended his hand. As I grasped it he exclaimed in a firm, clear voice, in the Tsimshean tongue, with which he was familiar, " Ltha gwildum kowdiut, ltha

MAKAI

gwildum kowdiut " (" I am ready, I am ready "). I knelt beside him to speak a word of cheer, but as there was no response I felt his pulse and found that life was extinct. He had survived to convey to me his last message, which he did so distinctly that all in the lodge heard it. It impressed them deeply. They had never heard anything like this before. It sounded like a message from the other world. Thus Makai passed away, leaving a good record behind him. In accordance with his own desire his remains were interred with due solemnity in the beautiful island burying-ground which I had selected. He did not wish that his body should be encased in a totem pole or elevated on a mortuary platform. I conducted the burial service, and as a large number of Haidas had followed us, I gave an address over the open grave, to which they were most attentive. The idea of resurrection was new and strange to them. I had succeeded in forming an equivalent for the term in the Haida language, and with the aid of illustrations from the books of Nature and of Revelation they were enabled to understand it. The "corn of wheat" of the gospel and the "bare grain of wheat" of St. Paul's grand illustration of resurrection in Corinthians, carried the truth to more than one standing around Makai's remains. Thus the first-fruits of the Haidas were being gathered in.

A rumour now reached me of the outbreak of an epidemic, of that dread scourge the smallpox, amongst some distant tribes in Alaska. Knowing the terrible ravages which it had wrought amongst the Haida tribes on two previous occasions, I resolved to endeavour to introduce vaccination amongst them. I realised there would be a degree of risk and difficulty from the danger of inflammation afterwards, in some constitutions. In such case the medicine men would not be slow to accuse me of having introduced a poison with which I was endeavouring to kill them. Yet the assurance that I was making an effort to shield them against an enemy which had carried off nearly half

MAKAI

the Haida population, both on the islands and on the Alaskan shores, would, I believed, eventually give me another victory over the sorcery and superstition of the necromancers. Having at length succeeded in procuring a supply of vaccine lymph from the Indian Department of the Canadian Government, I invited a number of the Haidas to meet me in the Mission-room. I informed them of the danger in which they stood should the Kali-koustla (smallpox) again attack them, and the advantage to be gained by vaccination. I informed them of how the Iron people had suffered from its ravages in the past, until this remedy had been discovered. I endeavoured by every means in my power to induce some of them to submit to the operation, but in vain. They shrunk from it, evidently fearing that there was something mysterious in it. At length I resolved on trying the force and influence of example. Casting off my coat, I bared my arm, and vaccinated myself before them all.

I completed the operation, took up my vaccine and lance, and turning to them said: "Now since none of you would consent to be vaccinated, I have placed the medicine on myself. Should the Kali-koustla come now, probably numbers of you will die, as when it came formerly, but I shall escape." I was just leaving the room when a stalwart Haida who was a sub-chief sprang to his feet and exclaimed: "Etlagida lagging di ishin, tung kiwunsit alzeil kum di quothal ashang" ("Chief, it is good that you should place the mark on me also that I may not die"). I accordingly at once vaccinated him. His example was promptly followed by the others who were present. The rumour soon sped throughout the camps of the wonderful remedy; the scianawa of the Iron man which could effect what all their medicine men had failed to do, even to save them from the evil spirit of the Kali-koustla, and men, women, and children came crowding in upon me, so that for several days I could scarce find time to eat, so great was the rush for vaccination. But alas for the results. Though I had taken

MAKAI

the precaution of warning them that it would probably become painful and swollen in a few days, yet I was not prepared for the storm of indignation which arose. Some of them became very unwell; not only the arm but in several cases the shoulder and neck became inflamed and swollen, and as the effect followed the cause so quickly they feared the worst, and threatened to shoot me, should the symptoms increase. I was now as fully engaged in endeavouring to soothe and allay the symptoms which had arisen, as I had been before in vaccinating. One case especially caused me grave anxiety. The swelling and high fever which accompanied it was intense. The medicine men declared he would die, and that my bad medicine was worse than the smallpox. I prescribed such remedies as I knew would subdue the inflammation and allay the fever, and he began to recover. The same treatment proved successful throughout. The medicine men were baffled and ashamed. And many more came from both north and south to obtain the virus with which the medicine man of the Iron people could defeat the common foe, which they all feared so greatly. But as soon as one difficulty had been surmounted another arose.

Visiting a chief believed to be dying, I found he had called his sister, and delivered to her a slave girl, who was to act as his nurse on his reincarnation and birth, as her child. He believed that after his death his spirit would again return in the first child born afterwards in his family. He strictly charged his sister to superintend his nursing, and to be careful that he received no injury. I was thus led to inquire concerning this belief, and found it was entertained generally by the Haidas. I have since discovered that it is not peculiar to the Haidas, but has been held by the coast tribes generally. Very often the name of the deceased is given to the new-born child in recognition of this belief. It is but another testimony of the innate desire of man for immortality. But the Divine revelation has brought life and immortality to light. I introduced in my teaching

MAKAI

the great truth set forth by the Apostle in the fifteenth chapter of 1st Corinthians, "to every seed its own body," and the truth of the resurrection proved the most effective antidote to this error. I found also that it was not unusual amongst them to cast offerings of food into the fire to supply the wants of the souls of departed friends. From the terms used to denote this custom, and also that of seeking to propitiate the spirits which they associated with the forces of nature, we derived the terms both in the Haida and in the Tsimshean languages by which to render the word "sacrifice."

A great "potlatch" or distribution of property was now about to be made at an encampment between Virago Sound and North Island named "Yatz." To this all the Haidas to the north of the islands, as also the Haidas of Prince of Wales Island in Alaska, had been invited. I accordingly resolved on a mission to that point also. The old trader, over whom a great change had passed, I invited to accompany me. He had abandoned all his heathen sympathies, had been duly united by marriage to the Tsimshean woman with whom he had lived for many years, and had requested to be received into the Church of Christ. His wife also had gladly received the truth and was baptized. Both of them were now endeavouring to show the heathen a good example. This was helpful to the work of the Mission, as native races are always powerfully influenced for good or evil by the whites who reside amongst them. We set out in a good canoe with a crew of five Haidas, and crossing the inlet coasted along the north of the island. Towards evening a sudden squall arose and quickly lashed the sea into foam-crested waves. We were compelled to seek shelter in a little opening between the rocks, where we found a sandy beach. Here we decided to encamp for the night. After our evening meal and prayer, we cut away the undergrowth and spread out our mats and blankets. Whilst thus engaged our old friend the trader, who was looking on, anxiously inquired, "Must we lie down there?" "Yes," I

MAKAI

replied, " it will be all right when we have spread our mats and blankets." " I fear to lie down where there are so many reptiles," he replied. " Oh," I assured him, " they are harmless, only field-mice and frogs, so that you need not fear."

We accorded our friend a place to sleep in the centre with Chief Cowhoe on one side, whilst I lay on the other. In the middle of the night, I was suddenly aroused by a loud whoop, and at the same moment I received a violent blow in the face. I sprang to my feet, believing we were attacked. Chief Cowhoe and the other Haidas had seized their guns and stood at bay, peering around for the enemy. The campfire had gone out and it was dark. " Who struck me?" inquired Chief Cowhoe indignantly. Before I could reply there was another yell, and instantly our friend, who was yet lying down, began to rain blows around him right and left, whilst he continued to cry out in rage and terror. He was in a nightmare from which with difficulty I aroused him. Cowhoe was angry, as he had received a blow from which he was still ailing. I assured him that I had been struck also, and informed them of the cause, as they feared he had gone mad. On fully recovering consciousness he apologised and informed us that he had had a bad dream, in which he saw the vermin of the camp gradually crawling towards him, and this it was that had caused his fright and outcry. " Had I not been at hand," I replied, " I fear you would have fared badly, if I may judge from the faces around." " Oh," he replied, " I could not sleep for some hours because of our surroundings, and when at length I slept I dreamed that a large snake was creeping towards me and endeavoured to crawl into my mouth, and it was in my efforts to prevent it that I must have struck out." I explained this to the Indians, and they instantly burst into roars of laughter at our friend's expense. We all settled down to rest again, thankful that it was not worse.

It is much safer to encamp in the open air on the Queen

MAKAI

Charlotte Islands than it is on the mainland. There are no wolves on the islands, nor are there any grizzly bears, both of which are numerous in many places on the mainland. On several occasions I have had to keep watch throughout the night owing to the bears and wolves which snorted and whined around my tent. On another occasion I was compelled to sleep on the branch of a tree for safety. But it was not from the denizens of the forest that the Haidas feared an attack, but rather from some of the tribes who had come over from the Alaskan shore to attend the great " potlatch." For they had not forgotten the wars of the past in which they had been compelled to abandon their own encampment on North Island and the isles to the west of Graham Island, and to seek refuge on the shores of Prince of Wales Island to the North of Dixon Entrance, which island now forms a part of south-eastern Alaska. On the following morning we re-embarked, being anxious to reach the camp, but we had not proceeded far when we found we were followed by a large shark. Its large fin towered high above the stern of our canoe and caused considerable uneasiness amongst our crew, but to Squire it was a cause of terror. Being a very heavy man, he was seated in the bottom of the canoe, and with much difficulty he kept turning and twisting from side to side, in order to look around at this strange follower. At length, tired of his efforts, he appealed to me to tell him if it was yet following us. He was much distressed, as he feared it would attack and upset our canoe. We had a fresh halibut on board which the Haidas stated was the attraction, as the shark scented it.

At length the Haidas became disconcerted, as it pressed on our canoe, and one of them seized his rifle to shoot it. But the others called on him to desist as, if only wounded, it would probably capsize or smash our frail craft. But Cowhoe, who was steering, called for the sail-pole, stating, as he did so, that he had heard from the old hunters that a blow dealt fairly on the head would stun the shark, and

MAKAI

cause it to sink. Standing up, with the sail-pole in hand, he brought it down with all his might, the heavy end, which was slightly sharpened, striking the shark fairly on the head. It lashed the water powerfully with its tail, dashing it over us, and with a swirl disappeared in the depths, and troubled us no more. In the Haida language the shark is termed a "kahtow," or the mother of the dogfish, and is so named from the resemblance between them.

In a few hours we arrived in sight of the encampment, where there was evidently a very large gathering. The canoes were hauled up in orderly lines along the beach, and from the sail-pole each waved either the Union Jack or the Stars and Stripes. A westerly breeze was springing up which floated them proudly, and the union of the colours indicated a union of hearts. May it ever be thus. If the Indian tribes can thus bury the disputes of the past and scatter the swan and eagle's down over each other, their most treasured emblems of peace, how much more should we, who profess the possession of a higher civilisation, endeavour to keep the "unity of the spirit in the bond of peace." May the same colours be found united on every sea as the safeguard of peace. In the van of the world's progress may they ever be united in disseminating the light of truth, and distributing the leaves of the Tree of Life, which alone can effect the healing of the nations. The peaceful settlement of the disputed boundary line by the United Commission is a cause for thankfulness. It has at least shown the world that there is a better way of settling disputes than by the reckless expenditure of means, and the cruel sacrifice of lives, until one or the other, or sometimes both the combatants are bankrupt in funds and broken in power.

We were well received by the united gathering, and the largest lodge was opened and prepared for a service. Not only was the interior well filled, but around the outside of the building and on the roof large numbers assembled to

MAKAI

hear the message of life and salvation. The hymns in their own tongue were a great attraction. The prayers to the Great Chief above (Sha Lana nung Etlageda), of whose name they had only heard in their ancient legends, astonished them. And to hear in their own tongue the wonderful works of God, had introduced a new theme for discussion around their camp-fires.

The darkness and ignorance of heathenism was passing away, and on these long benighted and fierce islanders, the true light from the Sun of Righteousness was rising. After a very busy day, we were glad to retire to rest under our canoe-sail. During my visit I was kept fully engaged in prescribing medicines for the sick and imparting instructions to inquirers.

On our return trip, as we encountered rough weather, we ran into Virago Sound and Harbour to visit the encampment there. There were no Haidas in camp. They had all gone to the gathering which we had visited. Their lodges and totem poles resemble those of Massett. The camp is well sheltered and stands in a good position, being convenient both for halibut and salmon fishing, and also near to the resorts of the fur seal.

This harbour would seem to offer special advantages for a naval station, corresponding to that of Esquimalt on the south of Vancouver Island. It commands Dixon Entrance, which separates the Queen Charlotte Islands from Alaska, and is, as its name indicates, the entrance from the Pacific to the coast of the mainland and Prince Rupert.

The abundance of halibut in these waters is surprising. I have seen an old man and his wife push out in their canoe, and in less than two hours return to shore, heavily laden with fine large fish, of which some would weigh from eighty to a hundred pounds. These they cut up lengthways in thin slices, which they hang up in the same way as clothes, to dry in the sun. This halibut, as dried by the Haidas, is a favourite article of food amongst the coast tribes, and is bartered to them by the Haidas for the olachan grease, which is generally eaten with almost all their food, especially with dried fish, herring-spawn, and a species of sea-weed.

Halibut, dried or fresh, formed our principal food on the islands, with occasionally a piece of bear's meat when in season, and also water-fowl. There are no deer on the islands, though they abound on the mainland, and on the islands of the coast, both of Alaska and British Columbia. Probably on this account there are no wolves on the Queen Charlotte group. This fact induced me to endeavour to introduce deer, and on one of my visits to the mainland I offered to purchase live deer from the Tsimshean hunters. I succeeded in procuring seven, to which one was afterwards added, and which was captured by a steamer on her voyage up the coast. The Hudson's Bay Company carried them across to the islands on their steamer free of charge. These deer throve and increased for several years under the protection of an officer of the Hudson's Bay Company, who succeeded the first trader, and who was also a magistrate. But after his death the Haidas shot them off, until I fear they were annihilated. Had they been preserved, they would have served as a food supply on the islands, and it would be quite worthy the attention of the Government to renew the stock, seeing there are no wolves to injure them, as on the mainland.

Sheldon Jackson, the pioneer missionary to Alaska, conferred a lasting benefit on the Esquimaux there by introducing the reindeer from Siberia. These not only supply the natives with milk and food, but enable them to perform long journeys without having to carry provender for them, as they scrape away the snow, and eat the moss, latterly known as reindeer moss (*Cladonia rangiferina*), which they find underneath. Continuing our return voyage, we were again compelled to encamp on an exposed point for the night, as the wind had increased to a gale, so that it was impossible to proceed. It continued rough throughout the night, and had abated but little the following day. We hesitated to embark, but our friend the trader was most anxious to return. Acting against our own judgment, in our desire to oblige him, we ventured. It was an arduous struggle against wind and wave, and our progress was but slow despite our best efforts. When at length we reached the entrance to the Massett Inlet, out of which the wind was blowing a gale, the tide was near to the full. Steering close in to the shore, we succeeded in reaching a point from which we could sail across the inlet close to the wind. We had not proceeded far when the tide turned, and shortly after our sail was rent to pieces with the fury of the blast. We had gained the mid-channel, where the current was fast carrying us seaward, and our Haida crew gave free expression to their feelings: " We shall all be lost ! " cried the man who had gathered in the fragments of the torn sail, " and you will have been the cause, Squire, for selling such bad stuff. I got that sail in your store just before we left," and he looked at the trader as though he would like to have thrown him overboard. The latter groaned as he turned to me in despair, and cried, " Oh, what can I do ? "

" There is but one thing you can do," I replied, " pray ! " And instantly he burst forth into prayer, but the burden of his petition, repeated again and again, was for forgiveness for having embarked in such a craft, with a vow that if spared to reach the shore, he would never set his foot in a dugout again.[1] Though in imminent danger, as we were being fast carried out to the open ocean where the waves must speedily overwhelm us, yet I could scarce repress a smile at such a prayer. " Squire," I cried, " do you consider it sinful to embark in a canoe ? " " Oh, I do not know what I am saying, pardon me," he replied. I reminded my crew that there was a return eddy shoreward

---

[1] " Dugout" is a term often given by the whites to the Indian canoe, because each canoe is hewn out of one tree.

MAKAI

on the further side of the current, and if we could only gain this we should succeed, unless we were swamped in making the shore. Thus encouraged they paddled as for life, and we found we were making increased progress, as we got under the lee of the land. To encourage our white friend, I informed him that I could discern what appeared to be people watching us from the shore. It turned out, however, to be but driftwood.

We reached the shore quite exhausted, but thankful for our deliverance. Not a word was uttered by Squire, who appeared as though overcome by fear, and when I called some hours after to ascertain how he was, his wife and daughters inquired as to what had occurred, as he had not spoken nor had he eaten anything since his return. I related what we had passed through and gradually induced him to join in the conversation, which broke the spell which appeared to bind him. "Oh," he exclaimed, "I have told you before you are a desperate man, and you will die in the water!" "But you forget," I replied, "that it was your anxiety to return which forced us to embark, as both my Haida crew and myself had decided to wait for a lull in the storm." Squire kept his vow thus made in the hour of peril, as nothing would induce him to embark in a canoe again for a trip, however short. But though he refused to accompany me again to sea, he endeavoured to assist our efforts both by precept and example, and thus he manifested the reality of the change which he had experienced. He had decided to retire from the service of the Hudson's Bay Company, and as the time drew near for his return to the mainland his anxiety to undo, if possible, whatever he had erred in increased. He requested permission to inaugurate a weekly prayer meeting in his own house, to which I gladly assented. I had already instituted such a meeting every Thursday, and it was not unusual now to hear several of the leading chiefs as well as a number of the young men leading in prayer for themselves and for

MAKAI

their fellow-tribesmen. It had originated in a social gathering shortly after the erection of the Mission-house, when I invited all who appeared desirous to forsake the old life and follow the new way. I reminded them that they had now heard the Gospel message in their own tongue, and that I should be glad to know what they thought of it, or whether they believed it. When I had ceased speaking the leading chief, Weha, whose reply to me on my first visit at the meeting held in his lodge was summed up in the words, "You have come too late," rose to reply. He had long since changed his opinion, and his face bore a very different expression now as he replied. "At first when I heard the words of the Great Father the Chief of Heaven (Shanung Etlageda) it did not reach my heart. Then it seemed to lay hold on me, and whether in the forest or on the ocean I could not forget it. The wind in the trees sounded His word, the waves on the shore re-echoed it; I could not sleep at night thinking of the evil deeds I had wrought in the past. But then when you told of His mercy and of His love in sending His only Son (Il keet-an-shwan-shungs etil Shalana) Jesus Christ to lift our heavy load from off us and to bear it on Himself, I saw and believed it, and now I am glad both by day and night. I am no longer under the shadow of the mountain, but I live in the sunshine on the summit." He was followed by several others, amongst whom was the young chief Cowhoe. The Testament which had been given him by the good Captain was no longer a sealed book to him, for he knew and rejoiced in many of the precious truths it contained. Edenshew, too, influenced by his son Cowhoe, was seeking the Way of Life.

Steilta's successor, the chief of the eagle crest, had early decided for the truth, and had stood firm despite much opposition from some of his tribe. At their own request I registered their names, together with the names of thirty others, as catechumens. There were others who desired to be registered, but as they had not wholly abandoned all heathen practices, their application was postponed. The medicine men were eager now to seize every opportunity to oppose and discourage all inquirers after the truth. This was shown in the case of a gun accident which happened to a young man, one of the most earnest of the catechumens. He had learned to read, and had obtained a Bible before leaving on a hunting and fishing expedition, in order to improve his own knowledge and to benefit his companions in the chase. As he himself expressed it, "I do not know very much yet, but I have learned that the Word teaches, 'And let him that heareth say Come,' and so I am able to obey that, and will try and call my friends to come also."

This he did faithfully, but on his return, whilst unloading his canoe, he seized a gun to lift it out with the muzzle towards him. In doing so he gave it a slight pull forwards, and the trigger striking the thwart of the canoe the gun was discharged. It was heavily loaded with shot, which tore through and carried away the greater part of the flesh of the forearm from the bone. A messenger arrived in haste to inform me he was bleeding to death, and we hastened to his assistance. Together with my wife, we were enabled to dress the wound and arrest the hæmorrhage. He made a good recovery, though it left a bad scar. This, like every mishap to an inquirer, the medicine men hastened to attribute to the new teaching and its influences, but it only served to lead to further inquiry, and to strengthen our adherents in the faith.

CHAPTER XVII

INTRODUCTION OF LAW

"Be darkness at Thy coming light,
Confusion, order in Thy path,
Souls without strength, inspire with might,
Bid Mercy triumph over Wrath."
MONTGOMERY.

THE time was now ripe for the introduction of law in the community. The teachings of Christianity had prepared them for it, by the illumination of their understandings. Many of them evinced concern for the welfare of their forefathers and friends who had passed away without the knowledge which they now possessed. I was enabled to satisfy and assure them in regard to this, by reminding them that the Great Chief above would judge righteously according to the measure of light and knowledge possessed by His children.

"Your forefathers," I informed them, "with the knowledge and light they possessed were enabled to discern a man by his actions, as to whether he was bad or good. This is evident from your own language, for you speak of one man as 'Etlinga lagung,' a good man, whilst you say of another 'Eetlinga dahaung-ak,' or, a bad man. These terms were not made by you, nor yet by me, they have come down to you in the language used by your forefathers. And why did they thus distinguish as between man and man? Was it not because of their actions that they were thus designated as bad or good? And if your forefathers could thus judge, and classify men by their actions, how much more the Great Chief on High, who knows the thoughts and

INTRODUCTION OF LAW

intents of men's hearts. He will render to every man according to his deeds, and according to his righteousness."

This argument from their own language enabled them to understand it more clearly than from any other illustration given. As the Hudson's Bay Company was about to appoint another officer to take charge of their trading post on the islands in the place of our old friend now resigned, I wrote to the Attorney-General of the Province begging that the officer when appointed might be requested to accept a Commission of the Peace. I had been frequently called upon to settle all manner of disputes which arose in connection with their slaves, or out of the fire-water feasts, or from gambling, or other causes, and in adjudicating in these disputes I was compelled to call upon the offenders to find bail for their future good behaviour. This was generally paid in blankets or furs, so that I had quite a stock of such property awaiting the arrival of a properly qualified officer of the law, to decide them definitely.

Some of these cases were serious, where life had been endangered and threatened; others were more amusing, as in the case of two men who were engaged in fishing near Tow Hill, on the north-eastern coast of the islands. One of them, who was no longer a young man and was affected with a stiffness of the neck, sighted a black bear when wandering along the shore from the camp. Not having a gun, he hastened back, and called upon his companion to bring his gun and follow him quickly. He then returned on the track of the bear, which he was eager to keep in sight.

Bruin, suspecting he was followed, retreated into the forest quickly, followed by Cogese Haung, as the older hunter was called. He followed hard and fast on the bear's trail until he came to a fallen tree, over which he scrambled, only to find himself right in front of the bear, which had evidently selected this position to await his pursuer.

The hunter, thus taken at a disadvantage unexpectedly, and being unable to retreat as the bear was on him, suddenly

HAIDA TOMBS

At Massett, Queen Charlotte Islands, B.C. The side-posts are solid and sunk in the ground. The horizontal piece is hollow, and contains the corpse. These tombs are now falling through decay.

TOMB OF INDIAN CHIEF

He belonged to the Kunhadda Crest, represented by a frog.

INTRODUCTION OF LAW

dived under the tree over which he had just crossed. The opening under the tree was large enough to admit his body. Bruin thrust in his claw to pull the old hunter out, and inflicted an ugly wound on his arm. Suddenly remembering his hunting knife, which he had in his belt, he pulled it out, and as Bruin thrust in his paw again, the hunter struck at it with his knife. This was repeated again and again, knife against paw, and claw against knife, until blood flowed freely from both bear and hunter. Just then, while as yet the issue was uncertain, a loud whoop was heard. It was from the other hunter, a young man, who, following with his gun, desired to locate his companion. The old man gladly responded to the cry, and as he advanced shouted out loudly again, informing him of the relative positions of himself and the bear, lest he might also be taken unawares, or lest he might shoot him by mistake. Meantime the bear continued to endeavour to pull the old hunter from his refuge, so that when his friend came to his rescue his arm was badly lacerated with the claws of the bear. Approaching the fallen tree the hunter peered over, and aiming his gun, shot the bear through the heart.

It was a good fur bear, and when brought to the trading post the hunter received some twelve dollars for it, of which he handed but one dollar to the old man, who had first sighted it, and was thus injured by following it. As we had dressed the poor fellow's arm, and he was still under our care, he complained to me, and I called the young hunter and demanded that the amount received should be equally divided. As he had not spent the entire amount, I had no difficulty in procuring the balance for my old friend, and I believe it hastened the healing of his injured arm as much as our dressings. I made the young hunter feel ashamed by putting his selfish act before him in its true light. This is a fair illustration of how many of their troubles arose, and of the necessity for a way in which to settle such difficulties amicably and equitably.

INTRODUCTION OF LAW

I was glad, therefore, on the arrival of the officer who had been appointed, A. M'Kenzie, Esq., to find that he had been offered and had accepted a Commission of the Peace.

"But," exclaimed he, as he informed me of it, "of what use can it be here, where there is neither law nor order, and how can law be enforced?"

"It would have been of no use here when I arrived," I replied, "but the Gospel has prepared the way for the law, and now there will be no difficulty. As soon as you are at liberty to open court you can do so in my large Mission-room, and I can bring forward several of the leading men, whom you can swear in as special constables—men in whom I have every confidence, as they have stood by me through evil and through good report." He was astonished, and replied, "Why, I have always heard that these Haidas were the terror of the coast, and I should not have accepted the position but that I knew you were here."

"Well," I replied, "you will now see for yourself the change which the Gospel has effected amongst them, a change which nothing else could have wrought. Very much remains to be done yet, but I feel that the worst has been overcome."

He was greatly encouraged by my statement, and accordingly court was opened a week after his arrival. I had selected and instructed my men, who were first called forward and sworn before a crowded room. Cowhoe was the first officer sworn, and to him it was no mere form. He knew well the importance of the truths which the book he was requested to kiss contained. He could well say, "The words of Thy mouth are dearer to me than thousands of gold and silver." He was followed by Steilta, the young chief, whose predecessor had declared that had he lived he should have been "first in God's way," and whose remains were the first to have Christian burial. After the peace-making which had taken place in regard to the slaves, he had come out on the side of the truth, and had witnessed a good confession.

INTRODUCTION OF LAW

Next came Kinas-Kilass, a name famed in Haida story, where his forefathers were always represented as first in fight and adventure. He, too, had proved himself worthy, and his courage was undoubted. He was amongst the first who had been registered as catechumens. The fourth was as fine-looking physically as the others, and each of them were over six feet in height, but this last was the only one whose face was tattooed, which caused him to look fiercer than he was. When all had been duly sworn, the court was opened, and case after case was disposed of until I had got rid of all the pledges which had been stored away. This occupied us several days.

These freebooters had formerly declared, when I warned them that slavery was unlawful, that they owed no allegiance to any sovereign or state, and when I ventured to show them their islands on the map, had declared indignantly that I was lying, and rushed out in anger. The insignificance of the Queen Charlotte Islands, in comparison with the American continent, aroused their ire. Now they were becoming a law-abiding and peaceable community, and the slaves, whose condition had greatly improved, were fast being adopted into the families of the owners.

It was at this juncture that I decided to make an effort to induce them to cleanse the camp by burying the dead, whose remains were scattered broadcast. I called together a number of the chiefs and leading men, and put before them the necessity for such a step for sanitary, social, and Christian reasons. There were some dissentients, who urged that the customs of their forefathers were good enough for them, and that they did not wish to forsake them for the customs of the Yetz hahada or "iron people." I reminded them of what they had suffered from the ravages of the smallpox, and how they had submitted to be vaccinated, and that, in order to be free from this and other diseases, it was necessary to bury the dead and clean their encampments. Several of the chiefs expressed their desire to see my proposal

INTRODUCTION OF LAW

carried out, as they began now to feel ashamed of the manner in which the remains of their deceased ancestors and relatives were scattered throughout the camps.

My difficulty, I found afterwards, was to persuade any to assist me in this work. For each one shrunk from interfering with the remains of the dead relatives of others, and as they were all thrown together, they could not discern their own. At length I succeeded in obtaining a number of the slaves. These I directed to dig deep pits, near to the largest deposits of the dead. In these the remains were interred until the chief thoroughfares were cleaned. I rewarded the slaves for the good work they had done, and for the first time we had the pleasure of being able to walk through the encampment without the unpleasant associations which had generally accompanied it.

Whilst thus improving internally, there was also an increasing desire to improve their standing and relationship with those against whom they had carried on their raids, and whose camps they had devastated in the past. A long-standing quarrel between them and an Alaskan tribe was now peaceably settled. The Haidas had been in the habit of making periodical raids on all the tribes of the mainland in succession. Now it was against the Tlingit, then the Nishkas, and after that against the Tsimsheans they fought. Then they would make an expedition away far to the south, on the east or west of Vancouver Island, returning after some time with many slaves and much booty. In addition they frequently fought amongst themselves, the northern tribes against the south, or sometimes against the tribes on the west coast. In their attack on the Nishka tribes, which led to a war between them, they had to ascend the Nass some twenty miles from the mouth. The aggressors who inaugurated the strife were the Haidas of Yehling, an encampment near to Rose Spit, on the northeastern promontory of the islands.

It was rumoured that one man of their tribe who was visit-

INTRODUCTION OF LAW

ing the Nishkas had been killed. At once Gaioutlins and another chief summoned their men to prepare, by drinking salt water, which was always the custom, as already explained, when about to start on a warlike expedition. This was done under the directions of the medicine men, and was generally continued for several days. Then the large war canoes were launched and having embarked they pulled out to sea, chanting war songs in which those on the shore joined. Such was the expedition which led the attack on the Nishkas. They gained a point not far from the villages overnight, where they drew up their canoes under cover, and having set a watch, lay down to rest to await the dawn. Early in the morning, with the flowing tide, they swept up on the sleeping villages, and landing, rushed to the attack. It had been arranged that half the warriors of each canoe should attack a lodge, whilst the remainder should guard the canoes and be ready to receive and bind the captives. With their base thus protected, the others stealthily advanced on the lodges. All this was but the work of a minute or two, as the Indian dogs in the camp, of which there were many attached to each lodge, had at once raised the alarm. But to little purpose, for as the first Indians aroused rushed out to learn the cause, they were either struck down or seized, and passed to the canoe-men, who bound them and threw them into their canoes. Those who offered the most vigorous resistance were for the most part slain, though several Haidas fell in the attack, and many more would have fallen, but that they retreated as quickly as they had arrived; for the men of the other lodges which had not been attacked were fast rallying to the support of their friends. They were too late, however, to rescue those who had been captured, as the canoe-men had kept the canoes afloat, and as the retreating warriors cast their captives into the canoes they sprang in after them, and with a loud whoop they were at once well out on the river, with a fair wind and a falling tide. Some of their captives, however, made such vigorous struggles for freedom on the passage down the river,

INTRODUCTION OF LAW

that the canoes were in danger of being upset or broken. Fearing to face the open ocean with such desperate captives, they landed at a convenient point at the mouth of the river, and slew all who had thus resisted. Their scalps they left hanging on the face of a bluff hard by, and this incident has given the name of Kincolith, or the Rock of Scalps, to this place, which has long been our leading Mission station on the river.

Once fairly out on the ocean, the Haidas had no further fear of being followed, and they reached their encampments chanting songs of victory. It was not to be expected that the Nishkas would long remain passive after this fierce attack. They were anxious to avenge their friends who had been enslaved. But they had to prepare their fleet to face a voyage of over one hundred miles before they could look their enemies in the face, and this required time. At length they started. Favoured by a strong down-river wind, which continued and carried their fleet out to sea, and past the outer islands, their courage rose as they sighted the mountains of "Lak Haida," Queen Charlotte Islands, rising on the western horizon. But the watchful Haidas were on the alert. Some of them who were out hunting the sea otter in their canoes first descried the Nishka fleet while yet far distant, and hastening shoreward gave the alarm. But more than half the fighting men of the camp were absent, having been invited to a great feast of the "Ahtiwass Hahada" on the northern inlet. A fleet-footed messenger was despatched to apprise them, whilst those in camp prepared to meet the attack.

Meanwhile the necromancers were not idle. They were engaged in casting offerings on the waters and supplicating the Scanawa of "Nee-kwun," the Spirit of the Storm, to rise and lash the waters off the Rose Spit into fury to overwhelm the advancing foe. For often when food was scarce and they had thus sought its aid, had not a whale been cast up on it to appease their hunger? So superstitious were they in regard to the supernatural powers possessed by the "Un-unā,"

INTRODUCTION OF LAW

or Spirit of the Storm, that on one occasion when crossing the waters of Rose Spit in a canoe with a chief and his son, the lad happened to expectorate in the water, upon which his father became very angry and threatened to cast him overboard if ever he should so insult the Un-unā of the bar again. When I ventured to remonstrate with him in regard to it, and to point out his error, he replied that such an offence would not have been overlooked when he was young, as many had forfeited their lives by similar offences, which might bring destruction on our canoe.

Probably the medicine men, who were also weather prophets, had discerned the signs of an approaching squall, for just as the Nishka fleet approached the shore on the northwesterly side of the promontory, a sudden storm broke, which prevented part of the fleet from landing. Those of them who had succeeded in reaching the shore rushed upon the village, as the Haidas had taken to the cover of the forest as they approached, and finding the lodges blockaded from the interior, at once made preparations to fire the town. To prevent this the Haidas opened fire from their hiding-places, but the Nishka warriors, having been reinforced by the crews of several canoes which had succeeded in effecting a landing, were thus enabled to return the firing, whilst the remainder continued to set fire to lodge after lodge in succession.

Whilst the village was burning the skirmishing was continued for some hours, and numbers fell on both sides. The Nishka also discovered a storehouse belonging to the leading chief, which stood concealed in the forest behind the village. This they raided and burnt also. In the meantime the smoke of the burning camp had been sighted by some of the Haidas of the Massett Inlet, who at once informed their guests. They surmised the cause, and hastily embarked and hurried to the aid of their fellow-tribesmen, but several of the Nishka canoe-men, who were anchored offshore in readiness to retreat, gave the signal to those on shore. They succeeded in embarking under a harassing fire from the

INTRODUCTION OF LAW

Haidas, which wounded several, but as the squall had abated and a steady west wind was blowing, they soon left the scene of the combat far astern. Though they had failed to recover their friends who had been captured, yet they were in high spirits at having been enabled to burn the settlement, and thus carry the war into their enemy's camp, where they had hitherto considered themselves secure.

The Haidas again attacked the Nishkas, and succeeded in burning a part of one of the lower villages, but were repulsed. On their return down from the Nass on this occasion they encountered four canoes, which they attacked and overpowered, killing some of the occupants and capturing the remainder. The Haidas had thought these were Nishkas, but it turned out to be Tsimsheans whom they had thus attacked. This aroused the Tsimsheans, and a large fleet set out against them. They succeeded in effecting a landing, but found the encampment which had formerly been the headquarters of the tribe which attacked them deserted. Fearing a united attack from both the Nishkas and Tsimsheans, they had removed to Massett. To this camp the Tsimsheans followed them, and a fierce fight took place, in which a number were killed on both sides. After this, the Haidas made a raid on the Tsimsheans when they were encamped on the Lower Skeena, and succeeded in capturing some and slaying others. This led the Tsimsheans to prepare another expedition against the islanders, in which they succeeded in capturing a party of women who were out berrying. They also killed several men, whilst a number escaped to the forest.

For some time after this the Haidas were continually engaged in raiding and skirmishing along the coast of the mainland. No place was free from their ravages. At Kshawatlins, near to where the new terminal city of Prince Rupert now stands, between Metlakahtla and the Skeena, they surprised and captured several canoes laden with salmon. There were twelve Haida war canoes engaged in this raid, and they succeeded in capturing several Tsimshean canoes and over

INTRODUCTION OF LAW

twenty prisoners. But although the Tsimsheans were taken by surprise, and were unprepared to fight, yet they sold their lives dearly, and a number of the Haidas were shot in the attack.

On a small island in Lake Kshwatlins may be seen the remains of the fortification to which the Tsimshean fishermen fled on the approach of the Haidas. The Haidas now began to realise that they had continued the war too long, and were winning a bad reputation, which might work to their injury. One of the leading war chiefs proposed a peace. His proposal was at first opposed by some, but the majority were in favour of a change. Gaowtlins was also for peace. Messages of peace were sent to the Tsimsheans and Nishkas, with the announcement that the peacemakers were coming. These carried the swan and eagle's down. They were received with joy, and the dancers were welcomed in the camps, where they scattered the down over the Tsimsheans first, and then presented them with peace offerings of slaves and other property. They then carried the swansdown to the Nishkas, whom they propitiated in like manner. Almost all those captured were returned. For a subchief whom they had killed a number of slaves were given in exchange. The Nishkas, in return, loaded their canoes with boxes of olachan grease, which is much prized by the Indians as an article of food. The war chant was changed to songs of peace along the coast and out to the islands. For a time there were but few slaves amongst the Northern Haidas. But this peace was not permanent. Ere long the signs and sounds of strife again arose. This time the Southern Haidas were the aggressors.

It remained for the advent of Christian Missions to lay the foundation for a lasting peace. And on many of the old battle-grounds, where formerly tribe fought against tribe, and people against people, we have witnessed Haidas, Tsimsheans, Tlingits, and Nishkas joining with heart and voice in singing the praises of the Prince of Peace in the angelic anthem which announced His birth, "Glory to God in the highest, and on earth peace, good will to men."

CHAPTER XVIII

A TOUCHING PARTING

" The wall of foam far out to sea
With a roar like thunder swept our lea,
Whilst tossed about with wind and wave,
We laboured hard our craft to save."

W. H. C.

AS heathen, the Haida custom was to issue invitations early each year, and to assemble as many of the tribes as possible to one point or encampment for the dance and potlatch. It was generally arranged some weeks previously which camp should be the rendezvous, and due preparation was made to receive and entertain the guests. Sometimes in a large camp there would be several totem poles carved and awaiting erection. Of these, one or more would be mortuary totems for deceased chiefs, and the others crest totems erected by the chiefs or leading men to signalise their succession to a title or chieftainship.

Like the Indians on the mainland, the Haidas are fond of music and singing, and not the least part of the programme was the chanting of their own praises or that of their guests. In every tribe there was one or more well known as leaders and instructors in the chants and songs of the tribe. Time was kept by rude drums which were formed like large square or oblong boxes of well-seasoned red cedar wood, covered with skin. This and a cedar trumpet which was much used by the medicine men, with their rattles, were their only instruments. They made more noise than music, and as their chants were more monotonous

A TOUCHING PARTING

than melodious the true melody and compass of the voice was not exercised. In the first services which I conducted, I had to be both choir and choirmaster, as there was no one to assist me but my wife when present. I was sometimes disconcerted by a loud remark or a burst of laughter from my congregation, as they criticised the singing of the "Yetzhahada" to one another. After a little, when I had translated and composed some hymns and chants in their own tongue, I taught them to sing them, and they were both surprised and pleased at the improvement in their vocal powers. It acted as a charm also in drawing many to the services who otherwise might not have attended.

Ere long I was encouraged to hear the songs of Zion when passing through the camp, or along the shore, or at times from their canoes, when returning shoreward after dusk. It was this which led me to propose to them to receive their friends with a new song, when next they assembled for their festivities. Great was the surprise of their guests as they arrived, arrayed in paint and feathers, to find nearly one hundred young people drawn up on the shore clean and decently attired, with several banners borne by youthful standard-bearers, who, as soon as the canoes touched the shore, burst forth at a given signal in the anthem, "How beautiful upon the mountains are the feet of him that bringeth good tidings." This newly-formed choir preceded the long line of chiefs and their followers to the guest-houses, where they were welcomed by the dancers, who from their carved coronets surmounted with the receptacles for the peace-making swansdown, scattered the emblem of peace over their guests. All the guests expressed themselves as much pleased with the change.

The rush of naked slaves, with their bodies blackened, into the water before the advancing canoes to cast the offerings of their chiefs before the new arrivals was a sight witnessed no more at Massett. From that time onward the more joyful Christian greeting gradually took the place

A TOUCHING PARTING

of the heathen custom, and the slaves became free in the true sense that "He is a free man whom the truth makes free."

The visit of a "Yetzhahada," or white man, was marked as a red-letter day in our experience on the islands. Consequently we were not a little surprised and elated when Professor Dawson of the Canadian Geological Survey Department arrived one day on a schooner. He had come in the interests of his department to make a cursory survey of the islands, and was accompanied by his brother. For his worthy father's sake, the late Sir William Dawson of Montreal, whose contributions to science, as well as his championship of the faith, have won for him a lasting fame, not only in Canada but throughout the world, as well as for his own sake, we accorded him and his brother a hearty welcome. We also gladly afforded them every facility in our power in their investigations and inquiries. We had the pleasure of entertaining them for two Sundays, as they made Massett their headquarters while surveying the inlet and the vicinity of Virago Sound. It was from this survey that the first correct map was prepared of Queen Charlotte Islands, and it was by him that the name of "Collison Bay" was given to the water thus marked on the east coast of the southern island. He informed me of it on his arrival. His conclusions as to the geological formation of the islands, as also of the large areas which he surveyed and reported on in the north-west, have been for the most part verified by the discoveries made since. He was one of those men who in a short lifetime succeed in effecting more than many who live their threescore years and ten.

Vancouver, the great navigator, whose name has been worthily perpetuated on the shores of the north-west coast, was another striking illustration of this truth. For he was only forty years of age when he passed away rather suddenly in Surrey, England, whilst engaged in the preparation of his journal for publication. He had entered

A TOUCHING PARTING

the Navy at the early age of fourteen years. I have seen a photograph in the possession of a brother missionary, the Rev. A. J. Hall of Alert Bay, of Vancouver's grave. Mr. Hall had engaged to address a missionary meeting at Petersham whilst in England on furlough some years ago. He found on his arrival at St. Peter's that he was in advance of the hour fixed for the meeting, and so wandered into the churchyard, where he was surprised to find engraved on a tombstone there the name of "Captain George Vancouver." It was partly covered by moss, which he had to scrape off before he could make it quite legible. There was a movement in both Victoria, Vancouver Island, and also in Vancouver City several years since to erect monuments in memory of this brave navigator, but as far as I am aware nothing has yet been done. Surely it is high time that some worthy memorial should be made to commemorate the discoveries of the early navigators on this coast, of which Captain George Vancouver stands highest. Such a memorial would serve to enlighten and stimulate the youth of our coast in future generations.

Vancouver does not appear to have visited the Queen Charlotte Islands. His principal aim was to discover if possible the long-discussed North-West passage, which led him to follow up the coast-line of the mainland in the hope that such a passage might be found.

In the spring of 1879 we were favoured by a visit from the Right Rev. W. C. Bompas, D.D., who has well been entitled "The Apostle of the North." His long journey from the interior across the mountains and British Columbia, and his race with winter down the Skeena, are too well known to require further reference here. He came to the coast acting under a special commission from the Right Rev. George Hills, D.D., then Bishop of British Columbia, to set in order such things as required episcopal supervision and administration. This arrangement had been agreed upon by the Church Missionary Society, which supplied the necessary funds.

A TOUCHING PARTING

The same causes which necessitated his visit had also induced the Committee of the Church Missionary Society to request me to return to the mainland and take up again the work at Metlakahtla, which I had resigned in order to open the Haida Mission. As the Bishop only remained at Massett whilst the steamer was discharging, he was but a day on the islands and could not learn much of the work. True to his custom and practice, when we invited him to take up his quarters for the night in a bedroom specially prepared for visitors, he declined, and instead begged that he might be permitted to spread his blankets on a mat just across the doorway. I urged him to occupy the bedroom which had been made ready for him, but to no purpose. "To sleep on a bed in a bedroom would tend to unfit me for my future itinerancy in the forest," he declared. "Well, Bishop," I replied, "do not lie down across the doorway, as you may be disturbed there, but spread your blankets on the mat in the corner instead." This he did, and appeared to enjoy his rest, though I must add that we could not enjoy ours because of our distress at the good Bishop's discomfort.

As he had brought over a young man, a half-breed who had been teaching at Metlakahtla, to take temporary charge of the Mission during my absence, I had to inform the Haidas of my intended departure from them for a short time. Great was the commotion throughout the camp when they learned the situation. The Mission-house was crowded with my people anxiously inquiring how long I would be absent. Many touching speeches were made, but the most affecting was that made by Nakadzoot, formerly the leading necromancer with whom I had so often crossed swords during the past. "We feel," said he, "as the disciples must have felt when the Saviour was about to leave them, and to ascend up where He was before."

The chiefs had all their flags flying and cannon loaded, and as we proceeded to the shore to embark we had to pass through a double line of Haidas all with hands outstretched

A TOUCHING PARTING

to say "Good-bye." The chiefs came out with us to the steamer and saw us safely on board. When the anchor was weighed, and the whistle sounded, instantly a volley from the cannon mounted in front of the lodges of the chiefs, awoke the echoes in the valleys around, and the good captain, Lewis, who had declared his fears on our first arrival that we should all be murdered, declared now that he could never have believed, had he not seen it, such a change could have been effected amongst such a people as the Haidas. He continued a faithful friend until his death in 1903.

After a hurried visit to Metlakahtla, I accompanied Bishop Bompas to the Nass in a large canoe. Neish-lak-annoish, chief of the Ketlahn tribe, who was the owner and captain of the canoe, was steering. I was paddling, seated on the thwart next to him, whilst the Bishop was paddling in front of us. His vest and shirt were rent from under the arm downwards, and as he lifted his arm in paddling, every stroke revealed the rent. "What is the matter with the Chief?" (Bishop) inquired our steersman, who was evidently ill at ease on observing the plight of the Bishop. "There is nothing the matter," I answered. "Nee wila walshka wil bak-beak na wish-washt ka"—"See, then, how his clothes are torn," he replied, upon which I had to make an apology for the Bishop by informing the chief of his long journey through the forest of many weeks and moons in order to reach the coast. It evidently gave the chief food for thought, as he had nought to say further for the next few miles, and after paddling and sailing for fifty miles we reached Kincolith, where a warm welcome was accorded us by our good friends the Rev. R. Tomlinson and his wife. Here, after an examination which lasted a week, I was ordained to priest's orders by the Bishop. He must have found my Latin and Greek rather rusty, as I had read but little of either since leaving the examination halls of my Alma Mater.

I realised that an examination of the Tsimshean and Haida languages would have been more in line with my work just

A TOUCHING PARTING

then. However, the Bishop expressed himself as highly pleased with the result, which was more than I had expected.

It was greatly to his own credit that notwithstanding the many long years of his wilderness life in the several dioceses of which he was the pioneer bishop, in the north, he continued to keep up his study of the classical and Eastern languages and was one of the best Sanscrit scholars of his time. He had endured much hardship as a good soldier of Jesus Christ, and could truly say with the great apostle and missionary to the Gentiles, "In journeyings often, in perils of rivers ... in perils of the Gentiles ... in perils in the wilderness, in labour and travail, in watchings often, in hunger and thirst, in fastings often, in cold and nakedness." And may we not add for him, "Beside those things that are without, there is that which presseth upon me daily, anxiety for all the Churches."

In narrating to us the straits to which both Indians and missionaries had been sometimes driven for food, having been compelled to eat the skins of the animals which they had taken for their fur, and even to boil and gnaw their moccasins to preserve life, I inquired, "Bishop, have you or any of your missionaries there endeavoured to cultivate the potato?" He replied that he feared it was too far north for anything of this kind to mature. I advised him strongly to endeavour to induce the missionaries to give it a trial, and some time afterwards I was informed that it had been tried and proved a success.

A similar idea prevailed among the pioneer miners in the Yukon in the early days of the gold excitement there, but afterwards it was found out that potatoes and other vegetables could be cultivated successfully and profitably. Indeed it was discovered by some that a potato patch in those days, when the cost of provisions ran high, was almost as profitable as a good claim.

When after a brief stay on the Nass the Bishop set out on his return journey to travel across the mountains to his

A TOUCHING PARTING

distant diocese, he was accompanied by the Rev. R. Tomlinson and myself up the river to the head of canoe navigation, from which we accompanied him some way on the trail. Here, in the forest, together with several of our Indians and the Bishop's Indian carrier, we bowed in prayer. We commended the Bishop to the guidance and protection of Our Heavenly Father in his journeys and labours for the Gospel, after which he dismissed us with his blessing, and with a hearty " Good-bye " we parted.

He had but one Indian lad to accompany him, and as they had to carry their blankets and provisions, with one or two small vessels for cooking, as also a gun and a small axe, the Bishop was fairly well laden when he started. Finding they had more than they could well pack, at the last moment the Bishop handed us his greatcoat to be given to whomsoever we deemed most worthy of the gift. We knew how much he would miss this, especially when encamped at night in the mountains, but he parted with it cheerfully.

It was just the same spirit which led him in his first diocese, when with several of his missionaries engaged in making out their orders for supplies, which were limited to so many pounds for each, the Bishop overheard a young missionary complain of his inability to include some articles which he desired. He at once cut off several articles which he had ordered for himself to enable the new arrival to procure what he wanted, though, as the good Bishop informed me, the following year, when the supplies arrived, the man for whom he had thus denied himself was on his way homeward bound, and the articles he had ordered were of no use to the Bishop.

Shortly after our return I found that the young man who had been sent out to succeed me in the Haida Mission, Mr. George Sneath, had arrived at Metlakahtla, and as the Committee of the Church Missionary Society had entrusted me with the superintendence of the Haida Mission, I at

A TOUCHING PARTING

once made preparations to accompany him to introduce him to the people, and to install him in the work. Accordingly I secured a large canoe in which to convey him with his outfit and provisions across to Massett. I selected a crew of five Tsimsheans, all skilful canoe men, and inured to the dangers of the ocean, as they were fur seal hunters.

Before leaving, I inquired from my successor as to his fitness for the journey, and whether he suffered from sea-sickness. He replied that he had no fears whatever. And indeed his record served to confirm his statement. He had been sent out first to the East African Mission, where his health had broken down, which compelled his return to England.

"On my return from East Africa," he informed me, "I was wrecked in the Bay of Biscay, and was tossed about for some twenty-four hours in an open boat before being picked up, but I never was sea-sick."

"Why," I replied, "you are just the man for the Queen Charlotte Islands Mission. The Committee have done well in sending you here." And I related some of my experiences in my canoe voyages to him, as I had made some fourteen passages at that time between the islands and the mainland, as well as many voyages up and down the coast and on the rivers.

We left Metlakahtla early one fine morning, and succeeded in reaching Ziass, or Little Dundas Island, before dark. Here, where the fur sealers generally encamp when hunting, we took up our quarters for the night. As there were a number of fur seal hunters in camp, I conducted a service for them and my own crew. Returning from the service to our hut, I remarked one of my crew leaning on the stern of our canoe with a very dejected countenance. On inquiring if he was sick, he replied, "No, I am not sick in body, but my heart is sick. We are to start out in this canoe to-morrow, but I fear we shall never reach the islands." "What leads you to think so?" I inquired. In reply he laid hold of the bow of the canoe, and shook it. As he did so, the canoe quivered and bent. "Look at that," he said, "the timber

A TOUCHING PARTING

is too weak for the size of the canoe." The Indian was correct. I called the crew and the owner of the canoe together, and pointed out the defect, and it was agreed that the canoe should be ribbed and strengthened before setting out. Accordingly the following day they procured a number of cedar branches, which they planed off on two sides, and nailed them about twenty inches apart the whole length of the canoe, which so strengthened it that it was unlikely she would split in a rough sea. In addition I engaged another Indian, a fur seal hunter, to accompany us, and requested those encamped there to advise us in embarking, as I trusted to their experience in regard to the weather.

Next morning at daybreak we were roused up, as the hunters informed us that the weather was propitious and the wind fair. We hastened to get everything on board, but just as I was about to embark, an old chief, who was encamped with the hunters, approached me, and pointing to a small black cloud in the south, he said, "Do you see that cloud? I was born on an island out seaward, and there I was reared, and we never ventured out on the ocean when we saw that sign." "And why did you not inform us of this before?" I inquired. "I told your crew," said he, "but they did not mind my word." On inquiring, I found that there was a division amongst them about the weather, but the majority were in favour of a start. It was about 4.30 A.M. when we set sail, and the wind continued to increase until soon the ocean was covered with foam-crested waves. I had taken our bearings, and handed the compass to the care of my friend Sneath, whilst I assisted in steering. As the storm increased, I observed him changing colour. His face became pale, after which he lay down on the goods in the canoe, and became so sea-sick that he dropped the compass amongst the freight, where it could not be found. Shortly after, I called his attention to his umbrella, a new silk one, which was in danger of being blown away. To this he paid no attention, being completely prostrated, and the next moment it was caught by

A TOUCHING PARTING

the gale and blown aloft, when it turned, and descending like an arrow shot down in the ocean.

We had now but one sail, as the second had been rent to ribbons, and but little of the remaining sail was left. With only less than three feet to the wind, and three of us steering, we were now labouring in a heavy sea. We frequently shipped volumes of water from the waves which broke over us, whilst with buckets we baled away to keep our frail craft afloat. Just then an ominous roar burst upon our ears, and a cry arose, "We are running on the bar!" True enough, for in a few minutes we were enabled to see the long line of breakers rising in a wall of foam on the ridge of the great sand spit. This extended seawards for several miles. Instantly the Indian who held the sail rope turned with a look of terror on his face. "It is of no use," he cried, "I can hold on no longer, we are lost." It was a critical moment, and lifting my paddle, I threatened to strike him if he relinquished his hold. I knew he was terror-stricken, and my action brought him to his senses again. This was the same man who had expressed his fears before we set out that we should never reach the shores to which we were bound. He was labouring under some illusion, and I feared lest his influence might prove infectious. Whether it was that he was suffering from heart disease at the time, or that the exposure and fright may have induced it, is not clear, but not long after our return from this voyage one night he was missing, and could not be found. The following morning his body was found not far from his lodge, where he had fallen. The cause of his death was evidently heart failure. One reason which led me to take him as one of my crew on this voyage was that indirectly he had saved my life on a former occasion.

The other members of the crew were doing their utmost in this hour of peril. "If we can but keep out from the suction of the bar," I cried, "we may succeed in getting round the point and then we shall be safe." This stimu-

A TOUCHING PARTING

lated all to work for life, and not another word was spoken. Each man held his breath, but I believe I was not the only one who prayed inwardly for help. And help was granted, as after a hard struggle, when well-nigh exhausted, we rounded the point of the bar, and ere long we were in comparatively calm waters. The wind, however, continued so strong that it lifted the seaweed off the shore and blew it like feathers over the tree tops. Now that we were under the lee of the land, we were out of danger, and we were indeed thankful for our preservation. We had made the passage from land to land in six hours, and would have effected it in less had not the loss of the compass caused us to fall too far to the south, and in the blinding spray the squall ran us well-nigh on the spit.

We coasted along the northern shore of the island to Tow Hill, which is a high rocky bluff standing alone on the shore line. It forms an excellent landmark, and will probably form the site of a lighthouse in the future, though it will be necessary to have some kind of a floating beacon off the extreme point of the Rose Spit to warn mariners of its dangers. It is so named after George Rose, M.P., a political writer and statesman and follower of William Pitt, and the name was given by Captain Douglas, an early navigator. It is named "Nai Kwun" or "House Point" in the Haida, just as Cape Ball on the east coast is named "Atlins kwun" or "Atlins Point." The Haidas have a fishing camp near to it on the shore, and here we were enabled to make a landing and prepare a little food, which revived us after our exertions. Our friend Sneath declared his experience when wrecked in the Bay of Biscay was but light compared to what he had suffered on this occasion.

Re-embarking, we pursued our journey, and reached the entrance to the Massett inlet, out of which the storm was raging from the south-east. We endeavoured again and again to make headway, but failed. Some of the young men of the camp sighted us, and signalling to them for help, a

A TOUCHING PARTING

number of them hastened to our assistance. Some of them poled, whilst others of them hauled our canoe with a stout rope, and thus landed us at Massett. The Haidas refused to believe we had come from the mainland, as they declared they feared to enter the forest for firewood, owing to the danger from falling timber. When at length I convinced them, and informed them of our perilous passage, they blamed the Tsimsheans, declaring that it was their lack of knowledge of the weather conditions which caused so many accidents amongst them.

In the meantime the fur seal hunters had given us up as lost. When the gale struck the island on which they were encamped, one of them climbed a tree which was generally used as a look-out post, but he could see no sign, and all agreed that no canoe could live through such a sea. Accordingly they brought back word to Metlakahtla that we were lost, and soon the wives and relatives of the men who accompanied me were seated outside their houses wailing in concert, as is the custom.

My wife, who was then at Metlakahtla, hesitated to believe it until one of the hunters arrived, and walking in placed my rifle on the table without uttering a word, and then went out. I had handed this man my rifle on the island, requesting him to bring it to Metlakahtla on his return to the mainland, as I did not require it. This he did, but as he believed we were lost he declined to speak, which led my wife to apprehend the worst. The day following, happily, the mail steamer arrived from Victoria, and as she intended to touch at Massett on her return from Wrangle, the captain agreed to call at Metlakahtla and report if we had not arrived at Massett, but if we had arrived in safety he would pass down with his ensign at the mast-head. Several days afterwards, to the intense joy and satisfaction of all, the steamer was sighted passing down with the ensign flying. We knew nothing of this, as when the steamer arrived at Massett we had left, and were well on our way to visit Skidegate and the

A TOUCHING PARTING

south, as I was anxious to introduce my successor to every encampment of the Haidas. On this trip we met with another startling experience, also in the vicinity of the Rose Spit.

We had embarked two young men—Haidas—belonging to Skidegate, who happened to be at Massett on a visit. As we stood off the bar and were about to sail round the extreme point, these men informed us that this was unnecessary, as there was a narrow channel or passage near the base, through which we could pass, and thus save ourselves some ten miles travel. We agreed to make this crossing if they could pilot us. This they volunteered to do. As we approached it, we failed to discover any opening in the line of breakers, and our pilots seemed to be as much at a loss as we were. We were now so near that we felt it would be difficult to retreat if we failed to find the opening. Just then our pilots pointed out a spot where there seemed a slight opening in the wall of foam. We paddled steadily for it until caught in the swell—when we were swept onward as in a mill-race, and left high and dry in the middle of the bar. Looking back, I saw an immense wave rushing towards us. "Out!" I cried, "two on each side," and suiting the action to the word, I sprang overboard, and seizing the canoe, whilst the others followed my example, I cried, "Pull all together and hold fast." "All!" The forelap of the wave struck us and we were lifted with the canoe and flung forward clear out on the far side of the bar. We were drenched with the wave, but we had saved our canoe, which would otherwise have been dashed to pieces by the weight of the wave had it broken over us. In addition the lighting of the canoe from our weight, together with the united lift which we were enabled to give, caused her to rise on the forewash of the incoming wave, whilst with two of us hanging over each side we balanced her and prevented her from capsizing. We were well drenched, but thankful at our narrow escape.

For a few moments no one spoke. The young lad, a Tsimshean, whom my successor had brought over from the

A TOUCHING PARTING

mainland to assist him in domestic duties, when he saw th great wave rushing towards us, had screamed in fear, and casting himself upon the steersman, who was nearest to him in the canoe, he threw his arms around his neck at the most critical moment and almost paralysed his efforts. With a vigorous effort, he threw the lad from him, just in time to assist us to escape. "Lthat kamkoadshka Shimoigit Lakaga agam," exclaimed the steersman, which translated is, "The Chief above has had mercy on us." I believe he expressed the feelings of all. Our Haida pilots had mistaken their mark and had missed the channel. There was not a word from either of them, and our Tsimshean crew were not in an accusing mood. But as I looked back at the great wall of breakers, I could understand why the Haidas, in the past, had regarded this place as an object of worship, and were accustomed to propitiate it by sacrifice and offerings. From this we made a successful passage to Skidegate, where we were again accorded a hearty reception, as also at Gold Harbour and other points. Here, as at Massett and vicinity, the Haidas regretted that I was about to make Metlakahtla my headquarters, but I promised them that they should not be forgotten or neglected.

Two enterprising white men had just established a small oil factory near to Skidegate, for the purpose of extracting the oil from the dog-fish, which abound in these waters. This oil, which is extracted from the livers of the fish, forms an excellent lubricant for machinery, and will command a ready sale. This was the first industry established on the Queen Charlotte Islands. I paid them a visit, and had a pleasant interview. I was glad to see a Bible amongst the few books they possessed. I wished their undertakings all success. Having conducted services at the several encampments, we returned again to Massett, and installed our successor in the work in the new Mission-house.

The Mission had now been firmly established. The language had been acquired and reduced to writing. I was

A TOUCHING PARTING

enabled to hand over several handbooks which I had compiled to my successor, to assist him in the acquirement of the tongue. Translations of hymns and prayers had been prepared, and were used at our services; also portions of Scripture, a catechism, and the commandments. The island burying-ground was now the "God's acre" of the Mission, and the dead were no longer unburied. The Haidas had learned to recognise and rest on the Lord's Day. Several of the leading medicine men had surrendered to the truth. Those of them who had derided the attempt to evangelise the Haidas, had been amongst the first to accept the Gospel message. The leading chiefs, including Weha, who had replied at my first interview that it was "too late," were now the chief supporters of the Mission. They, together with the principal medicine man, Nakadzoot, were registered as catechumens at their own special request. And some had passed away who had been baptized, and had given striking evidence, in their last hours, of the presence and power of Christ to sustain and strengthen them in the conflict with the last enemy. Moreover, the Gospel had been proclaimed both north and south, and at Skidegate a native teacher had been placed, who remained there until the Methodist Mission was established.

Amongst the Alaskan Haidas Missionary Gould had also commenced his labours in connection with the Presbyterian Missionary Society. These Haidas, being of the same nation and tongue as the Haidas of the Queen Charlotte Islands, were desirous to have a teacher, as they had seen and heard what had been done amongst their fellow-tribesmen at Massett and vicinity. The good seed of the Gospel was thus being sown throughout the Haida nation, and would ere long result in an abundant harvest and ingathering to the Church of Christ. Thus it was with courage and hope for the future that I embarked again to return to the work on the mainland. The young man whom I had left at Massett as teacher during my temporary absence, embarked

A TOUCHING PARTING

with us on our return to Metlakahtla, accompanied by his wife and two children. We were favoured with a fair wind from the west, and with two sails up, we fairly flew over the water. When some ten miles out from Dundas Island we came in sight of a large rock which was covered with a great number of sea-lions and walrus. Our course lay quite close to the rock, and as we drew near the roaring set up by these monsters of the deep was terrific. I took the precaution of warning my crew against firing at them as we passed, as when angered they have been known to attack and smash canoes, causing disaster to the occupants. But the temptation proved too strong for our native teacher, who, just as we passed within close range of the rock, discharged his rifle right in the midst of them. The bullet struck a large bull near the top of the head, and instantly the entire reef looked like a moving mass, as blowing and bellowing they fought and struggled to reach the water. They had evidently taken up their position on the reef at full tide, and as it had fallen considerably, they caused quite a commotion as they cast themselves into the sea.

Fortunately for us the wind seemed to freshen in the vicinity of the reef, for soon the sea around us appeared to be alive with these monsters of the deep. Some of them chased the canoe and rose again and again alongside of us, but with poles and paddles we frightened them off, and soon we had left them far astern. It was then that our captain, who was steering, addressed himself to our friend who had disobeyed the instructions not to fire. I knew it was coming from the look with which he had regarded the culprit the moment he fired. "Up willa wahl wa-ka-koad," said he. "That is the way fools act." "Ahlka ndaza wil ligi quildum ludapshga ka-koad ga." "They never consider before they act," he added, "and this is the cause of so many accidents. If you knew as much as I know, you would never have fired as you did. I have known when a wounded teipon (sea-lion) has wrenched a canoe asunder with his teeth and caused

A TOUCHING PARTING

the loss of all on board. I am an old hunter both on land and sea, and I have had many very narrow escapes, so you need not grumble at my reproof but accept it."

The silence with which the offender received the well-intended reprimand of the captain indicated his assent, and as though animated by the thought of having been so mercifully preserved in so many dangers during the journey now drawing to a close, we burst into a joyful song of praise in which all joined.

> "We are out on the ocean sailing,
> Homeward bound we swiftly glide,
> We are out on the ocean sailing
> To a home beyond the tide.
>
> "All the storms will soon be over,
> Then we'll anchor in the harbour;
> We are out on the ocean sailing
> To a home beyond the tide."

A. N.

CHAPTER XIX

THE HAIDAS AS MARINE HUNTERS

"And there we hunted the walrus,
The narwhale and the seal;
Ha! 'twas a noble game,
And like the lightning's flame
Flew our harpoons of steel."
    LONGFELLOW.

THOUGH the Haidas have been chiefly noted because of their warlike nature, as indicated by their continual raids upon other tribes, yet it must not be forgotten that they have even excelled as sea hunters. All the coast tribes have been more or less accustomed to hunting the various marine animals during the past, but owing to their natural position on the Queen Charlotte Islands the Haidas are as famed for their daring and ability in the chase on the ocean as they have been for their courage when on the warpath. They probably early discovered that the two pursuits of hunting and fighting harmonised, and that the most daring hunter was not likely to fall behind when face to face with the foe. And in their expeditions, whether for hunting or fighting, they found they required the same outfit: a good canoe, with bows and arrows, spears, clubs, harpoons, and golf-hooks, with which they could either attack an enemy or kill a whale. It was their industry and ability in the construction and preparation of their graceful canoes which enabled them to prosecute successfully both their hunting and fighting expeditions. Having made the passage from the mainland to the islands many times in their canoes, besides travelling up and down the coast in all states of the weather,

THE HAIDAS AS MARINE HUNTERS

I can testify to the efficiency of the Haida canoe in the water. The development of their canoe was gradual and was not attained by a single effort. At first it had a square bow, and as that part under the prow was only some two or three inches in thickness, and it was found that the wind and water held it so that it made it difficult to steer, consequently they designed to cut a large circular or oval piece out of this thin piece. Ultimately it was decided to do away with this part entirely, and the canoe assumed its present outline.

It is to be regretted that no provision has been made to preserve a sufficient supply of the best red cedar timber to enable the Haidas to continue their canoe building. In a few years this industry will have passed away and one of the most interesting features of Indian life will have been forgotten.

So identified were the Haidas with canoes and canoe building that we can hardly think of them apart from this attractive accompaniment. True, they were not the only canoe builders on the coast, as the Bela-bela Indians and also those on the west coast of Vancouver's Island turned out excellent canoes. But those of the former were wider in the beam and shallower, and in consequence were not such good sea-going craft, whereas the canoes of the west-coast Indians were much heavier in their build and lacked the graceful outlines of the Haida canoe.

In Captain Meares' voyages to this coast, he was greatly interested in the manner in which the Indians on the west coast of Vancouver's Island made their canoes. On p. 58, vol. ii., he states: " But the most laborious, as well as most curious, employment in which we saw the natives of Nootka engaged was the making of their canoes, which was a work of no common skill and ability. These boats are many of them capable of containing from fifteen to thirty men with ease and convenience, and at the same time are elegantly moulded and highly finished, and this curious work is accomplished with utensils of stone made by themselves. They even manufactured tools from the iron

THE HAIDAS AS MARINE HUNTERS

which they obtained from us, and it was very seldom that we could persuade them to make use of any of our utensils in preference to their own, except the saw, whose obvious power in diminishing their labour led them to adopt it without hesitation. . . . Their large war canoes were generally finished on the spot where the trees grew of which they are made, and then dragged to the water side. We have seen some of them which were 53 feet in length and 8 feet in breadth. The middle part of these boats is the broadest, and gradually narrows to a point at each end, but their head or prow is generally much higher than the stern. . . . They have no seats, but several pieces of wood about 3 inches in diameter are fixed across them to keep the sides firm and preserve them from being warped. The rowers generally sit on their hams, but sometimes they make use of a kind of small stool, which is a great relief to them. . . . Some of these canoes are polished and painted or curiously studded with human teeth, particularly on the stern and the prow."

This, then, is the manner in which the Indians of the west coast made their canoes a century ago. But the Haidas not only turned out larger canoes, but also much more ornamented. And the Haida canoes are furnished with seats fastened to the sides of the canoes with thongs of cedar bark, and supported by a piece of wood, which was carried on either side from bow to stern, and polished and painted. On each of these seats two rowers were seated, one at either end, so that a canoe with six seats would accommodate twelve rowers, who with their paddles could propel their craft through the water faster than a motor boat.

Whilst the Indians of the west coast of Vancouver's Island excelled in the pursuit and killing of the whale, which probably accounts, in a manner, for their heavier built canoes, the Haidas excelled all the other tribes in their pursuit and capture of the sea otter and the fur seal. Meares acknowledges that the hunting of the sea otter is attended with far greater hazard and trouble than the hunting of the whale. These

THE HAIDAS AS MARINE HUNTERS

marine animals were formerly very numerous along the coast, and especially in the vicinity of Queen Charlotte Islands.

The oldest Indians have informed me that it was the "thunder and lightning" weapons of the white men which chased away the sea otter and fur seal. So long as they were hunted only with bows, arrows, and spears they were numerous, but on the introduction of firearms they soon disappeared.

During my residence amongst the Haidas I had considerable difficulty every hunting season in settling the disputes which arose in connection with their sea otter hunt. Several canoes generally go out after the otter in company. Each canoe is manned by two or three men. One of these in each canoe is the marksman. As soon as a sea otter is sighted the marksman of the canoe nearest to the otter fires the first shot. If it does not kill the animal, it dives and will come to the surface again to breathe in about two minutes. A skilful hunter can surmise pretty well in what direction the otter travels while diving, and though he cannot expect to travel so fast in the canoe, yet they seize their paddles and endeavour to steer as near as possible. Then, when it comes to the surface again, the same process is repeated by the marksman in the nearest canoe firing the moment the head of the otter is sighted. It requires good judgment, a steady nerve, and good sight, especially on a rough sea, to make a successful shot. If the animal has been wounded by the first marksman, or, indeed, it may be twice shot before it receives the fatal blow, then there is difficulty in deciding how far each shot contributed to its capture. I had to spend many hours sometimes over a dispute of this nature before we could effect a settlement. And in every such difficulty the missionary was the court of final appeal. But if, as is often done, several canoes combine and agree to share and share alike, then there is no cause for strife, whether successful or unsuccessful.

Meares states, on pp. 24, 25, in regard to the sea otter:

THE HAIDAS AS MARINE HUNTERS

"This animal, like the river otter, is of an amphibious nature, but their peculiar element is the sea. They are sometimes seen many leagues from land, sleeping on their backs on the surface of the water, with their young ones reclining on their breasts. As the cubs are incapable of swimming till they are several months old, the mother must have some curious method of carrying them out to sea, and returning them to their hiding-places on shore, or in the cavities of rocks that project into the sea; indeed, they are known to sleep with their young on their breast, and to swim with them on their back, but if they should be unfortunately overtaken by the hunters, the dam and her brood always die together—she will not leave her young ones in the moment of danger, and therefore shares their fate.

"From the formation of their lungs, they are unable to remain under water longer than two minutes, when they are forced to rise to the surface for respiration, and it is this circumstance which gives their pursuers such advantage over them, though the wonderful swiftness with which they swim very often baffles the utmost attention and skill of the hunter.

"Nature has furnished the sea otter with powerful weapons of offence and destruction. Its fore-paws are like those of the river otter, but of much larger size and greater strength; its mouth contains most formidable rows of teeth superior to any other marine animal except the shark."

But it is its fur which has won for this animal so much attention. When in its perfection it is a beautiful black colour enriched with silver hairs, whilst the under fur is of a beautiful brown and velvet appearance.

Those animals which were formerly so numerous that they formed the chief clothing of the Indians, are now only found on the west coast of the Queen Charlotte Islands. And though efforts are being made to preserve the fur seal from annihilation, no steps have been taken to preserve the sea otter from the same fate. Its fur, and that of the black fox,

INDIAN HANDIWORK

The two large figures are carved pillars supporting the beams of an Indian house. Between them is a chief's dancing dress, on which a hat rests. On each side of the dress stand miniature totem poles.

THE HAIDAS AS MARINE HUNTERS

are now the most valuable on the market, commanding enormous prices. The bays and harbours of the west coast, as also the numerous channels separating the smaller islands of the Queen Charlotte group, offer a safe and ready refuge and breeding-ground for both the sea otter and the fur seal.

On one occasion I surprised the Haida hunters by bringing into the camp at Massett a fine full-grown fur seal which I had captured alive up the inlet. I had travelled some three miles or more and was about to return, when I sighted what appeared to be a large black dog lying on the shore near to the high-water mark. I proceeded to investigate it, when, as I approached, it raised its head to look at me. I then saw at once it was a fine fur seal which had evidently left the water at high tide and had laid down to bask in the sun, where I found it. It promptly started for the water, which it would soon have gained had I not instantly cast off my overcoat, and throwing myself upon it, I wound the coat around its head and flippers. It struggled hard to free itself, and in doing so it succeeded in tearing the lining of my coat with its teeth. But I held on and shouted for help, when several Haidas who were in the vicinity came to my aid and carried it down to the camp. As I approached the Mission-house I was followed by quite a procession, all eager to see the captive which had been secured in such a novel manner, for my assistants recounted the use I had made of my overcoat, and all wanted to see it also. As I had only dried fish to offer it, it would not eat, and though I had salt water brought in for its use, it only lived one week. I had it skinned, and presented the skin, which was very fine, to a friend. The Haidas informed me that they only remembered one similar instance of the capture of a live fur seal on the shore by an old chief who had died a short time before.

Of a people who spend so much of their time on the water, and who thus excel in marine hunting, it is scarcely to be expected that they would prove very efficient as hunters in

THE HAIDAS AS MARINE HUNTERS

the forest. And, indeed, the land animals in the islands are neither as numerous nor as fierce as those found on the mainland. For instance, there are no grizzly bears on the islands, nor are there any wolves; the lynx and the wolverine are also missing. This would seem to be a safe and suitable country for deer, yet this animal, though numerous on the mainland, is not found on the islands. A few caribou of a somewhat different species from that found in such numbers in the northern interior of the mainland have been discovered on Graham Island, which is the most northerly of the entire group. But the Indian hunters who discovered them shot them on sight, and it is to be feared that they were the last of a species which is now extinct, as no more of them have since been seen on the islands.

It may be that a small herd may yet be found on the western mountain range. If not, it will be the duty of naturalists to explain the causes which led first to the existence of these animals on the Queen Charlotte Islands, and afterwards prevented their increase. I had long known caribou existed on the islands, as in the year 1877 an old hunter brought in the skin and antlers of one of them to the Hudson's Bay Company's store for sale. The old trader believed at first that this animal had been shot on the Alaskan coast, but as no canoes had recently arrived from the Alaskan islands or coast, I made inquiry and found that it had been shot near North Island on the north-west coast of Graham Island. It is not far from the same place where the last two were shot and brought to Massett.

But not only have the Haidas been famed as canoe builders and hunters, they have also acquired a reputation as skilful artists in carving, not only in wood and stone, but also in ivory and gold and silver. Probably their early efforts were confined to the first mentioned, as indicated by their totem poles, some of which are elaborately carved, though crumbling to dust from age. Their stone weapons and tools, and also war clubs, formed from the bones of the whale, all prove that

THE HAIDAS AS MARINE HUNTERS

the art of designing and carving has long been practised among them. I have in my possession a war club, formed from the jaw-bone of a whale, carved to represent a fish. This very staunch and effective weapon was used when fighting at close quarters, and the ornamental carving proved that it belonged to a chief.

The Haidas of Skidegate possess a deposit of black stone in the vicinity of their village, from which they obtain material to keep them engaged, during their spare moments, in designing and carving a variety of articles for sale. Miniature totem poles for mantelpiece ornaments, of various sizes, large and small dishes, sometimes inlaid with abilone and ornamented with rows of the teeth of marine animals and fishes and many other designs, are carved, and then smoothed by rubbing them with the dried skin of the shark, which is superior to sand-paper. During the winter this tribe of Indians continue to prepare a stock of ornamental articles from this black stone, which takes a fine polish, and brings them a good sum of money when sold at various centres. The possession of this stone is quite a treasure to them, as it tends to preserve and improve the art of carving and designing amongst them, besides bringing in a revenue.

Thus it will be seen that the Haidas excelled in the arts of peace, and did not spend their time in idleness and ease, and though they have won a name for bravery and valour on the warpath, yet they deserve distinction on account of their skill in hunting, both on the ocean and in the forest. To such a people it was to me an ambition and inspiration to convey the blessed news of that tree of life the leaves of which are for " the healing of the nations."

CHAPTER XX

THE FIRST BISHOP OF CALEDONIA

"The people that in darkness sat,
　A glorious Sight have seen,
The Light has shined on them who long
　In Shades of Death have been."
Morison.

WITH the assistance I had given him, my successor in the work was not slow in acquiring a sufficient knowledge of the Haida tongue to enable him to continue the work which I had thus been called upon to relinquish. A few months after his arrival and my return to the mainland in November 1879, the Right Rev. William Ridley arrived at Metlakahtla, having been appointed and consecrated as the first Bishop of the new diocese of Caledonia, which was the ecclesiastical title given to the northern part of the province.

On my return to the mainland I found my fellow-missionary, Duncan, had completely broken down in health. In consequence of this, I had to undertake the entire charge of the Mission at Metlakahtla. Between the 1st of April 1879 and the 10th of March 1880 seventy-two adults and sixty-three children were baptized. The adults had been prepared by Mr. Duncan and myself, and the greater number of these were presented to our new Bishop for baptism. They were baptized on Sunday, 25th January, and 1st February 1880. There were at that time nearly one thousand Indians at Metlakahtla. The following year Mr. Sneath reported that the Haidas continued to attend the services well, and were also sending their children to the schools.

THE FIRST BISHOP OF CALEDONIA

Shortly after this Mr. Sneath resigned and took up Mission work amongst white settlers in the State of Washington. One morning, during his first year's work there, when about to start on horseback to conduct a service at an outlying station, he decided to take a little medicine in the form of a powder which had been prescribed for him by a physician there. Being hurried, he neglected to mix the powder in a little water, but proceeded to swallow it from the paper in a dry state. By some mishap the powder was drawn into his windpipe, and several children who happened to be in the room at the time, saw him writhing and struggling, but supposed he was doing it for their amusement, and only laughed in innocent glee. In his struggle for breath he fell on the floor, and when the people of the house entered, they found life was extinct. He had been suffocated. Thus by neglecting a simple precaution, a valuable life was cut off quite suddenly, just in his prime, and his labours lost to the great cause to which he had devoted himself. It was my melancholy duty to communicate the sad news to his friends in England through the secretaries of the "Church Missionary Society." The Rev. Charles Harrison was appointed to succeed him in the Mission. Accompanied by his wife, he left London on 21st October 1882 and arrived at Metlakahtla in December. As there was no communication with the islands during the winter months, they remained at Metlakahtla until 30th March 1883. This delay proved of great advantage to the missionaries, as it enabled me to assist them in acquiring the rudiments of the language, and they were made acquainted with missionary methods and labours. It also afforded them an opportunity to study the Indian character and customs. For though the Haidas differ considerably from the Tsimsheans in their national characteristics and peculiar customs, yet they have much in common, notably the crest system with all its ramifications and associations, and our newcomers never forgot the lessons learned in the time of waiting.

THE FIRST BISHOP OF CALEDONIA

They arrived at Massett on the last day of March 1883. Early the following year Mr. Harrison was enabled to baptize fifteen persons, including two chiefs. It was an illustration of the old saying, quoted by the Divine Master Himself: "One soweth and another reapeth."

In a service which he conducted weekly for old people, he was surprised at the style in which they turned out. Many of the congregation, both men and women, attended with rings in their ears, rings in their noses, small pieces of silver stuck in their chins, bracelets on their wrists, and beads and anklets on their ankles. But this was little to what he might have witnessed, several years previously, in the early days of the Mission. The small pieces of silver which he thus refers to were substitutes for the labrets which were inserted in the under lip. This custom was common amongst all the tribes on the north-west coast, and many such labrets, made of bone or stone, projected from the lower lip from one to two inches, and tended to disfigure the features of the women who wore them greatly. The higher the rank of a chieftainess, the larger the labret which she was entitled to wear. While as yet but a child, the chief's daughter had her lower lip or the part immediately under it pierced, and a piece of bone or silver inserted in the opening. This ceremony was signalised by a potlatch, at which a large amount of property was distributed to those invited to the feast. On each occasion of the enlargement of the labret, the same ceremony was repeated, so that a large labret or life ornament represented much property given away, and a proportionate high rank or status attained.

A similar ceremony was observed in the boring of the ear, especially of the sons or nephews of chiefs. Consequently it was not uncommon for a man of rank, if insulted by an inferior, to point to his own ear and remind his insulter that he never had his ear pierced, which was equivalent to saying, "You are a person of very little consequence." The civilising and enlightening influences of Christianity have induced

THE FIRST BISHOP OF CALEDONIA

them to abandon the disfigurement of their features, which caused them no little pain, and added but little to their beauty.

In September of the following year, 1886, the Mission-house which I had erected was accidentally burnt down, and, with it, the missionaries lost all their furniture and effects. The Haidas, however, quickly rallied to their assistance, and erected a temporary dwelling, which served to accommodate them until a new and better Mission-house had been erected.

Mr. Harrison had been enabled to complete some necessary translations, and had baptized eighty Haidas, thus bringing the total number of baptisms up to 178, of which some twenty-three had been confirmed by the Bishop.

A large and better church building now became a necessity, as the old damp house had become dilapidated and could no longer accommodate the numbers attending the services. On Sunday, 17th January 1886, a special collection was taken up for this purpose. Over one hundred trading blankets were handed in, and a considerable sum in cash promised. These blankets, which were issued by the Hudson's Bay Company in payment for furs, had formerly been largely used in the potlatches. Now, however, they were put to a new use. They were valued at $1\frac{1}{4}$ dollar each, or about five shillings. As they were piled up inside the communion railings, they presented the appearance of a trading store rather than a church.

On the 7th of May the following year, 1887, the new church was opened and consecrated. The opening collection amounted to one hundred and fifty dollars. On the same day the Bishop baptized eighty-two persons, confirmed sixty-three, and united eighteen couples in the bonds of holy matrimony. There were now eighty-six communicants at Massett. In reference to this occasion the missionary wrote: "When the Bishop came to Massett, there were only some fifty persons in the village. I sent one canoe south, and another north, to call the Indians to Massett to

THE FIRST BISHOP OF CALEDONIA

be present at the opening of the new church. Some of them were sixty miles from home, hunting and fishing. As soon as they heard the news, they left their fish and furs behind, and hastened homewards. From the east and the west, from the north and the south, the Haidas came, until they numbered three hundred and sixty on the day of dedication. Tired and stiff, weary and worn, they arrived, canoe after canoe full of Indians, men, women, and children, in order to witness the setting apart of their church to the services of the Almighty God. Some of them had walked a distance of thirty miles, weary and footsore, in order to be present to receive baptism and confirmation. Some only got back to Massett in time for the afternoon service, and all with one heart glorified God, the Giver of all good things, for His bountiful gift of " St. John the Evangelist's Church."

"At 10.30 A.M. the choir came and stationed themselves in the garden in front of our house. The churchwardens also were present; twenty chiefs also at this time were present in a cottage about two hundred yards from the Mission-house. The church is situated half-way between the two houses. When the Bishop was ready, the choir, numbering thirty-two, marched two by two slowly down towards the church, singing "Onward, Christian Soldiers," &c. After the choir came the two churchwardens carrying their wands of office, followed by myself and the Bishop.

"During this time the twenty chiefs marched up from the cottage two and two, and the processions met at the church door. Two of the most prominent chiefs handed the donation paper to the Bishop, asking him to dedicate the church and to set it aside for the services of God for ever. The Bishop, having replied in the affirmative, the chiefs proceeded to their seats in the church, followed by the choir, who went to their places in the chancel. The Bishop and I then took our places, and the dedication service was read, and the church set apart to the service of God accord-

THE FIRST BISHOP OF CALEDONIA

ing to the rites and ceremonies of the Church of England in Canada. After a hymn, a collection was made, and the Indians, though poor, gave tangible evidence of their sincerity, by augmenting the offertory to the sum of $150, or about thirty pounds sterling."

Thus it will be evident that the long conflict of Christianity with heathenism was past. Once more the truth had triumphed and the harvest of the good seed which had been sown in weakness was being reaped, and to both sowers and reapers on the islands was fulfilled the truth of the words, "They joy before thee as the joy of harvest and as men rejoice when they divide the spoil."

In September 1890 the Rev. C. Harrison retired from the Mission and returned to England. I paid a visit to Massett at that time, and received a hearty welcome from the Haidas, who were all rejoiced to see me. I found George Cowhoe dying. His face was radiant with smiles when he saw me enter, and he held my hand as he expressed his joy at seeing me once again before he passed away. On the little table beside him lay the copy of the New Testament which had been given him by Captain Prevost of H.M.S. *Satellite*, and from which I had been enabled to guide him to the truth. From its pages he had been led to Him who is "the way, the truth, and the life." Beside it lay the Bible I had given him, with some copies of translations. He knew his time was short, but he was strong in faith and hope. We had an interesting conversation in regard to the great change which had passed over the Haidas. I sang and prayed with him, and then bade him "Good-bye," but I remembered a line with which I had long been familiar, and which I rejoiced to know was true:

> "Yes, we part, but not for ever,
> Joyous hopes our bosoms swell,
> They who know the Saviour, never
> Know a long or last farewell;
> Joyful meetings lie beyond this parting vale."

THE FIRST BISHOP OF CALEDONIA

He only lived a few days after my visit, and continued to pray and praise till his departure. I visited the island burying-ground, where, after much conflict, I had been enabled at length to inter the dead, and here I recognised the last resting-places of many whom I had known as fierce heathen, but who had experienced the transforming power of the Gospel, and had died in the faith of Christ. Near to the new church, and here and there through the camp, I pointed out the places where we had interred the heaps of dead which formerly lay unburied.

In September 1891 the Rev. J. H. and Mrs. Keen arrived to take charge of the Haida Mission. Bishop Ridley accompanied them to introduce them to the Haidas, and to induct them in the work. On this occasion the Bishop baptized eight adults and confirmed a like number. The new missionary was no novice. He had laboured previously in the North-west American Mission. He made rapid progress in acquiring the language, as he was able to read the services in Haida on the fourth Sunday after his arrival, and to preach in four months without the aid of an interpreter.

That the Haidas were continuing to advance in civilisation is evidenced by the fact that Mr. Keen found that two of the young men had purchased small harmoniums, whilst several others had obtained other musical instruments. They had also succeeded in forming a brass-band, consisting of eight instruments and two drums. Like all the other tribes on this North-west coast, Mr. Keen found the Haidas very fond of music; consequently the brass-band occupied a high place in their estimation.

As every Indian encampment has now its own band, it may not be out of place here to state the origin of this accomplishment. In 1870, on the return of Mr. William Duncan from his first furlough to England, he was delayed in San Francisco, awaiting the departure of the steamer for Victoria, Vancouver's Island. During this delay he met a friend who

THE FIRST BISHOP OF CALEDONIA

was much interested in his mission amongst the Indians. This gentleman had a complete set of band instruments at his disposal, which he offered as a gift to Mr. Duncan for the Metlakahtla Mission. These were gladly accepted, and conveyed up the coast by Mr. Duncan. He had them hung up around the room which he used as office and study. Here they remained unused for several years.

In 1879 I was one day consulting with Mr. Duncan, when it occurred to me to make a suggestion regarding the instruments. "You are about shortly to visit Victoria," I said; "why not endeavour to find a musician who will come up here for the winter and instruct some of the young men in the use of these instruments? And," I added, "I am prepared to board and lodge him, and otherwise assist." Mr. Duncan readily agreed to my proposal, and on his visiting Victoria shortly afterwards, he succeeded in finding a very capable musician, a German, who had formerly been bandmaster in a Prussian cavalry regiment. As he had the winter months at his disposal, he accepted the offer and came up the coast. We selected a sufficient number of young men, all of whom were most eager to learn, and under such an ardent and proficient instructor they made rapid progress in both theory and practice. Before the winter was over their confused medley of sounds gradually became blended and harmonious. It was a proud moment for both the master and his pupils when they came forth and rendered several airs with proficiency. Little wonder that they had succeeded so well, when both the instructor and his pupils were almost music mad. For often in the midnight hours, when all were asleep, this disciple of Orpheus would rouse the household by springing from his bed to the floor with a bound, as though just released from some dread spell, and seizing his violin, would discourse some sweet strain on it for a short time, and then betaking himself to his bed again, would sleep peacefully till the morning.

When he had completed his term of engagement, he nomin-

THE FIRST BISHOP OF CALEDONIA

ated one of his pupils to succeed him as bandmaster. This, the first Indian brass-band on the North-west coast, excited the wonder and admiration of all the tribes around, and on the arrival of visitors of distinction the band generally turned out to serenade them. The Indians are quick to imitate, and the next encampment which procured a band was Kincolith, which was the second mission station established on the North-west coast. Here they succeeded in raising over six hundred dollars amongst themselves, with which they procured a complete set of band instruments from San Francisco. They then engaged the lately appointed Indian bandmaster from Metlakahtla to instruct them in turn, paying him exactly a sum equal to that paid the German instructor. This band was speedily followed by another at Port Simpson, which was the third in order; and now every Indian encampment, whether up the rivers or along the coast, can boast of this accomplishment. Its tendency has been to civilise and elevate the Indians, and it has kept many of the young men engaged during the long winter evenings. Many of them are not only skilful performers, but can transpose and even compose music. It is incumbent on the missionary to welcome and foster whatever tends to the uplifting and improvement of the people amongst whom he labours, whilst carefully guarding against whatever tends to degrade or defeat his mission.

That I was not forgotten by the Haidas is evidenced from one of the first letters written by the Rev. J. H. Keen during his first year's labours amongst them, in which he states: " In their prayers at prayer meetings they always, unprompted, remember Mr. Collison, the founder of this Mission," and he adds: " Such a scene as this presents indeed a striking contrast to many a one which even the younger men have witnessed in this very village. Among those who offered prayers at our meeting on Thursday last was Chief Edenshew, who, as a younger man, headed many a savage raid on the neighbouring tribes." Edenshew

THE FIRST BISHOP OF CALEDONIA

had long opposed the truth, but the prayers and example of his son Cowhoe had at length resulted in his conversion. So that the bread so long since cast upon the waters was yet being found, though Cowhoe had passed to his reward.

Edenshew's first contention with me was in regard to his slaves, as he feared my mission was to set them free. Next he assailed me respecting the witchcraft of the medicine-men, and lastly, his complaint and regret was that he had failed to marry the Queen's daughter, which failure often troubled him. This matter was first suggested to him in the following manner. Amongst the early navigators who had touched at Queen Charlotte Islands, there was one named Captain Douglas. During the time his ship was anchored in Virago Sound, or cruising around the north of the islands, Edenshew spent most of his time on board. Captain Douglas made blood relationship with him, and gave him his own name. When about to leave the coast, he invited Edenshew to embark with him. "If you accompany me to England, the country of the Iron People," said he to Edenshew, "you will receive many gifts, and perhaps you may marry Queen Victoria's daughter."

"And I refused to go with him," said he, "because I was young and foolish, and preferred leading in the raids on other tribes and capturing slaves."

I generally soothed his feelings of regret by reminding him that had he gone with his friend, the captain, he would probably have been dead, whereas now he had lived to a good age. "And," I added, "you might not have married the Queen's daughter after all, as only kings and princes can hope to attain to such an honoured position."

"But am I not as king here?" he replied, "and always have been," and then he would rehearse some adventure of the past in which he always came off victorious.

Mr. Keen reported the number of baptized Indians at Massett in 1892 as three hundred and sixty-five and forty-five catechumens, with seventy communicants, whilst the

THE FIRST BISHOP OF CALEDONIA

school register recorded the names of ninety-seven pupils enrolled. A native branch of the Church Army had also been organised. Mr. Keen's knowledge of the language enabled him to confer a great benefit to the Mission by his translational work. He succeeded in translating the Gospels of St. Mark, St. Luke, and St. John, together with the Acts of the Apostles, and the first Epistle to the Corinthians from the New Testament, and the books of Genesis and Psalms from the Old Testament; as also portions from the Book of Common Prayer and hymns. But his experience of the unpopularity of translations of the hymns and canticles for the service of praise in Public Worship was identical with that of other missionaries amongst the languages of the mainland. The native Christians all prefer the hymns and chants in the English, and all hold to their English Bibles and prayer-books. Nevertheless, the translations are of great value to the Mission teachers in imparting religious instruction, and also to the native Christians in enabling them to grasp the true meaning of the English versions.

After some eight years' successful service in the Haida Mission, the Rev. J. H. and Mrs. Keen embarked for England on furlough, and, as they had experienced the isolation of island life very intensely, at his own request he was transferred to the Tsimshean Mission at Metlakahtla, where he took up residence on his return from furlough in 1900.

In August of the same year my son, the Rev. W. E. Collison, who had been previously ordained by Bishop Ridley, was appointed to take charge of the Haida Mission. Having been the first white child born at Metlakahtla, where he lived until his twelfth year, he was thoroughly acquainted with the Indian manners and customs, and spoke their language, both the Tsimshean and Nishka, as one of them. In 1887 he proceeded to England to further his education. Prior to this he had been under home tuition. He returned to British Columbia in 1893, having been absent seven years. On his return, he appeared to have completely forgotten

THE FIRST BISHOP OF CALEDONIA

the native language with which he had formerly been so familiar. But some three weeks afterwards, when conversing with his brother, who was reproaching him in Nishka for having forgotten it, suddenly his memory was aroused, and he was at once enabled to speak in the Nishka as freely as possible.

On his departure to take charge of the Mission, he was accompanied by his sister, who was the first white child born on the Queen Charlotte Islands. A Valedictory Meeting was held at Kincolith when they were leaving, at which many Nishkas were present, and joined in wishing them "God-speed" and success. Thus, on the very spot which derives its name from the slaughter of the Nishkas by the Haidas during the conflicts of the past, the Nishkas were now engaged in joining in prayer for the success of those who were thus proceeding to their former foes, with the message of the Gospel of peace.

They made the passage by a small coasting steamer, the *Chieftain*, and encountered rough weather in crossing to the islands. A number of friends crossed with them, including the Rev. J. H. Keen, Indian Agent W. Morrow, and others. Miss Collison suffered from sea-sickness, and as the waves washed over the decks and into the galley, putting out the fires, no food could be prepared. But the warm and hearty welcome with which they were received on reaching Massett cheered and encouraged them, and caused them to forget their misery.

As soon as the steamer was seen approaching, a large number of canoes filled with stalwart Haidas went out to meet her, and, on anchoring, they gathered around to extend a hearty greeting to the new arrivals. What a contrast to the arrival of their parents on the same shores as the first missionaries, just twenty-four years previously! Then there was no friendly hand extended in welcome, but dark faces, besmeared with paint, scowled at us, as we passed along seeking a shelter. And the captain's warning, "You will

THE FIRST BISHOP OF CALEDONIA

all be murdered," was still sounding in our ears when we reached the shore. But these dark days had now passed, and everything had become changed.

They were escorted to the shore by a fleet of canoes, where large numbers of the Haidas were waiting to welcome them. Chief Edenshew had passed away, but his son, Mr. Henry Edenshew, a fine young chief, who was now acting as a teacher and catechist, extended them a warm invitation to his house. Here his wife hastened to entertain them, and they quickly forgot the trials of their rough passage and its accompaniment of sea-sickness in the hot dishes of steaming halibut and tea placed before them.

By a strange coincidence, it was my daughter's birthday when she thus landed at her birthplace. She thus wrote in regard to it: "I think they must have known that it was my birthday, and that I had come to celebrate it amongst them, as it was just twenty-three years from the day when I was born, within one hundred yards of where I was being entertained and welcomed. And truly it was well worth all the difficulties through which we had passed, to experience such kindness and to enjoy such a welcome as our Haida friends had given us."

It was a great pleasure to the Haidas, especially to the women, to welcome thus one who had been born amongst them, and who had now returned to aid her brother's effort to lead them onward in the new life on which they had entered. And as to her brother who had now entered upon the work, everything reminded him of those dark days when he had shrunk from the presence of the medicine-men, and had often fled to hide himself on their approach. It was for this he had been spared and raised up again when his life was despaired of from the attack of typhoid fever caused by the noxious effluvia from the unburied dead. Then heathenism reigned throughout the camps. Now Christianity was triumphant. His sister continued to assist him until the following year, when he found a worthy helpmeet in a lady who had

THE FIRST BISHOP OF CALEDONIA

laboured in the Tsimshean Mission for several years as an honorary missionary, and now under their united efforts the Haidas have continued to advance in civilisation and the Christian life.

Just now a new and important crisis has arisen. The Queen Charlotte Islands, the old home and haunt of the Haidas, have been found to offer many attractions to the enterprise of white settlers and capitalists. Gold, copper, and coal have been found in sufficient quantity to warrant the investment of capital in their development. The timber, especially the red and yellow cedar, which enabled the Haidas formerly to construct the finest war canoes, and thus gave them the mastery of the coast, is among the best in the province. The comparative mildness of the climate, tempered as it is by the Japanese current, is sufficient to attract a farming population, whose chief object will be the raising of stock and green crops to supply the demand which will be made by the population of a large city. To such dimensions Prince Rupert, the Pacific terminus of the second trans-continental railway of Canada, is sure to grow. For though second in the order of construction, the Grand Trunk Pacific Railway will most likely be the first in importance, commanding, as it does, the shortest route between Europe and the East. Bishop Berkeley's well-known line, "Westward the course of Empire takes its way," is invested now with a wider meaning than ever before.

Since the victory of Japan over Russia, "the Land of the Rising Sun" has forced her way into the front rank amongst the nations. And, under her influence, China is awaking from the sleep of centuries. Let the Christian nations see to it that they seek not only the extension of their commerce and the development of trade, but that they unite in taking advantage of the improved facilities to send to these rising nations and empires that which has tended to elevate and strengthen themselves. It has been shown in the foregoing pages what the Gospel has done for the Haidas.

THE FIRST BISHOP OF CALEDONIA

Then, again, the Queen Charlotte Islands offer unlimited advantages as a centre for the deep-sea fisheries, which are only waiting for development. This will naturally attract a fishing population around its shores, to gather in the harvest of the ocean. Much of this will find a market in the cities of the coast and the interior, and much more will be transported by the special accommodation provided by the great trans-continental lines to the markets of the East and Europe.

How will all these great changes affect the native population? Prior to the evangelisation of the Haidas, they had been decreasing rapidly. Drink and disease, imported by themselves in their annual visits to the cities of the South, both provincial and American, had wrought sad ravages amongst them, and had reduced their numbers to less than one-fourth of what they had been. The new order of things has stayed the plague, and a slight annual increase has resulted. But with the influx of population from every quarter, and of various nationalities, both Christian and heathen, and a greater demand for their labour in the various industries, greater temptations will assail them, to which, if they give way, they must again suffer.

We would earnestly ask our white friends and fellow-countrymen, who may be brought into contact with the native races of the country, that they endeavour, by word and by example, to encourage them to walk worthy of the high vocation wherewith they are called, that so they may become worthy subjects of our great Dominion, and citizens of the coming Kingdom of truth and righteousness, which shall endure for ever.

CHAPTER XXI

THE NASS RIVER

> "Ye whose hearts are fresh and simple,
> Who have faith in God and nature,
> Who believe that in all ages
> Every human heart is human,
> That in even savage bosoms
> There are longings, yearnings, strivings,
> For the good they comprehend not,
> That the feeble hands and helpless,
> Groping blindly in the darkness,
> Touch God's right hand in that darkness,
> And are lifted up and strengthened."

I WAS no stranger to the Indians of the Nass River when I first entered upon the work and went to reside at Kincolith as the headquarters of the Mission. I had visited this station and had touched at every encampment on the river as early as the year 1874, when I accompanied the Rev. R. Tomlinson on an evangelistic tour. Mr. Tomlinson was then in charge, having succeeded the Rev. R. A. Doolan, who was the pioneer missionary on the Nass. Afterwards, when Mr. Tomlinson resigned, in order to open the Inland Mission to the Giatiksheans, Mr. H. Schutt, a Missionary Schoolmaster, was appointed to the charge under my superintendence. During his tenure of office, and also of Mr. David Leask's, a half-breed teacher who with his wife held it for a time, I continued to visit the Mission occasionally to examine the catechumens, and to administer Baptism.

On my first visit I was singularly impressed with the natural beauty of the river and the valley through which

THE NASS RIVER

it flows. The mountain ranges, crowned with snow, flank the valley on both sides, receding away into the distance. The shades of colour from the snowline downwards add greatly to the beauty of the scenery. The blue and purple of the mountains surmounting the dark green of the spruce and cedar, change to the lighter green of the cottonwood and willows on the lower stretches of the valley. Here and there on the lofty mountains standing behind the front ranges, an occasional glacier adds additional grandeur to the scene.

A romantic feature, which adds greater interest to the river, is the footprints of Thaimshim, the great wonder-worker of the past, whose deeds are linked with the traditions of both the Tsimsheans and the Nishkas. Indeed, so closely are the deeds of Thaimshim associated with the Indians of this river, that it is not unusual to hear these tribes referred to by the same name, or as the people of Thaimshim.

The first place where we meet with his exploits is between Nasoga Gulf and Iceberg Bay. Tradition asserts that this was at one time an open channel, but as it afforded an easy approach to the Tsimsheans and Haidas to the olachan fishery on the Nass, which the Nishkas were opposed to, Thaimshim came to their aid and hurled a mountain into the channel, thus stopping the passage and rendering access to the fishery more difficult. That it was at one time an open channel is probably true, but owing to land slides and the action of the tides, together with the discharge from the rivers, it has gradually filled in, converting into a peninsula the land which had been an island.

A few miles further up we are shown the crag on which he rested on the shore when he wished to feast on the salmon. Here he called on the salmon to come up to him, which they tried to do but failed. He then formed a succession of bowls in the rock right up to his seat, which enabled the salmon to jump from one to another. Thaim-

THE NASS RIVER

shim then opened his mouth wide and the salmon jumped in, one after another, until he was satisfied. But the size of the hollowed basins in the rock scarcely fulfil the expectations aroused by a being who has been moving mountains. His prowess is restored, however, in our estimation when, farther up, a sharp peak of about one thousand feet in height is pointed out as his walking-stick, which he left there when on his way up the river. There are many such traces of his adventures and traditions of his exploits on the river and along the coast.

Another most interesting feature of the Nass River is the great lava plain situated about forty miles from the mouth on the eastern bank. When I first ascended the river in 1874, I ascertained all I could about this volcanic eruption from several of the oldest Indians of the Upper River tribes. I was led to do this from the fact that I detected many signs which indicated its recent origin. Sections of trees and roots, the wood of which was still in good preservation, I found partly encrusted with the lava. The old man from whom I received the first account of the eruption was evidently over eighty years of age, and was moving himself on all fours with the aid of a pair of deer horns which he grasped in either hand, as he shuffled along the camp. He informed me that the eruption occurred when his grandfather was a boy.

"The river did not always flow where it does now," said he. "It flowed along by the base of the mountains on the farther side of the valley some miles away. It was there the people were encamped when the Nak-nok of the mountain became angry and the fire-stone flowed down. They were all busy in catching, cleaning, and cutting up the salmon, to dry in the smoke. Whilst they were thus engaged, some of the boys were amusing themselves in catching salmon, and cutting openings in their backs, in which they inserted long, narrow stones. Then, setting them free in the water, as the salmon swam near the surface, the boys clapped their hands and called them finback whales.

"While they were thus enjoying their cruel sport, the ground began to tremble, and suddenly the mountain vomited forth fire and smoke. We knew then that the spirit of the mountain was angry with the boys because of their cruelty to the salmon. Then, when we saw the Nak-nok of the Mountain rushing towards us clothed in fire, we fled for our lives. All that day we fled, and at sunset, as we looked back, we saw the spirit cloud with its huge wings outspread following us. We reached the foothills on this side, which we ascended, and there we took refuge, as all were exhausted, and could run no farther. The river of fire-stone, swept on by the cloud spirit, drove the river before it across the valley, until it also reached the base of the foot-hills. Here it heaped up, the river which quenched and cooled the fire-stone, boiling and thundering, and leaving it heaped up along the bank as it is to-day.

"As night fell, the spirit cloud disappeared in the darkness, but the whole valley was on fire, which continued for many days, until all the trees, and even the ground, were consumed.

"It was then that we separated and settled in the two encampments of Giatlakdamiksh and Giat-winikshilk. Before the mountain vomited forth the fire-stone, we were all one encampment on the upper side of the valley, but from that time we became two camps."

This was the account of the great lava eruption, as detailed by the oldest resident of the nearest village to the scene. That it was the traditional account as held by all, I verified by passing along to the farther end of the village, where I again inquired from two other aged men, evidently patriarchs of the tribe. Their account agreed with that of the first, even to the names of three of the lads whose cruel treatment of the salmon was believed to have been the cause of

THE NASS RIVER

the eruption. The leader of the offenders was named Ligishansh; the others I took no note of, as there were several. I was rather pleased at their idea that the cruel sport of the boys had caused the trouble, as they have no term in their language for cruelty, and I have frequently had to use my influence against it in various forms.

In confirmation of this Indian tradition of the probable date of the lava eruption on the Nass, the following incident may be added. Some years ago the Dominion Government sent from the Geological Office in Ottawa an experienced geologist, to examine and report on the aspect and formation of the country between the Upper Nass and the Stikeen Rivers. In an interview with this gentleman, I mentioned the existence of the lava plain as a subject worthy of his investigation as a geologist. I informed him that from the Indian tradition, and my own investigation, I concluded it could not be more than some one hundred and fifty years since the eruption occurred. He was rather amused at my information, and declared that he had examined several such eruptions in the North-west, and every one of them was probably two thousand years old, and he added he had but little doubt that this was of the same duration.

"Well," I replied, " Mr. M., you are a professional geologist, whilst I do not pretend to know very much in this branch of study; nevertheless, I decline to surrender my conviction in regard to it, until you have examined it. If, after examination, you are still of the same opinion, then I shall submit my opinion to yours, only requesting that you will give me your reasons for your decision."

This he promised to do, and having procured two Indians from me to join his party as guides, he started. Some weeks afterwards I received a letter from him, dated from the Geological Office at Ottawa, in which he stated that, not only was my conclusion correct, but he saw such evidence of its recent occurrence, that he considered that, if anything, I had over-estimated the number of years which

THE NASS RIVER

had elapsed since it occurred. The mountain on which the crater is situated, and from which the lava flowed, stands on the opening to the She-aksh or New River Valley, a few miles from the Nass, of which the She-aksh River is a tributary.

It is not generally known that the Indians on the Nass River were more or less familiar with white men before many of the tribes around them. This was owing to the first advent of the Hudson's Bay Company on the Northwest coast. The Company selected a projecting point on tide water, near the mouth of the river, and here in the year 1831 they erected a trading post. It was of the character of a fort, built with a view to defence, in case of attack, as all the Company's posts were, with a strong stockade all around it, as the natives could not be trusted in those days. But there was a power more to be dreaded than the Indians, which the Company's officers had not considered. It was the strong Nass winds, which sweep down the river day and night for nearly three months, when the cold is most intense, thus not only rendering their exposed position untenable, but preventing the Indians from approaching the fort during this time to trade. The river freezes down to within a few miles of this point, and remains in the grasp of the Ice King for several months. The ice is generally from two to four feet in thickness.

The generation of Indians who remembered the first advent of the " Omukshewas," or white men, have almost all passed away. Many of them are buried right on the site where the fort formerly stood. This point, which was formerly known as " Fort Point," is now known as " Cemetery Point," and forms the " God's Acre " of the Kincolith Mission Station. The oldest chief on the river, who only died lately, aged eighty-three years, informed me that he remembered the coming of the white men. He was then a child of some five or six years, and was taking his first lessons with bow and arrow. Another veteran who died lately took much pleasure in reciting and singing the songs

ON THE NASS RIVER, B.C.

The crew are resting in a backwater after struggling with the strong current. The general shape of a large Indian canoe is here well shown. The bow is on the left of the picture.

THE NASS RIVER

the Indians sang when one of the Company's ships was seen approaching the mouth of the river:

> " Ho ! ho ! ho ! Angland's ship a-ho !
> Hip, hip, hurray ! "

In 1834 the Company moved the fort to a place thirty-seven miles farther south, on a spacious and well-sheltered harbour known amongst the Indians as " Laklquaha-lamish," or " Rose Island," but now more generally known as " Port Simpson." It was so named in memory of Captain Simpson, who died after establishing the Hudson's Bay Company's fort on the Nass, and whose remains were removed to the new site when it was established.

The late Captain Walbran, in his excellent work entitled *British Columbia Place-Names*, 1909, on page 396 gives an extract from Dr. Tolmie's diary, which describes vividly the departure of the Hudson's Bay Company from the Nass to occcupy Fort Simpson. It is as follows: " Fort Simpson on the Nass was finally abandoned 30th August 1834, a Saturday night; and such a Saturday night the Indians never had before, as the Tyees (chiefs) of the Company had made them a parting present of a twenty-five gallon cask of rum, and with this aid to festivity, the Indians duly celebrated the event.

" No sleep could be obtained on the *Dryad* anchored a short distance from the shore, a drunken orgy of the wildest kind taking place; firearms were discharged, and shrieks and yells filled the air. Among it all could be heard the ripping and hammering of timber, and when the short summer night was over, the destruction of the fort was nearly complete. On the tide suiting in the morning, the *Dryad* sailed."

Thus Port Simpson, which then and for many years after was known as " Fort Simpson," was first established in the autumn of 1834. From this time onward the Tsimshean tribes of Indians continued to move from their old encamp-

THE NASS RIVER

ments at Metlakahtla and vicinity to settle around Fort Simpson.

About the year 1849 a peculiar religious excitement arose among the Indian tribes of the interior, known as the "Pe-ne." It had its origin amongst the Babine Indians in the vicinity of Stewart. A French Roman Catholic missionary, known as Father Nobili, had visited that point, amongst others, and had conducted a Mission there of a few weeks. Not long after his departure, some of the Indians, principally the medicine-men, commenced to imitate the teachings of the missionary, combining it with their own heathen practices.

In the Rev. A. G. Morice's *History of the Northern Interior of British Columbia*, pp. 234-5, he states of this movement: "After Father Nobili's departure, numerous pseudo-priests or would-be prophets sprang up from all places, who, on the strength of dreams, real or pretended, claimed supernatural powers, preached after a way, made people dance when they did not know how to make them pray, gave new names to their adherents, and otherwise counterfeited the work of the missionaries. And," he adds, "all villages of any importance, especially in the north of New Caledonia, boasted at a time the presence of some such self-appointed priest.

"The Babines were not to be outstripped in that race after notoriety. Their champion was a certain loud-mouthed man known as Uzakle, whose pretensions were the ultimata cause of a wonderful religious movement among the natives of the extreme North-west, both Tsimsheans and Denes, a commotion which can rightfully be compared to the Messiah crazes of later days." The good Father is quite correct, for not only did the movement affect the Tsimsheans and Denes, but the Nishka tribes on the Nass River, the Klingits of south-eastern Alaska, and even the Haidas on the Queen Charlotte Islands, joined in it.

An old man who was quite blind, and whose memory of

THE NASS RIVER

the "Pe-ne" was very vivid, went through the entire performance for my benefit on one occasion, in my headquarters at the Nass Olachan Fishery. He commenced with a low, mournful chant, crossed himself, prayed, sang again, and danced. With it he also combined the incantations of the Shaman, or medicine-men. But he had quite a different account of its origin. He stated that a hunter of his tribe had gone away alone to his hunting-ground to set his traps. Whilst engaged preparing his traps and snares in his little hunting lodge, a strange visitor entered. He addressed him in a strange tongue, pointed upwards, crossed himself, sang the chant, prayed, and then departed, as he had come. The hunter believed his strange visitor had come from the Spirit land, and so overcome was he that he remained motionless in his lodge and forgot all about his hunting. When his friends came in search of him, they found him prostrate from fasting, as he had eaten nothing from the time his strange visitor had left him. He described the visitation graphically to his tribe, by whom it was eagerly taken up, and soon they were engaged in repeating it night and day from tribe to tribe all along the river, chanting and dancing and praying, often till daybreak.

It was a strange combination, not wholly devoid of good. It revealed the religious desire in man. It was a reaching out for something above and beyond them. It was a longing for that which alone can give satisfaction. Tennyson's well-known lines perhaps best express the state of the Indian at this period:

> "But what am I?
> An infant crying in the night,
> An infant crying for the light,
> And with no language but a cry."

CHAPTER XXII

ANKIDĀ ENCAMPMENT

"We feel we are nothing—for all is Thou and in Thee,
We feel we are something—*that* also has come from Thee;
We know we are nothing—but Thou wilt help us to be.
Hallowed be Thy name—Hallelujah!"
—TENNYSON ("The Human Cry").

ONE of the most picturesque of the Indian villages of the Lower Nass River is Ankidā. It stands on the lower end of an island situated in mid-stream.

A line of large Indian dwellings stand facing the main branch of the river. In front of each of these lodges two or more totem poles stand. These are elaborately carved from base to top with their grotesque crestal figures. These totem or crest poles are of different height, as the rank of each of the chiefs here is indicated by the height of his totem.

Some years since a sub-chief attempted to break this law by erecting a totem higher than that of the leading chief. The latter warned the offender, and called upon him to reduce the length of his pole. This he refused to do, knowing it would cause him shame amongst his fellow-tribesmen. The offended chief then determined to enforce the law, according to Indian custom, and so, loading his gun, he shot the offender as he emerged from his house.

This same chief afterwards defied the law by aiding in the importation of intoxicating liquor amongst his tribe. But a large force of native constables from Metlakahtla succeeded in capturing him at Fishery Bay, and he was

ANKIDĀ ENCAMPMENT

brought, bound hand and foot, to Metlakahtla for trial. The missionary, the Rev. R. Tomlinson, then in charge of the Nass River Mission, fearing serious trouble over the seizure of the chief, repaired to the camp to endeavour to preserve the peace. But some of the women of the tribe, led by the chief's wife, seized the missionary as a hostage, and detained him until he succeeded in convincing them that his detention could not benefit the chief's case in the eyes of the law. He was then liberated. After a short term of imprisonment and fine, the chief returned to his camp a better because a wiser man.

Ankidā derives its name from the old method of catching the olachan there. This was done with a long stick, of which one end for two feet or more was fitted with iron or wooden spikes well sharpened. Armed with such an instrument as this the Indian fisherman sat in his small canoe or dug-out and used the stick in much the same manner as a paddle. In a shoal of fish he generally succeeded in impaling a number at every stroke, which he turned into his canoe. This spiked stick is known as the "kidāh," and its general use by the Indians of this encampment during the olachan fishing gained for it the term Ankidā, or the place where the kidāh is used. In the same way the Indian encampment at Hazleton on the Skeena River is known by them as "Kitanmaksh," "maksh" being the old term for torch, as the Indians there generally fished for the salmon with torches by night.

Ankidā occupied the central position amongst the Indian encampments on the Lower Nass, prior to the establishment of Missions.

There were four other villages in the near vicinity, but none of them were so conveniently situated for both the olachan and the salmon fishing as this encampment. For this reason also it figured first in the conflicts of the past, having been attacked both by the Haidas and also by the Tsimsheans. It was probably owing to this that its chiefs

ANKIDĀ ENCAMPMENT

had gained for themselves the reputation of being fierce and more warlike than those of the surrounding tribes.

But the teachings of Christianity had changed the character of the leading chiefs, and even the once proud Klaidak, who had slain his fellow-chieftain because he refused to shorten his totem pole, and afterwards had defied the law, at length surrendered to the power of the Gospel and was received into the Church of Christ. And even those of them who refused to abandon what they designated as the ways of their forefathers, were yet induced to forsake the worst features of heathenism and to adopt more civilised habits. The successor to the head chief mentioned above was one of these, and as the title was hereditary he was known by the same name. I early gained an influence with this chief, who always welcomed me and my crew to his great lodge.

On one occasion I visited him whilst he was engaged in a great "potlatch." It was Sunday, and his lodge was filled with his guests, all arrayed in the paint and feathers. It was customary in these days to await the arrival of the Indians from the upper river and from the interior for the olachan fishing before issuing the invitations for a "potlatch." This plan secured a large and representative attendance. Great piles of blankets both in bales and singly were heaped up around, whilst wash-basins full of silver currency were placed here and there ready for distribution. The preliminary rites had been performed, including the dance of peace and the scattering of the swansdown. This was evidenced by the clouds of down which were floating everywhere, and which soon made us appear as though we were partakers in the ceremony. On intimating to the chief my desire to conduct a short service, he at once assented, and ordered his young men to prepare a place for me and those who accompanied me.

The "potlatch" was discontinued, those who were outside pressed in on hearing the singing, and I addressed them for

ANKIDĀ ENCAMPMENT

some twenty minutes. Their interest was intense, and I have seldom had a more interested congregation. Some of them, who were strangers from the interior, were interested not only in the subject but also at hearing a white man speaking in their own tongue. But seizing as an illustration the ceremony they had just been engaged in of the scattering of the swansdown, which amongst them is regarded as the symbol of peace and good-will, I proclaimed to them the truth that the Great Chief above had made peace for man by sending His Son to be the propitiation for our sins, and through Him had sent down His Holy Spirit to convey His peace to us.

Some years afterwards this chief abandoned heathenism and was baptized, as also all his tribe. He had a marble bust carved, life-size, of himself, copied from a photograph, and this was mounted outside his lodge for several years before he died. It is now erected over his grave. I was invited to officiate at his funeral, which was attended by large numbers of his friends from all the tribes which had gathered at the fishery.

One very striking feature of the funeral was the total absence of the old-time graceful canoe. All the Indians attended and followed the remains on gasoline launches, of which there were many. There were also five Indian brass-bands, which discoursed the "Dead March" in turn, and other sacred airs. A solemn service was held in the church at Lagkalzap, from which the remains were conveyed to the deceased chief's old encampment at Ankidā, where he was interred in accordance with his last request. After the funeral I was requested to initiate two young chiefs to succeed my old friend, who had thus passed away. It was an interesting ceremony, introduced by myself some years previously, to supplant the heathen mode of instituting a chief. The two young men came forward, accompanied by the other chiefs, who formed a semi-circle around them. After inquiring as to their purpose in thus presenting the two men, and having received favourable replies to my questions, I addressed them in a few words on the responsibility of the office of a chief, and then taking the sash and insignia from one of the chiefs I passed them to another chief, who crossed it upon the breast first of one and then of the other, at the same time calling them by their new titles. They were then led to seats placed for them amongst their brother chiefs, after which three cheers were given for each of them.

A chief then advanced and presented me with a copper tomahawk which had long been a favourite weapon with the old chief whom I had just buried. In presenting it he said, " Well, chief, you have laid our good old Shimoigit (chief) Klaitak to rest, and you have strengthened our hearts by filling up the vacancy thus made by instituting two of our brothers to take his place, so we have agreed to ask you to accept this, which was long preserved by the old chief, and which was a favourite weapon of his when he went out on the war-path in the years gone by, when his arm was strong and his eye clear. He always regarded you as his friend, and therefore we are pleased to present you with this as a token of his regard for you."

In accepting it I held it up before the assembled audience of over two hundred, and replied: " Chiefs and friends, I am thankful to accept this weapon as a trophy of your old chief. I can assure you that I shall never use it as he did on the war-path, but I shall be happy to exhibit it to your children, and explain to them how much more pleasant it is to tread the paths of peace than to have to fight on the war-path as your fathers were compelled to do."

Instantly the entire audience rose to their feet and gave me a hearty cheer, to which I bowed an acknowledgment and passed out, proud of my presentation, which I have added to my museum of Indian curios.

The old chief whom I had thus known for so many years, and whom I had been privileged to lead from heathenism

ON THE NASS RIVER, B.C.

The river is frozen over with ice several feet thick. The Indians are engaged in setting nets beneath the ice to catch the olachan. A sleigh stands ready to convey the fish away.

ANKIDĀ ENCAMPMENT

into the light of the truth, sent for me about two years previous to his death, and related to me the following tale, which I committed to writing on the occasion:

The Chief's Story

There was great excitement in the central encampment on the Lower Nass River. In response to an invitation which had been sent out some weeks previously, the tribesmen were assembling from every camp on the river. Some great event was about to take place. The canoes which had been sent to summon the chiefs were manned by young braves, who cried aloud in front of the various camps, that the head chief had discovered the " Gan sha-goibakim-Lakah," or that which enlightened the heavens, and was about to lead an expedition to procure it.

It was further announced that the leading chief of every crest and clan who joined in the expedition should receive a share in this wonderful discovery.

An ambitious hunter of the tribe who had ascended the highest mountain on his hunting-ground in quest of the mountain goat was overtaken by the sunset when near the summit, and was compelled to seek shelter and rest in a cleft of the mountain for the night.

He was not without food, as he had shot a young sheep early in the day, which he had skinned; and then having rolled up the choicest portions of the meat in the skin, which he had first scraped and cleaned carefully, he had cached it in a crevice of a rock where the wolves and wolverines could not find it.

To this natural food depot he now descended, and having abstracted a choice cut he kindled a fire, and impaling his steak on a stick, which he sharpened for the purpose, inserted it firmly in the ground leaning towards the fire, where it was soon frizzling and roasting.

Whilst waiting in pleasant anticipation for his evening

ANKIDĀ ENCAMPMENT

meal, he drew his pipe from his belt, and having filled it, he applied a burning cinder and puffed away, with his gaze fixed on the fire.

Suddenly he was startled by the cry of a wolf near by on the mountain, which was quickly answered by a whole pack lower down. At once he realised what had occurred. This solitary wolf which he had first heard had discovered the portions of the sheep which he had discarded, and was summoning the entire pack to the feast.

Concluding that prudence was the better part of valour, he instantly seized his gun, and grasping the stick on which his evening meal was roasting he rushed up the mountain. Higher and yet higher he hastened, with the howling of the hungry wolves ringing in his ears. He was no coward, as he had often faced both the grizzly bear and the wolf in fierce conflict, and brought them down with his trusty weapon. But now the night had overtaken him, and he knew he could but fire at random in the darkness and waste his ammunition, which was precious.

Meanwhile, the wolves had ceased their howling, and he knew they were engaged in devouring the remains of the sheep which he had killed, as an occasional angry yelp indicated the struggle which was taking place over it. Still he continued his upward flight, and had now reached a point where hunter's foot had never trod before. Nor could he climb higher, for a glacier hung like a curtain from the crags above him.

Brought thus to a stand, he looked around and discovered an opening, into which he passed. To his surprise and satisfaction he found it was a lofty opening, with the roof sloping upward and outward. And as he gazed he was attracted and astonished by what he supposed at first to be numbers of icicles, suspended from the overhanging roof of his shelter, but on closer examination he found they were not icicles but stalactites, of which several had fallen to the rocky floor underneath and been broken.

ANKIDĀ ENCAMPMENT

A miner could not have been more delighted on discovering a gold-mine than was the hunter on the discovery of this gallery of crystals. For he had often heard thrilling tales of the discoveries of such treasures in the past, and how some chiefs had become great and wealthy by purchasing numbers of slaves with them.

He was not much further troubled with the fear of the wolves, so elated was he with his great discovery. Besides, he knew that they had descended the mountain again. They had followed his trail to the fire which he had left burning right in the centre of the narrow pass, and fearing to pass it they united in a final concert of howling, and then retreated down the mountain.

He then unbound his rabbit robe, which he had carried slung over his shoulders, and wrapping himself in it he placed his gun near to his side and lay down to rest till the day should dawn.

But sleep he could not. His mind was too full of his discovery, and as he lay looking upward he could see the starlight flashing from crystal to crystal and illuminating the roof of his shelter with the rays.

At length he slumbered and dreamed of wolves and crystals until he saw the pack of wolves rushing up in an attack on his treasures, from which he awoke with a start, to find that the day was breaking. He arose quickly and hastened down to where he had kindled his fire overnight, and finding a few sparks still burning he quickly replenished it and fanned it into a flame. Hastening back to where he had hidden the meat he took a portion from the natural safe in which he had placed it, and returning to the fire he roasted it, and feasted on it for breakfast. This he concluded by a draught of water from a stream which trickled down the mountain near by. Thus refreshed he started on his return journey to the camp, where he related to the astonished tribesmen the story of his great discovery. This, then, was the cause of the gathering described before. It

ANKIDĀ ENCAMPMENT

was to acquaint the chiefs of the neighbouring villages of the news of the discovery, and to devise plans for obtaining possession of the prizes. It was at length decided that a strong and very long basket should be constructed, together with some new bark ropes, and that a slave named Zidahak, who was famed for his ability in climbing to dizzy heights, should be lowered in this basket from the top of the mountain to the gallery where the glistening crystals hung.

While these preparations were being made Zidahak was the hero of the hour, and in the enjoyment of his honours he quite forgot he was a slave. The lucky finder was also rewarded with many presents, and promises of more when the crystals were brought home. For this purpose a number of the strongest of the braves from each tribe was selected to accompany Zidahak to the mountain top, and to lower him down to the treasures. Many were the charges he received as he took his place in the basket to be lowered down, to the much-desired gems. A signal was agreed upon, which Zidahak should give when ready to be drawn up, and this done he was gently pushed over the edge of the precipice. Hand over hand he was gradually lowered downwards and yet downwards until but little of the rope was left, and they began to fear that it would prove too short to reach the prize.

But just when within a few feet of the end, a jerk of the rope thrice repeated from below indicated that he had reached the spot, and securing the rope to a spur of rock they sat down to await results. Meantime Zidahak was not idle. Now with his right hand and now with his left, and occasionally with both hands, he was pulling off first the largest stalactites within his reach and then the smaller, and packing them in the basket around his feet and legs.

Higher and yet higher he packed them, without reflecting for a moment on the weight which he was adding every minute to his load. And now, as the basket was quite full, he placed several under his arms, and then gave the signal

ANKIDĀ ENCAMPMENT

agreed upon for hauling him up. Slowly, inch by inch, the basket began to move upward, creaking under its weight.

Now he could hear the shouts of the young men above as they heaved away in concert on the strained rope. And still they toiled on, trusting to Zidahak to guide the basket in its ascent and keep it clear of the projecting ledges of the rocky steep. This he endeavoured to do, and was successful in his efforts until near the top. Just here was a sharp projection, and as the pull on the rope was more inward now, he was unable to keep the rope off the rocky ledge. Suddenly a strand of the rope was severed by the sharp ledge of rock, and he cried aloud to warn them of the danger. But instead of trying to devise some means of repairing the damage, and fearful of losing the prize now that it was almost within their reach, they all united in a strong pull together. Instantly the rope parted and all the party were thrown on their backs, whilst the basket with the unfortunate slave and all his hard-won treasures was hurled downwards several hundred feet. His body, together with the stalactites, bounded and rebounded from rock to rock and from ledge to ridge, until arrested about midway down the mountain.

And here they found him, a mangled mass, but on unfolding his inner garment, or what remained of it, they found six of the smaller but more perfectly formed crystals lodged, three under each arm, where he had clasped them even in his death fall. Of the others only broken scraps could be found here and there scattered down the mountain.

After the young men who had formed the expedition had cremated the remains of the faithful slave Zidahak, they hastened to return to camp with the six stalactites thus preserved. There was much mourning and lamentation in the camp when the sad news was announced, but the sorrow was not for the unfortunate slave Zidahak, but rather for the treasures which had been lost with him. The six crystal stalactites which had been preserved were exhibited

ANKIDĀ ENCAMPMENT

for several days in the lodge of the leading chief, and hosts of Indians from all the tribes entered to examine and admire them. And as they did so, they generally ended their examination with exclamations of sorrow for the crystals which had been lost. "Alas now, how sad that such a number of these costly crystals should have been lost. Iowa. Alas!" But not a word of regret for poor Zidahak. A meeting of the chiefs and their councillors was then convened, when the crystals were named and distributed to the leading chiefs as follows:

The first crystal was named "Aizuli," or the "Eldest," and was presented to Chief Neishlishyan, or the "Grandfather of the Mink." Of this crystal a chant or song was composed by the music-master of his tribe, which was sung on special occasions, as when a great potlatch was made.

The second stalactite was named "Tka-ga-Koidix," or the "Coming of the Whole." This was presented to Chief Gadonai, and a song was also made for it.

The third crystal stalactite was named "How-how-imshim laub," or the "Lion Stone," and was presented to Chief Klaitak, the predecessor of the chief who narrated the incident. A chant was also composed by the music-master of the tribe for this crystal.

The fourth crystal was named "Daow-im Lakak," or the "Ice of Heaven," and was presented to Chief Gwaksho, who was the chief bear hunter on the river, and killed a bear on one occasion without any weapon but his teeth.

The fifth crystal was named "Kalga Lagim Lakan," or the "Great Fire Glass of Heaven," and was presented to Chief Neish lak-an-noish, who was a Zimshean chief, but had married a Nishka chieftainess. This chief was famed for his skill as a carver and designer, in gold, silver, and wood.

The sixth and last of the crystal stalactites was named "Gwe-yel," and was presented to Chief Ginzadak, who after a hard life of raiding and fighting with other tribes at

ANKIDĀ ENCAMPMENT

length became a Christian, and witnessed a good confession to the end of his days.

A great song was composed by the music-masters of the camps in commemoration of the finding of the crystals, and the circumstances connected with it. This song was named "Maouk," and was sung annually by the tribes when they assembled for the potlatch, or Yiaak, on the lower river. They were generally known as "Giat-tkadeen," or "The People of all the Valley."

Such was the story as related to me by Chief Klaitak. The "Lion Stone" crystal which had been presented to his predecessor was now in his possession, and as I was desirous to see those ancient treasures my request was granted, and the young chief, in whose charge they had been placed, favoured me with a view.

They were carefully hidden away in a strong chest in his house, and no one was admitted but myself on the occasion. It was evident from the care with which he exhibited them to me that he still considered them as crown jewels.

The stalactites were from eight to twelve inches in diameter. They were hexagonal in shape, and looked like cut glass. As I examined them, I was pleased to remember that not only the old chief who had told me the story, but also nearly all the chiefs to whom they had been originally presented had heard an older story of greater and more enduring treasures than these, and of the sea of glass mingled with fire in the heavenly mansions of which the Apostle declares: "Eye hath not seen, nor ear heard, nor hath it entered into the heart of man to conceive the things which God hath prepared for them that love Him."

CHAPTER XXIII

THE SKEENA RIVER MISSION

"Though the mills of God grind slowly,
Yet they grind exceeding small.
Though with patience He stands waiting,
With exactness grinds He all."
—LONGFELLOW.

THE Tsimshean Indians are inseparably connected and identified with the river Skeena. Some of the early navigators proceeded to give a name to this river, as they named also other places on the coast, without inquiring from the Indians, or seeking to ascertain what the native names were. By so doing the only key to the early history of the country was discarded, as much may be learned from the original names given by the Indians centuries before. The original name of this river, as given it by the Indians, is "Ikshean." To this the name "Skeena," by which it is known to the Whites, does not appear to bear any resemblance.

The late Captain Walbran in his interesting work of *British Columbian Place-Names* states, on the authority of Dr. Ridley, late Bishop of Caledonia, that the name Skeena is an adaptation of "Kshian," the Tsimshean name of the river meaning a "divide."

"Kshian" does not mean a "divide," but a "flowing out." "Iksh" as a prefix always implies "out of," as "ikshadowlth," meaning "gone away out." Comparing the two terms we have "Ikshean," made up of "iksh," out of, and "shean" or "shyen," which means "the clouds." This indi-

THE SKEENA RIVER MISSION

cates the clouds as the source of the river. Tsimshean also is made up of "tsim," in, and "shean," the river Skeena. Hence it is evident that they derive their tribal name from the name of the river. The first syllable "ik" is dropped from "Ikshean," which is their term for the Skeena, and the word "tsim," or "in," substituted. We therefore have "Tsimshean," which translated literally means "in the shean." They are therefore "the people of the Skeena."

This is just where their old encampments are found at the head of tidal water in the Skeena River. Not only so, but they carried the names of their respective camps to which they formerly belonged with them when they removed to Port Simpson, Metlakahtla, and other points on the coast. There were originally ten tribes, each of which occupied their own encampment as follows:

> The "Kishpagalots," or "People among the elderberry bushes."
> "Kinnadoiaksh," or "People on the rapids."
> "Kitseesh," or "People of the salmon traps."
> "Kitsatlal," or "People of the willows."
> "Kitlahn," or "People of the salmon roe."
> "Kitandoh," or "People on the other side."
> "Kitwilgiauts," or "People whose canoes are afloat."
> "Kilutsa," or "People on the inside."
> "Kinagangeek," or "People where the flies abound."
> "Kitwilikshaba," or "People on the starting-place."

These tribes or clans had each a winter encampment on the salt-water on the Metlakahtla Channel, to which they moved for the winter. Here they were never frozen in, which they would have been had they remained on the river. In addition they had an abundance of fresh food in the fish, crabs, and shell-fish with which the Metlakahtla waters abounded, besides deer and water-fowl. But in moving from the river encampments on the Skeena, to the winter encampments, they usually broke the journey at a sheltered bay near the

THE SKEENA RIVER MISSION

mouth of the river, known now as Port Essington. It was so named by Vancouver, who anchored off it in his voyage of discovery in 1793.

But the Indians had named this bay long before Vancouver had visited it. It was known as "Spa-ukshūt," or the autumnal encampment, because they encamped here on the way down the river. Later on, after all these tribes had almost deserted the Skeena and made Metlakahtla and Port Simpson their permanent encampments, the Kitsilass (people of the canyon) Indians began to move from that rocky habitation and to take up their residence at Port Essington. This movement was accelerated by the establishment of one or two trading stores there, as the ability to procure the white man's goods in exchange for his furs was a powerful attraction to the Indian hunter. It was just this that had drawn the Tsimshean tribes to abandon their summer and winter encampments on the Skeena and at Metlakahtla, and to settle around the Hudson's Bay Company's establishment at Port Simpson.

In July 1875 I visited Port Essington, and conducted the first services there for both whites and Indians. I found a number of white miners in camp *en route* to the newly discovered gold-fields of Omineca. Mr. Cunningham, a pioneer trader who had just established a trading post, kindly placed his dwelling-house at my disposal for a service, and assisted in every way to make it a success. The rooms were filled, and many had to remain outside. I deputed a native teacher to conduct services with the Indians, which he did in their own tongue. After the service I performed a marriage ceremony, and baptized several children. I was appealed to also to act as peacemaker in the settlement of a dispute. Mrs. Cunningham kindly volunteered to open a Sunday-school, for which I engaged to send her a supply of books. Thus the Mission was inaugurated on the Lower Skeena.

The following year the Methodist Missionary Society

THE SKEENA RIVER MISSION

entered upon the Indian work at Port Essington, whilst the Rev. H. A. Sheldon was appointed by the Bishop to carry on the missionary work of the Church amongst the whites there. Mr. Sheldon had proved his zeal by volunteering to open a Mission amongst the miners on the Upper Stikeen; but as the mines there did not prove a success they were abandoned, and he at once removed to Port Essington, where he laboured with much acceptance until his death. He was drowned by the foundering of his canoe on the Skeena, near Point Lambert, and almost within view of his Mission. He was accompanied by three Indian lads as his crew, and Mrs. Cunningham as a passenger. The canoe was labouring in a heavy tide rip, when a squall struck them from the sea. This caused it to spring a leak, and the water poured into the canoe. Fearing to be immersed, Mrs. Cunningham, who was seated in the bottom of the canoe, suddenly stood up, and as the canoe was nearly full of water it capsized, and all were precipitated into the sea. The only lad that was saved stated that the missionary had a paddle in his hands when the canoe capsized, but this he threw to one of the Indians to assist him to keep afloat. He then raised his voice in prayer for the Indians and disappeared whilst still praying for them and the Mission.

Mr. Sheldon's body was not found for some weeks, though a reward was promised to any person who might find it. I endeavoured to encourage them to search for it, and it was at length discovered and interred under the shadow of the church he had erected and which he loved so well. The members of his congregation united in procuring a stained glass window, which was put up in the building "in memoriam." But this memorial was destroyed with the church by a great fire which swept away a large part of the town. Mr. Sheldon's memory, however, is preserved in the minds of many whose esteem he won by his efforts to guide them into the way of truth. His latest breath was spent in prayer for his work and for his people as his spirit passed to his

THE SKEENA RIVER MISSION

rest and reward. He was succeeded in the work at Essington by the Rev. Michael Brown, who with his friend Dr. Haddon ministered to the spiritual and bodily needs of the ever-changing population at Port Essington. Mr. Brown was compelled, after several years' labour, to resign on account of his wife's health. He afterwards took charge of Cedar Hill church and parish, near Victoria, where he died.

In July 1880 I ascended the Skeena River from Metlakahtla by canoe to open the first Mission on the Upper Skeena amongst the Gitikshan tribes. With five Tsimsheans and a medium-sized canoe we were twelve days in poling up the river to Skeena Forks, which was afterwards named Hazleton. As the Skeena is larger and more rapid than the Nass, it was with difficulty that we succeeded in propelling our craft up some of the rapids, and I never relaxed my efforts to assist my crew until we reached our destination. The Skeena was then, as it is now, full of salmon at this season of the year, and the bears usually gather on the sand-bars and fish out the salmon with their paws. At one point I shot a black bear, for which my Indians were grateful, as we had been subsisting almost wholly on fish for ten days. The following day being wet compelled us to remain in camp, when Bruin was skinned and cut up, and the flesh served out, roasted, broiled, and in soup for the three meals. The occupants of another canoe which encamped with us were also invited to partake of the improved fare, and the increased numbers afforded me a larger congregation for our evening service. On one sand-bar we saw a number of black bear feeding on the salmon with one immense grizzly, the track of which I measured and found it to be a span and a half in length, or about thirteen inches. They are very dainty in their choice of salmon, and have been seen to catch numbers of them and cast them away one after another until they find one of which Bruin approves. Of this he will partake of a few bites, and then cast it aside and fish for another.

In this way large quantities of salmon are left lying along

THE SKEENA RIVER MISSION

the banks and on the bars of the rivers, which become very offensive later in the season. The mosquitoes were very annoying, especially in some places where they were protected from the wind, and this was too often forgotten by our Indians when selecting a camp. It was interesting to witness the plan adopted by my crew to protect themselves from these pests, and secure rest and sleep during the night. They first cut a number of strong osier rods of ten or twelve feet in length. These they sharpened at both ends, and then by pushing first one end into the ground for eight or ten inches, then bending it over they push the other end into the ground in the same manner. It is thus bow-shaped, with the centre of the bow four or five feet from the ground. Then another rod is fixed in the same manner, but at right angles to the first, thus crossing it at the centre. Then other rods are inserted in the spaces between, until a cage has been completed. The canoe sail is then brought and thrown over the whole, and sand is placed on the skirts of the sail where it rests on the ground. It is necessary at this stage that one person should be admitted to kill all the mosquitoes which may have entered. This done, I was invited to enter quickly, followed by my son, who accompanied me, and by the five members of my crew—seven in all. We were all packed closely together, as herrings in a barrel. For a short time there was a feeling of satisfaction at our deliverance from the clouds of bloodthirsty mosquitoes, the united buzz of which rose and fell like a number of hives of bees as they surged around our cover, seeking in vain to find an entrance.

But for me there was no sleep. The heat was so intense that I was bathed in perspiration, as though in a Turkish bath. Added to this was the sense of suffocation. I struggled and endured until the first dawn of daylight. Then with a rush I raised the skirt of the tent near me and dashed out, despite the cries to restrain me which arose from all within. I felt I could survive amidst the mosqui-

THE SKEENA RIVER MISSION

toes, but that I should be smothered if much longer in that hot bath of heated breath and steam. I rushed to the fire, and gathering the still burning cinders together, I added fresh fuel, and then stood in the smoke, with closed eyes and mouth, content to gasp now and again for a mouthful of air. But my crew were ill at ease. In my exit I had admitted too many of the enemy. Murmurs of disapproval of my actions, with occasional groans, intimated their unrest, and soon this gave way to a united roar as they too burst from their cover and rushed for the smoke. An early cup of coffee, which we drank with the cup in one hand and a branch in the other to beat off our assailants, prepared us for another start. We soon got into a breeze on the river, which swept our foes away, and with their departure we forgot our miseries.

My arrival to open the Mission at Skeena Forks was most opportune. A pioneer trader, who had been trading there with the Indians for furs, had failed, and was about to leave. I at once secured his little shanty and the large log-building in which he had carried on his store business, at a low rent, with a promise to purchase. I pulled down the shelves and counter, and with the lumber constructed seats and a platform, thus preparing it for public services, as well as for day-school use. With an old crowbar hung by the door, for use as a bell, I summoned my congregation to service, and soon had good congregations, and thirty-five scholars registered on my school-roll.

My chief trouble arose from the Indian gamblers, who plied their craft from early morn till eve, right in front of my Mission-hall. I warned them against continuing it on the Sunday, but they paid no heed. On the second Sunday, however, they had no sooner seated themselves to commence their noisy game when I charged upon them to seize their gambling outfit. They realised my object, and grabbing their effects fled up the hill, with their blankets trailing behind them. I informed them I would seize their sticks

THE SKEENA RIVER MISSION

and mats should they attempt to play again near the Mission buildings. Concluding that prudence was the better part of valour, they did not transgress again, but carried on their games on the hill behind the camp.

Thus the Skeena Mission at Hazleton was inaugurated, and I continued to carry it on until the approach of winter, when I hastened to return to the coast to make arrangements for my work there.[1] On our way down the Skeena by canoe my crew selected what they considered a good encampment for the night, with a sandy beach and a supply of firewood. But they failed to notice that a high spur of rock abutted on the river, leaving only a narrow pass of two or three feet between rock and river for man or beast to pass up or down. This was close to the upper end of our camp. I occupied one tent with my son, a child of six years, whilst the second tent was occupied by the canoe owner, who was also the steersman, a chief of the Kitanmaksh tribe, and his crew. We had only just turned in when a prancing and snorting arose around our tents, which gradually increased, until we feared our tent would be attacked. I realised what the cause was; we had encroached on the bears' right-of-way, the only road by which they could pass from one valley to another. As the snorting and rushing around the tents in-

---

[1] In the Rev. T. Crosby's book, lately published, entitled *Up and Down the North Pacific Coast by Canoe and Mission Ship*, on p. 227 I am reported to have said to the Rev. T. Crosby, in reference to the Mission at the Skeena Forks, now known as Old Haytiton, which I had just opened, "Mr. Crosby, we have no business here. You had the field before us." While refraining to say anything derogatory of a brother missionary who has passed away, I would just mention that my reply was qualified. Mr. Crosby had just been stating how they had visited this camp before, and had promised them a teacher more than a year previously, when I replied, "Then you evidently think, Mr. Crosby, that we have no business here, and that you were in the field before us?" He replied that this was just his view. I then informed him of my previous visit some two years before, and of Mr. T. Hankin's offer of a site for our Mission, and also of the cause of our delay in opening the Mission. I also invited him to give the address at our evening meeting, which he did, and explained to the Indians why he had failed to open the Mission there as promised.

creased, I decided not to make any movement, lest our Indians should say that the "Omukshewas" (whites) were afraid. Soon, however, I heard a commotion in their tent. A lantern was lighted and several guns were fired to frighten off these denizens of the forest, which had thus intruded upon our camp and disturbed our rest. For a time all was quiet, but soon they returned in full force and renewed their pranks. Fearing this time they would break through our tent, I arose, and having lighted my lantern, which I hung over the tent door, I discharged my rifle several times. The louder report of my Snider rifle had the desired effect. They retreated into the forest, and we were permitted to fall asleep, roused only now and then by the occasional howl of the hungry wolves in search of their prey. In the morning we found the beach around our camp covered with the tracks of bear, both black and grizzly, and also of other animals. I pointed out to the Indians how we had intercepted the bears by encamping on their trail, which they acknowledged, and the chief determined to set his bear traps just there on his return. He was a most successful hunter, as during my stay at his camp I saw him frequently returning from the chase with a burden of pelts. He was also a skilful canoe-man, and though the river was high, he steered us through the canyon without hesitation. He cried frequently to his crew to paddle with all their might, as, in order to enable him to steer clear of the great eddies which opened on every side threatening to engulf us, it was necessary to keep a strong headway on the canoe.

On our arrival at Metlakahtla a committee meeting was convened, at which, after the consideration of my report, Bishop Ridley decided to go up the Skeena accompanied by Mrs. Ridley and a native teacher, also a cook and general servant, and continue the Mission which I had thus opened.[1]

---

[1] In the report of the opening of this Mission as recorded on page 14 of *Snapshots from the North Pacific*, there is no mention made of my part in the undertaking.

INDIAN BRIDGE

An old Indian bridge spanning the Bulkley River (a tributary of the River Skeena) near Hazelton, B.C.

THE SKEENA RIVER MISSION

It was after the establishment of the Mission that it was named Hazleton. Prior to this it was known to the Indians as "Kitan-maksh," or the camp where the people fished by torchlight, and to the whites it was known as "Skeena Forks," from the junction there of the Bulkley River with the Skeena. There was a reason why I should thus have left my work amongst the Indians on the coast to open the inland Mission. Some two years previously I had been commissioned to accompany a brother missionary, the Rev. R. Tomlinson, on a tour into the interior to select a site for a Mission to the Kitikshean tribes of the Upper Skeena River. We travelled by canoe up the Nass River to the head of navigation, accompanied by four Indians and a boy, to pack sufficient provisions and covering for the journey. We also carried some seeds and gardening tools to test the soil of such sites as might be chosen, as well as to teach the Indians to cultivate their land.

On reaching the head of navigation on the Upper Nass, we sent back our canoe and divided our effects into packs for each of our carriers. We then started by the old " Grease Trail," which is over one hundred miles from the Nass to the Skeena River. One or two incidents which occurred on this journey deserve to be recorded. On our fourth day's march we met a tribe named the Galdōls, on their way to the bear hunt. The encampment of these Indians was situated midway between the Ominica and the Stikeen goldfields, and they had made it a custom to exact toll from miners passing from the one camp to the other. The Attorney-General of the Province had requested our missionary to warn this tribe against such illegal action. Here, then, was the opportunity, but it was felt that in order to detain them it would be necessary to entertain them to some food. This is Indian custom. Accordingly my companion approached me with the proposal that we should boil up a mat of rice which we had with us, some fifty pounds weight, to feast the party. I demurred, as I feared we should not be able to replace it.

THE SKEENA RIVER MISSION

Nor were we. The result was that both we and our Indian packers were well-nigh famished from starvation. At the first salmon-house we succeeded in obtaining a half bucket of potatoes from which the eyes had been cut for planting. These were boiled and served up for our midday meal, and at the next halting-place, which we reached at dusk, we only succeeded in obtaining one dried salmon. This but afforded a morsel for each of us, as we were indeed as hungry as wolves, and we were compelled to seek a camping-place where sleep would cause us to forget our need.

The following day we reached the Kishpiyouksh fishing camp, where we were treated to the first salmon which had been caught for the season. Being the first, it had to be cooked by a special process, as the Indians believe that otherwise the salmon would be offended and might perhaps desert the river. Consequently, instead of roasting or broiling the fish, it was placed in a large cedar box, which was half filled with water. A number of stones were then made red-hot in the fire, and one by one plunged into the water with the salmon. This was repeated until the fish was boiled, when it was served in a wash-basin. Although the dogs licked the stones repeatedly when they were taken out of the box, yet they were cleansed by passing through the fire before being placed in the box again. This process was an improvement, however, on what we had experienced a few days previously, when we had been treated to a meal of smoked bear's meat. Our host cut the meat to pieces by holding one end of it between his teeth, and then when it was cooked depositing it in a pan which he had scoured with an old moccasin. I took care to help myself to such pieces as had not touched the vessel which contained it. One penalty to which we were subjected in encamping in the salmon-houses was the dog nuisance. They were numerous, and the nights being cold when the fires went out, the wretched animals would insist on lying down upon us. But little rest could be had, as it occupied most of the night in kicking

THE SKEENA RIVER MISSION

them off our legs and feet. We learned the truth of the proverb that "He who lies down with dogs must rise up with fleas."

On our fifth day's march my companion, the Rev. R. Tomlinson, lost himself in the forest. We had just finished our midday meal and had started our Indians with their packs, when my friend handed me his gun, stating he would follow directly. I waited by the camp fire for some ten minutes or more, then hallooed loudly, but received no response. I concluded he had gone, and consequently started off to overtake him. But on reaching a soft place on the trail I failed to discover his tracks. I then returned to the camp fire, and not finding him, I fired first one barrel of the gun and then the other, in the hope that if he had gone astray he might hear the signal. But all without effect. The forest but re-echoed my signals. Fearing our Indians might mistake our disappearance, I now resolved to hasten forward in the hope that my friend had joined them. I soon overtook the last of them, and inquired if he had seen anything of the missing man. He scanned me deliberately with a suspicious gaze and then replied, "Who fired the shots that I heard, and how is it you have the gun which Mr. Tomlinson has always carried himself since we entered on the trail? You should know best where he is." It was quite evident that he believed I had shot my friend. I then hastened onwards to reach the others, and on informing them that my brother missionary was lost they replied, "How could Mr. Tomlinson lose his way. He has been over this trail before. You might get lost, but not he. Who fired the gun which we heard?" I saw at once that all were of the same opinion. They concluded I had shot my companion. So without further questioning I requested them to pile their packs by the trail, taking only a few provisions, and to return with me for a search. We had not proceeded many miles when on entering a wide valley we descried a figure hastening forward. We soon discovered it was a man, and truly the lost man. He had become engrossed in watching two armies of ants at war. And their wonderful skill and order had so attracted him that he forgot all else.

When at length he remembered himself and hastened to return to the path of duty, he rushed off in the wrong direction. Every step led him farther astray, until he realised that he was lost. Lost in the forest! Can we realise what it means? Not a forest which may be measured by acres, but a boundless forest full of mist and mystery. Little wonder that so many travellers, miners, and prospectors have lost their reason, and then their lives, in the mazes and gloom of the forest. Little wonder that as our friend felt his strength failing from ineffectual efforts to find his way, he cast himself on his knees in prayer for guidance. Nor did he ask in vain. He arose calm and collected, and pursued his way until he reached a lake. There was a trail around it, which he followed. It was a trail made by wild animals coming to the lake to drink. This he followed until he found a trail leading from it, which connected with the main trail at a point which we had passed over in the morning. This he recognised, and rejoiced to realise that he had found his way again. And only those who have passed through the same experience can tell what the joy is. It is indeed light and liberty. It is more; it is deliverance from death. For this is certainly the fate of any one who when lost in an American forest without any means of sustenance fails to find a way out again. Many men perished thus during the Yukon gold excitement. Their bones lie bleached under the trees and by the lonely rivers which meander through the forest glades.

That incident, however, brought before me vividly the danger of merely circumstantial evidence. Had my friend been lost on that occasion, I fear that the evidence would have been sufficiently weighty to have convicted me. It

THE SKEENA RIVER MISSION

was asserted by the Indians truly, that Mr. Tomlinson knew the trail well, having passed over it several times, whereas this was my first journey. Therefore they rejected the idea that he could have lost his way. It was true also that he had never permitted anyone to carry the gun but himself from the start. Also that I had fired off both barrels, the reports of which they had heard, and they concluded that we had disagreed over the mat of rice which had been used up to feast the Indians whom we had met. All this would have been witnessed against me.

We continued our march from the Kishpiyouksh, or "the people hidden between," and in two days reached the Kishgagass encampment near the Babine lake. This tribe continued to follow the custom of cremating their dead, which was formerly followed by the Tsimsheans and Nishgas. Several funeral pyres were still burning, and the plain extending away from the village was covered over with piles of charred wood where the dead had been consumed. I had well-nigh been guilty of a breach of Indian law at our last camping place, just before reaching the village. As my men were busy putting up our shelter sail, and I in lighting our camp fire, I looked around for fuel, and finding a heap of charred wood I proceeded to appropriate it. One of our party sighted this and hastened to inform me that the body of a child had been cremated on it a short time previously. I did not require any further information, but dropped it instantly with a shudder.

It was while encamped at this village that we felt the loss of our mat of rice so acutely. There was no fresh food procurable, but the chief in whose house we were encamped had a pit of salmon roe opened, which had been covered up for nearly six months. This is the strongest dish which the Indians indulge in, and the odour can be detected afar off. A portion was prepared for us and our party on the Sunday morning, and all were invited to partake. A large dish was placed before us and our host, who was in rather a nude

THE SKEENA RIVER MISSION

condition, not having taken any pains to dress himself for the occasion. My brother-missionary having dipped his spoon in the dish, took a stand with his back to the company, who were now all enjoying the meal. For him enough was as good as a feast, as he had no sooner tasted it than he hastened to return his spoon. In doing so he inquired whether I should not desist also, but being weak from hunger I informed him that I should continue to the bitter end, which I did, to the astonishment of "mine host," who found it necessary to bestir himself to keep pace with his guest. Had I not done so I should have been unable to have taken my part in the services of the day, as our own provisions had run out.

After the Sunday services, the first which had ever been conducted there, we instructed them on the Monday in gardening, and how to plant potatoes and vegetables. We presented the chief with a set of tools, to be loaned out to any of his tribe desirous of using them. This tribe has since abandoned heathenism and become Christian, largely through the teaching of a native Christian from Kincolith, who with his wife have laboured there faithfully for some eight years. The Mission has been under the superintendence of the Rev. John Field, who has laboured with much acceptance for many years at Hazleton in the Mission which I inaugurated in 1880. The headquarters of this Mission will now be at New Hazleton, on the line of the Grand Trunk Pacific Railway, which is rapidly opening up the country for settlement. Near to Hazleton, on the Bulkley River, which flows into the Skeena at this point, is an encampment of the Hagwilget Indians. This tribe has long been under the teaching of the French Roman Catholic Mission, and though so near to our Skeena River Missions, yet there has been no friction, as they speak a different tongue. They are one of three branches of the Dinne nation of the interior which have endeavoured to seek an outlet to the coast.

The other two branches are the Tahltan tribe on the Upper Stikeen, near Telegraph Creek, and the Zitz-Zaow

THE SKEENA RIVER MISSION

Indians, already mentioned, which had succeeded in reaching tidal waters on Portland inlet. One of the principal features of the Upper Skeena to the Indian mind is a mountain near Hazleton, named by them "Tum Lak Ahm." In their tradition of the Deluge, the canoe in which their ancestors were preserved rested on this mountain. The Tsimsheans, Nishgas, and Kitiksheans all claim to have descended from the occupants of that canoe, and thus declare their common origin. That these three divisions all speak dialects of the same tongue would appear to confirm this assertion. Formerly all travelling and freighting of goods on the Skeena River was by Indian canoes. A large freight canoe usually carried two tons of merchandise, and required a crew of five Indians to pole it up the river. Accidents were not infrequent, especially when the river was in flood, notwithstanding the ability of the Indians and their experience of river navigation.

A white trader named Youmens, who had established a trading store at this point, had chartered a large canoe to bring up a cargo of goods, but the canoe was capsized in the canyon and lost with its entire freight and several of the Indian crew. One of the latter was a son of a sub-chief of the Hazleton tribe. He at once demanded an indemnity from the trader for the loss of his son. This the latter refused, declaring that he had lost both canoe and cargo, which amounted to a large sum. The Indian was indignant, as by their own laws he was entitled to blood-money, or a property indemnity. Some three years passed away when a similar accident occurred, and a second son of the same sub-chief was lost in bringing up a cargo for the same trader. Again the bereaved father appealed to the trader for remuneration, but only to be denied as before. Smarting under his loss and shame, as his fellow-tribesmen chaffed him for permitting his second son to work for a man who had refused his appeal on the loss of the first, he determined on vengeance. Two days after receiving the sad news, as the trader was seated in front of his store bartering for some furs, this chief came along with his blanket around him, and seizing the trader by the hair of his head, pulled him back and stabbed him through the heart.

When the news reached the Government a party was despatched under the Chief of Police to apprehend the murderer. They wisely decided to proceed by the Nass River and across country to the Skeena. They succeeded in obtaining an Indian guide, the son of a Nishka chief, who led them in the early morning to the house of the murderer, whom they seized in his bed, and casting him into the canoe were well out on the river before his tribe was aware of what had occurred. A hue-and-cry was raised, but it was too late, as the canoe swept out of sight borne along by the rapid current, and they knew it was useless to seek to follow. The culprit was duly tried and condemned to death, but he died in the prison before the day fixed for his execution. The young Indian who had thus rendered the expedition a success was rewarded by the Government, which forwarded him a silver watch accompanied by a testimonial acknowledging his faithfulness and ability. This testimonial he has framed and hung up in his house. It reads as follows:

"The Government of British Columbia having learned that you rendered valuable assistance to the law officers of the Crown in connection with the recent arrest of the murderer of the late Youmens on the Skeena River, forward herewith for your acceptance a silver watch and chain in token of their appreciation of your services in the cause of law and order as opposed to barbarism and crime. Signed on behalf of the Government of British Columbia.

(Signed) JNO. ROBSON,
Provincial Secretary.

To JOHN W. MOUNTAIN,
Indian Chief."

This man is now a chief, and is one of our leading Christians. But the best part remains to be stated. A surviving

THE SKEENA RIVER MISSION

son of the murderer afterwards became a Christian, and having proved himself a clever student became our native teacher in the Mission there. He proved faithful in that office for several years until his death, and thus did much to remove the stain which his father's act had wrought.

That Youmens might have prevented such a catastrophe, and saved his own life by a small payment, is evident on comparing the action of the other trader in the same camp. This man was in the habit of putting out poison for foxes in balls of fat, as they were rather numerous, and their fur valuable. On one occasion, however, a young Indian was out on the trail when his dog discovered one of these poisoned baits and devoured it. He soon developed signs of poisoning, and his owner fearing that the dog had something in his throat, endeavoured to pull open his jaws to examine him. In doing so, his dog bit him, and he also soon developed symptoms of having been poisoned. He hastened back to the village, and was just able to relate what had caused his ailment, when he expired. As the Indians knew of the poison having been thus distributed, they at once concluded it was this which had poisoned both the dog and its owner. They therefore proceeded to impeach the trader, and on learning the facts he invited them to his store. Here he counted out to them one hundred trading blankets, valued at one dollar and a quarter each, also a little tobacco and matches. With this amount they were perfectly satisfied, and peace was preserved between them. Had he not done so, his life would have been the forfeit.

Such was the state of the Indians of the upper Skeena when the first Mission was established there. Some years afterwards the first *steamboat*, a sternwheeler, was put on the river by the Hudson's Bay Company. This was followed shortly after by others operated by local companies. It was a great achievement, proving the triumph of steam and skill over the forces of nature as developed by the rapid currents of the Skeena, rushing through its rocky canyons. What

THE SKEENA RIVER MISSION

an advance this was over the canoe! The Indians looked in wonder at what they named the "white man's fire canoe," and the oldest amongst them who had declared when they had seen the first saw-mill, that they wished to die now that they had witnessed the water cutting the wood, were so overpowered by this new development that they inquired eagerly why it was that the white man died? And now they are permitted to witness the next advance. This is the wonderful "iron horse" which rushes snorting and whooping through forest and plain, piercing the mountains and spanning the rivers in its track.

Even to the white pioneers who have long been contented to use the Indian trail and dug-out, with their ingenious monkey bridges spanning the rivers, these rapid and wonderful developments have seemed as a dream. But to the natives, who have but lately emerged from the Stone Age, the change is overwhelming. The question is, will they survive it? The great change in their mode of living, in their dwellings, in their food and clothing, is well calculated to try them greatly. But they may adopt and accommodate themselves to all this if they will only hold aloof from the evils of our civilisation. It is the "firewater" with all its attendant evils which will prove the destruction of all who give way to it. We rejoice that evangelisation has preceded civilisation, and that so many have been won for Christ and the truth before these great changes have occurred. And though they may not long survive the great inrush of our civilisation, and the new population, yet we know they will have a name and a place in that Kingdom which shall never be destroyed, but which shall endure for ever.

CHAPTER XXIV

THE ZITZ-ZAOW TRIBE

> " Light for the forest child :
> An outcast though he be,
> From the haunts where the sun of his childhood smiled,
> And the country of the free ;
> Pour the hope of Heaven o'er his desert wild,
> For what home on earth has he?"

WHILST the Tsimsheans, Nishkas, and Haidas were thus being gradually gathered into the Church of Christ, there were other bands of Indians and remnants of tribes which had been almost annihilated in their continued conflicts with one another during the past.

Not the least interesting of these was the tribe known as the Zitz-Zaows, whose encampments and hunting-grounds were situated on Portland Inlet, which now forms part of the boundary line between British Columbia and Alaska. This band of Indians, I discovered, was a branch of the great Dinne nation, which inhabits the north-western interior, between latitude 51° and 57° N. This agrees with Morice's delineation of the boundaries of the Dinne nation. These Indians have sought to find an outlet to the coast by three routes.

First they wandered down the Bulkley River to a point near its junction with the Skeena, where the Agwilgets are found. It is not generally known that the term "Agwilget" is from the Tsimshean, and may be rendered as the "steady-going people." When opening the Mission at Hazleton in 1881, I was brought into communication with this tribe and took down a limited vocabulary of their nouns. A second branch of the Dinne is found on the Stikeen River at

THE ZITZ-ZAOW TRIBE

Tahltan, whilst the third division were these Zitz-Zaows on Portland Inlet.

As each of these three divisions had developed a different dialect in their progress to the coast, it might never have been known that they were of the same nationality, had not circumstances favoured my investigations in regard to them.

I found that of the dialect of each division some three-fourths of the words were different to the vocabularies of the others. This may be accounted for by the lengthened period of their separation from the parent stock, and from one another.

Of the three divisions, only one, the Zitz-Zaows, succeeded in reaching tidal waters; which they did when they struck the head waters of the Portland Inlet. They were probably the vanguard of their nation. But what a terrible toll was exacted of them for their venture! They found themselves surrounded by the more powerful tribes of the Tsimshean and Nishka Indians, as also the Klingit tribes of South-Eastern Alaska.

By these they were regarded as encroachers on their hunting-grounds, and consequently they kept up a continual warfare against them, waylaying them amongst the mountains and along the rivers, and shooting them down with their bows and arrows, or overpowering them at close quarters with their spears. For these coast tribes were fiercer and more warlike than the tribes of the interior, inured as they were from childhood to face the storms and perils of the ocean, in their well-constructed canoes, and ever on the alert for their yet fiercer foes, the Haidas. They were thus more than a match for these intruders from the east.

But a yet sterner foe compelled the shoreward progress of these children of the forest. They were often harassed with famine, especially in the early spring after a long winter, in which their food supplies were exhausted, and hunger was a foe with which they could not treat.

Their only escape was towards the sunny slopes of the

THE ZITZ-ZAOW TRIBE

Pacific. Here the streams abounded with salmon; deer roamed in the valleys and along the shores, whilst the goats on the mountains, in the late autumn, afforded an abundant food supply to the intrepid hunter.

One encampment of these Indians, the Lak-We-Yip, has been totally annihilated in their continual conflicts and skirmishes with the Kitikshean and Nishka tribes.

The Zitz-Zaows of Portland Canal fared but little better. On one occasion during the absence of the men of the tribe on a hunting expedition, the warriors of the Lak-Shale or Cape Fox tribe attacked the camp, and, having slain all who failed to escape, they impaled their bodies on sharp stakes, and stood them in a long ghastly line, on the shore in front of the encampment. What a terrible sight met the eyes of the returning hunters, as they found their women and children thus slaughtered! Naturally their first thought was of revenge, and after they had mourned over the bodies of their relatives and placed them away on the rocky headlands and islands around, they met to concoct their plans for revenge on their enemies.

Every stratagem of the hunter for catching bears and wolves, such as snares, pitfalls, and deadfalls, placed skilfully in the trails most frequented by the enemy, were called into requisition. To fire their camps at night in the dry season, and shoot them down as they fled, and to harass them in every way they could, until they had taken a life for every one they had lost. This was the policy to which they pledged themselves, and many a Klingit Indian bit the dust during the years that followed.

But it was not to be expected that their enemies should remain passive. It had stirred them up to further reprisals, and when their numbers had been still further reduced, a Nishka chief, with his clan of the Eagle sept, which also claimed hunting rights on the same inlet, laid the remnant of this tribe of Zitz-Zaows under tribute.

This position they accepted, as it also ensured them the

THE ZITZ-ZAOW TRIBE

protection of their allies, who supplied them with guns, powder, and shot, as also with blankets and provisions. For these necessaries they handed over all their furs at the chief's own valuation. That this estimate was far below the value of their furs, will be evident from the fact that this chief had then to sell the furs to the Hudson's Bay Company. The Indians have frequently informed me that when purchasing a Hudson's Bay Company's musket, the Indian was required to pile up the furs until it was level with the muzzle of a gun, and a martin skin was bartered for a bar of soap.

As the Nishkas had to sell their furs on such terms, their tariff with their tributaries may be easily estimated.

But better things were in store for both oppressor and oppressed when the missionary pioneers arrived on the coast. Duncan's action at Metlakahtla in establishing a trading store for the Indians gathered out of heathenism, secured for the Indian hunters a fair value for their furs, and though the Company at first opposed him, yet they found they had to conform to the new régime. And the standard thus set at the Mission soon came to be recognised all along the coast.

Under the advantages thus secured, the Zitz-Zaow tribe claimed the liberty of seeking freedom of action also, and I sent them several messages of encouragement after taking charge of the Kincolith Mission, inviting them to come and see me, and promising them medical aid for their sick, and protection from oppression.

In response to my invitation a large canoe arrived shortly after, bringing twelve men, the surviving leaders of the tribe. They were certainly as wild-looking a band of Indians as any I had met, veritable "children of the forest." They were hospitably entertained and cared for, and from this time onward they visited the Mission frequently, and often remained over the Sunday. They were induced to attend the services, and as several of them knew the Nishka language, they soon became familiar with the leading truths of Christianity. The chief Quiyah, a very sociable and agreeable

THE ZITZ-ZAOW TRIBE

Indian, encouraged his tribe to visit us, and after due preparation and instruction this chief and several of his people were baptized. After this they made the Mission Station their headquarters, and several of them erected suitable dwellings to reside in. In their wild heathen state they lived in huts, built with bark and branches, and subsisted principally on the flesh of the bear and porcupine, the mountain goat, and the ground hog.

We succeeded in inducing them to permit us to take one of their girls into the Mission for training, but on the third day after her entrance she was missing, and could not be found. Late in the evening she returned. She had gone up on a mountain near by in quest of porcupine, as she stated she could not subsist on the white man's food. She did not remain long with us, as she could not bear the confinement.

Later on this Indian, when a young woman, was attacked by a she-bear with her two cubs in the forest. She was quite alone, and had but a small axe with which she was gathering the inner bark of the young spruce trees. As the bear stood up to seize her, she sprang upon it and dealt it such a blow on the head that it tumbled over. Recovering quickly it sprang at her again and almost struck the axe from her grasp, but before it could repeat the blow she struck it again. It however succeeded in almost tearing her dress off her as it fell; and before it could return to the attack our huntress struck it again fair over the head, and with repeated blows despatched it. She then turned to the cubs which threatened her and quickly killed them both. I purchased the skin of one of these as a memento of her feat, which surpassed that of any hunter, as she was armed only with the axe. She has just lately repeated the feat and killed a second she-bear and cubs. This woman was the last of her tribe to be baptized and registered among our Christian congregation.

Some of their ideas and traditions are very different to those of the coast tribes. The rainbow was regarded by

THE ZITZ-ZAOW TRIBE

them with more than ordinary interest, as they believed it was formed of the spirits of their ancestors and friends who had departed this life. It was a bright and elevating idea as compared with many of the gloomy and fearful beliefs held by other northern tribes of Indians. And yet how far short it falls of the truth revealed in the inspired Word, which declares the " righteous shall shine forth as the sun in the kingdom of their Father."

But alas for my good friend the chief, who before he died found he could traverse the forest and sail down the inlets without any fear of an arrow from a concealed foe, yet death overtook him when least expected. When ascending a mountain, accompanied by one of his tribe, to place his bear traps in position, he was seized with a violent cramp. He was unable to proceed, so delegating his mission to his follower, he retreated again to the camp. Here they gave him a draught of the decoction of the bear cabbage (*Symplocarpus fœtidus*), which is poisonous if taken in excess. This was near midnight, and his friends lay down to rest. Some time after he was heard by them praying earnestly. In the morning they found their chief cold and stiff in death. The strong dose they had given him only hastened his end. Had he received proper treatment he would most probably have recovered. His remains were brought back to the Mission by the few remaining members of his tribe under a flag at half-mast. Many of his Nishka friends and brother chiefs embarked with the fleet of canoes and boats which escorted the remains to the rock-bound promontory on which the cemetery is situated.

His successor deserves to be honourably mentioned. In a letter lately received from our missionary amongst the Tahltan Indians on the Upper Stikeen, he states of the chief of that tribe : " The old chief is a dear old fellow, one of Nature's gentlemen, a rare character among the Indians." This brief character-sketch of Tahltan's chief describes exactly the present chief of the remnant of the Zitz-Zaow

THE ZITZ-ZAOW TRIBE

tribe, excepting the reference to his age, as this chief is comparatively a young man. He is not merely a hunter, but a prince of hunters. With a good eye, a steady nerve, and no fear, he can bring down his game at sight.

Not long since, while bear-hunting on his old hunting-grounds, he entered a small valley which was so completely surrounded by mountains that there was neither access nor exit but by the pass through which our hunter had entered. Instantly he halted, as though turned to stone, for a strange sight met his eyes. Six grizzlies were engaged in growling and fighting over the carcase of a black bear which they had evidently killed, and were now devouring. It was early in the season, and food was scarce, which caused them thus to indulge in such a carnivorous feast. Instantly, on perceiving the hunter in the distance, they charged upon him in a line, one after another.

Without retreating a step, he raised his trusty rifle, and, taking steady aim, he tumbled the leader over. This checked them, but only for a moment; they resumed their onward rush with a loud roar. Another well-aimed bullet reduced their number to four, just the number of cartridges left in his magazine. But, as they were decreasing the distance rapidly, every shot told, till but one remained, and this was only a few yards distant.

It was evident to the hunter that this was an old grizzly, both from his colour and from the slowness of his movements, consequently he permitted him to come quite near before he discharged his final shot. The bullet struck him in the vital part. It pierced his heart. One of his tribe, who was in the vicinity, hearing the repeated reports of the rifle, came rushing to ascertain the cause, and was surprised to see the long line of grizzly carcases right up to where they had been interrupted at their bloody feast.

This chief was united in marriage to a Nishka, a young woman trained in the Mission, as, owing to the crestal system, there was no woman whom he could marry in his

THE ZITZ-ZAOW TRIBE

own tribe. He has lately been elected to the office of churchwarden, and is most exemplary in his character and conduct. He has been greatly pleased to learn that he and his people are a branch of the Dinne nation of Indians, and that the Tahltan tribe, which is also a branch of the same, have abandoned heathenism and become Christians.

The Rev. T. P. Thorman, our missionary on the Upper Stikeen, informs me in a letter lately received: "I have baptized no less than fifty-one men, women, and children." This is the tribe amongst whom the Rev. F. M. T. Palgrave first commenced work in 1897, and laboured bravely as a pioneer missionary for five years at his own charges. As such, he had rough work in breaking up the fallow ground and sowing the incorruptible seed of the living Word. He was succeeded by the present missionary, whose journey in an open canoe up the Stikeen River in the late autumn nearly cost him his life. For some fourteen days he, with his wife and family, were exposed to a continual downpour of rain, which drenched them and all their effects. This resulted afterwards in a serious illness. But he struggled bravely against it, until compelled to surrender.

During this time he lost one of his children through a terrible accident, and, shortly after, he was called on to part with his wife. Yet, like a good soldier of Jesus Christ, as soon as he was restored he volunteered to return again to his Mission, and how delighted his converts were to welcome him amongst them again! Such courage and self-denial deserves to be rewarded. And it has been: in the number of converts he has been enabled to register, and in their affection for him, he is well satisfied.

Thus of the Dinne nation, the three branches which were making their way towards the western coast have all been met by missionary effort, and, whilst two of them have been evangelised by our Missions, the third has been taken over by the French Roman Catholic Mission, of which it forms the last outpost towards the coast.

CHAPTER XXV

THE NISHKA INDIANS AS HUNTERS

> "And they painted on the grave posts
> Of the graves yet unforgotten,
> Each his own ancestral Totem,
> Each the symbol of his household,
> Figures of the bear and reindeer,
> Of the Turtle, Crane, and Beaver.
> Each invested as a token
> That the owner was departed,
> That the chief who bore the symbol
> Lay beneath in dust and ashes."
>
> LONGFELLOW ("Hiawatha").

THOUGH the Zitz-Zaows, as has already been stated, were famed for their ability and skill as hunters, yet it is doubtful whether they surpassed the Nishkas in this respect. The introduction of the repeating-rifle and the breech-loading shot-gun has been of great advantage to the Indian hunters. In one season of about six weeks I have known our hunters to bring in some seven hundred and fifty bear skins.

Reckoning at even a lower rate for the other encampments on the Nass River, there could not have been less than two thousand bears captured in the one short season. This they never could have accomplished with the old muzzle-loading weapons. In addition there are fewer accidents now to the hunters. Under the old régime, often the hunters were seriously injured, and sometimes killed, in their encounters with bears. Many of the older men bear the marks of these encounters. Here is one who always wears his hat on one

THE NISHKA INDIANS AS HUNTERS

side of his head. His object is to conceal his ear, which has almost entirely been torn off by a bear which he had wounded. Here is another who was formerly very clever as a carver in both wood and metal. But a bear bit his thumb off and otherwise injured his hand, so that he can no longer exhibit his handiwork.

Many exciting tales of encounters with the denizens of the forest might be recorded, but the following, as related and described to me by the hunter himself, is, I consider, the most wonderful. He was visiting me one afternoon in February during a severe cold spell, and as I had a good fire burning to keep out the cold, my friend Gwaksho, who was a chief, drew near and permitted his fur robe to drop lower on his shoulders in order to enjoy the heat. As he did so I remarked that his shoulders and arms were covered with scars. I suspected that these had been caused by the medicine men of his tribe while he was yet a heathen, as one band of the craft known as the flesh-tearers were accustomed to rush around the camps howling like wolves, and would bite and tear the flesh off the shoulders and arms of those whom they might meet.

In answer to my inquiries as to how he had received such wounds, he informed me that they had been inflicted on him in a life and death struggle which he had with a bear some years previously. He had gone into the forest in search of a suitable red cedar tree from which to construct a canoe, and was accompanied by his son, then a boy of about seven years, when suddenly on crossing a large fallen tree he found himself face to face with a grizzly bear. He had left his gun leaning against a tree on disembarking from his canoe, and consequently had nothing with him but his hunting-knife. This, however, he had not time to draw, as, being at close quarters, the bear sprang upon him instantly.

As quickly, the hunter threw both his arms and legs around the bear's neck and shoulders, and pressing his head up closely under the bear's lower jaw, commenced to worry it with his teeth. His object was to endeavour to sever the bear's throat. He had good teeth, as all the Indians had formerly, prior to the introduction of the white man's bill of fare. The bear tried hard to dislodge the hunter and shake him off, and it was then that he succeeded in inflicting the numerous wounds, the scars from which had attracted my notice. The hunter was eager to draw his knife, but dare not relax his hold, as it would have given Bruin an advantage. At length he succeeded in severing the main artery and the wind-pipe, and was bathed in blood both from his own wounds and that of the bear. His little boy could not help, as, alas, he had no weapon.

With the artery severed the bear quickly weakened from loss of blood, and at length tumbled over, and at the same instant the hunter fainted. But only for a moment, as reviving again he called to his son for water. Pulling a large leaf of the skunk or bear cabbage (*Symplocarpus fœtidus*), he ran to a stream near by, and, filling it, hastened to return to his father. He drank eagerly, and directed his son to wash the blood from his face and eyes with the water remaining. With the aid of his son he was enabled to drag himself free from the bear, which was quite dead. More water was brought to wash and staunch the flow of blood, and leaves applied to the wounds.

Lacerated though he was, he was enabled with the aid of his son to reach the canoe, in which they drifted a few miles further down to another encampment of the tribe, when more effective help was rendered. Several weeks elapsed before he was able to get about again, but being of a strong constitution he was soon able to engage in the bear-hunt once more, but never left his gun behind again. He had preserved the fangs of the bear, which he presented to me.[1]

---

[1] This story of Chief Gwaksho's life and death struggle with a grizzly bear appears in the late Rev. Dr. Crosby's book. It is stated he received it from the late Bishop Ridley. It is incorrect, however,

THE NISHKA INDIANS AS HUNTERS

He succeeded to a chieftainship afterwards, and was living as a bigamist when the Gospel message found him, and when at length his heart opened to the message of the Divine love and mercy he was ready to accept the terms. He gave up one of his wives, and was baptized into the Church of Christ. He remained faithful unto death, and saw all his family following his example before passing away. His family and tribe erected a tombstone to his memory, on which figures of the bear stand to symbolize not only his crest or totem, but also his prowess as a prince of hunters amongst his fellow-tribesmen.

With the transformation which was thus progressing in the hearts and lives of the Indians, it was necessary that the change should be manifested in their encampments and dwellings. And this was being done. We had succeeded in leading our Christian Indians to pull down their old lodges and to erect new and improved dwellings. Ample scope was afforded them to develop their ability in their own designs in building, provided only they built in line, and each householder in the middle of his lot. This was necessary in order to preserve the proper distances between buildings to prevent the spread of fire. The work was crowned by the erection of a strong and commodious church in the centre of the encampment. This building was erected entirely by Indian workmen under the direction of the missionary. About half of the cost was subscribed by themselves and half contributed by friends. In this connection I have great pleasure in acknowledging the noble help given to my efforts by a lady in Ireland, who by both pen and voice succeeded in obtaining substantial assistance for this important branch of our Mission work.

But alas for the instability of all earthly enterprises!

---

both as to the chief's name and also as to the encounter. The chief got his legs around the bear's neck, as well as his arms, hence his lower limbs were untouched. All his wounds were received on his shoulders and upper arms.

THE NISHKA INDIANS AS HUNTERS

Before two years had expired we were overtaken by a great conflagration, which destroyed not only the new church but also some thirty of the improved dwelling-houses. This occurred on Sunday, the third day of September 1893. It broke out during the afternoon service and burned fiercely till midnight. Every effort was made to check the progress of the flames, but the water supply ran short, and the tide was far out. A high wind was blowing, and everything was very dry after a long spell of fine weather. In addition the majority of the men were away at the autumnal fishing stations.

The fire was supposed to have originated from a spark from the flue of a kitchen alighting on the bark roof of an outhouse in which hay was stored. I was the first to sight it from the chancel of the church when I had just sat down, having concluded the prayers, whilst a young man who was a native lay reader stood up to deliver an address from the lectern. He had just announced his text when I noticed a cloud of smoke arising from a back-house about a hundred yards from the church. I quietly signalled to two young men seated in the front, who instantly rushed out. The congregation took alarm, and moved out quickly but quietly. The preacher was left standing at the lectern, unable to comprehend the meaning of the outrush. From that time till midnight all were engaged in fighting the flames.

The burning shingles were lifted by the wind, which was blowing strongly from the west, and were landed on the roofs of the church and other buildings, a quarter of a mile distant. Every such burning brand kindled fresh flames, against which the fire fighters had but slight chances of success. Failing in our efforts to save the church, we hastened to carry out such articles as we could. Whilst doing so I was warned that the roof was falling in, and so I hastened to the Mission-house, which was now threatened. The fire had reached a point within one house of it, when I called on those whose dwellings stood beyond the Mission buildings to stand by me in an effort to arrest the flames, as should the Mission-house be overtaken nothing could save the houses which stood beyond it.

"Here," said I, "we have a good supply of water, and it is our only hope."

There were two wells of water, one of which I had dug myself, and the other which had been constructed by the Indians, and on these we depended for success. I directed several of them to cut down the upper part of the remaining house, whilst we kept up a steady stream of water on the burning building, which was two storeys in height. A number of cartridges exploded in the burning building, sending the bullets flying around us. Just then a messenger came running to inform me that the fire had overtaken a small trading store in which a one hundred pound keg of gunpowder was stored.

"Let all stand well away from it," I replied. "I cannot leave my post here." But, without waiting for my reply, one of them rushed into the burning building and succeeded in carrying out the keg of powder in his arms. By so doing this man risked his own life, but probably saved the lives of others.

We had now demolished the roof and upper part of the house adjoining the Mission, and by hanging a number of blankets steeped in water over the walls still standing, we were enabled to save the Mission buildings. But before we had fully succeeded in this, owing to the intensity of the heat and exertion, I swooned and fell over in a faint, from which I was recovered by some of my helpers pouring water freely over my head and face. The intense heat was caused by an outhouse full of packages of fish grease which caught fire and burned very fiercely, the burning grease running in streams from the burning building. A cry then rose that the water was exhausted. Seizing a piece of firewood, I broke an opening in the fence surrounding the Mission premises, and showed them the well which I had dug myself

THE NISHKA INDIANS AS HUNTERS

several years previously. This had been the means of saving the Mission-house from destruction on two previous occasions, and now it was to serve the same purpose again. For, encouraged by the fresh supply, the Indians rallied to the rescue, and soon we had the satisfaction of seeing the collapse of the burning buildings, and we knew that the Mission premises, together with half a dozen dwellings on the other side of it, had been saved. But what a scene of desolation we turned to! There remained but the two ends of the village. All the central buildings, including the fine new church, had been reduced to ashes.

At midnight we conducted a service around the burning embers of the church. Many were present who had lost not only their houses but also their furniture and food supplies, but their great grief was for the church rather than the loss of their own property.

One old chief, who had given one hundred dollars some time previously towards the purchase of a window for the chancel of the church, left his own house when in flames and, assisted by his daughters, rushed into the burning church and succeeded in carrying out the stained-glass windows, which were in sections and ready for erection. He suffered from exposure through the loss of his home and caught a severe cold, which resulted in pleurisy, from which he died. In his last hours he addressed his friends thus: "Do not grieve for the loss sustained by the fire. It has only purified us. I am ready to follow Jesus, naked if necessary."

He afterwards explained the meaning of these words. When he became a Christian some years previously he had retained his dancing-robe and head-dress, the insignia of his crest and chieftainship. These he had preserved in a box, which was consumed with its contents in the conflagration. Hence his reference to the fire having purified them. It was a revelation to the missionary; for the first time I understood the cause which had induced him on the occasion of his brother's death to return to the heathen camp and its

THE NISHKA INDIANS AS HUNTERS

customs. His wife, however, stood firm and refused to go back with him to heathenism. He remained there for one winter, and in the spring, accompanied by two of his friends, I visited him at the heathen camp. Addressing him, I said, "I have come to seek you at your wife's request. Your footprints are too deep at the Mission. They cannot be effaced."

Seeing his heathen friends assembling, I inquired of him where his box was. He pointed it out and I called upon one of my men to shoulder it, and requesting the second to take up his blankets and bedding, I passed my arm through his and together we made our way out and through the camp. The heathen party were so taken by surprise that they failed to recognise the situation until too late. A number of them rushed forward and endeavoured to obstruct our progress, but failed. He was evidently glad to escape, and received a hearty welcome from his wife and Christian friends. He never looked back again in his Christian course. His dying words had even a deeper significance than he intended to convey. The fire had purified us indeed. It tended to unite all more closely in a combined and determined effort to retrieve the loss.

Unfortunately there had been no insurance, but as help came in from friends towards the rebuilding of the church, I proposed to those who had been burned out to devote the funds thus contributed to their relief on the understanding that they should contribute liberally to the re-erection of the church. This they gladly engaged to do. This relieved the situation and prevented much suffering.

An appeal was made to the Indian Department of the Government, but no assistance whatever was granted, owing, as I was afterwards informed, to a false report having been made by a person who neither visited the people nor learned their state.

When the call was made for the re-erection of the church, the Indian congregation responded readily and liberally. Several of the chiefs gave as much as one hundred dollars

THE NISHKA INDIANS AS HUNTERS

each. A sum equal to that raised by the natives was contributed by friends in the Mother Country, and when our building fund was exhausted, our Indian workmen volunteered to finish the building by free labour. This they did, every man working from two to three weeks.

And at length a building in no way inferior to the first church was completed. The dwelling-houses also were restored on more sanitary lines, and with less danger from fire.

All the work of rebuilding was performed by our Indian workmen. They are almost all handy with their tools, and many of them are clever carpenters. Their dwelling-houses, public buildings, and the church all testify to this. One of my workmen, a young man who had seen the catalogue of church furnishings issued by an English firm, requested to be permitted to make a pulpit similar to a sketch shown there. He constructed a lathe, with which he turned the miniature pillars required, and completed the work in a masterly manner. He then added a small book-board, beautifully carved by himself, and afterwards a prayer-desk, similar in style to the pulpit. This last was his Christmas present to the church. In addition he is a musician, and acts as organist when required.

Another carpenter, who is also a chief, constructed a stand for the font. This is made of red cedar inlaid with yellow cedar so perfectly fitted and polished as to make it appear as one piece.

A third workman, who is quite an artist, executed the text around the arch of the chancel: "O worship the Lord in the beauty of holiness." And as there is no word quite the equivalent of worship in any of the Indian languages, I directed him to design and paint the figures of two angels, one looking upward in flight with hands clasped in a supplicating attitude; whilst the other figure, also in the attitude of flight, is looking upward whilst holding a harp in the left hand prepared to strike, whilst the right hand is uplifted in praise. These figures represent praise and prayer, which together constitute worship, so that while filling two vacant spaces over the chancel arch, they also convey to the Indian worshippers the meaning of the text underneath. The way in which this decoration is completed reflects much credit on the Indian artist, to whom it was a pleasure thus to embellish the house of God. And though not perhaps so cunning in handicraft as Bezaleel and Aholiab, yet who shall assert that they were not actuated by the same spirit?

CHAPTER XXVI

A REVIVAL

> "The dawn is not distant
> Nor is the night starless;
> Love is eternal; God is still God, and
> His faith shall not fail us;
> Christ is Eternal."
> LONGFELLOW.

IT was shortly after this great conflagration that an intense interest began to be manifested by the Indian Christians in spiritual matters. It spread rapidly to every encampment on the river. Even the heathen Indians partook of the same spirit. Services and meetings for prayer and the study of the Scriptures were held daily, and continued often till past midnight. As the canoes passed up and down the river and along the inlets, songs of praise might be heard in both the Indian and the English languages. Numbers both of men and women were to be found preaching and praying out of doors, at the fisheries and other encampments.

Fearing some abuse might arise unless the movement was properly directed, I convened a public meeting to which I invited the leaders of this unusual movement. I informed them of the organisation known as the "Church Army," the headquarters of which was in London, and that, as some of them were desirous to engage in open-air methods, and to use the drum and other musical instruments which was in accordance with Church Army regulations, I was prepared to write and obtain the rules, should they desire to inaugurate a local branch. To this they unanimously agreed, and at a

A REVIVAL

special service held in the old church, which was the oldest church in the diocese or on the northern coast, twelve men were admitted as an Indian branch of the Church Army. Philip Latimer, a senior Christian of many years' standing, and of most exemplary character, was appointed as first captain, with standard-bearers, lieutenants, &c. The organisation rapidly spread and increased, until every mission station in connection with the Church Mission has now a Church Army evangelistic band. And as the leading rule is that every member shall be a communicant, it has proved beneficial to the mission work and prevented schism. It affords an opportunity to every earnest Christian, whether male or female, to do something in the furtherance of the truth.

Amongst the trials in mission work during the past we must include loss of life from accidents on the water, owing to the fact that all travelling was by canoe. Four of our most intelligent and useful Indians, when on their return journey from Port Chester in Eastern Alaska, were all lost by the wreck of their canoe. The canoe was too heavily laden when they embarked, and their cargo was increased yet more by the carcase of a large deer which they had shot on the shore. In this condition they were overtaken by a sudden squall from the ocean off Cape Fox. They at once steered for a shelter known as Boat Harbour, but before they reached it, the sea was breaking in fury along the rocky shore. As the entrance to this small harbour is narrow, the waves roll off the rocks on either side and literally swamp the opening leading into it. They had just reached this entrance when they were submerged by an enormous wave, which broke over them from both sides, and shattered their frail bark, lashing them and their cargo under the foaming deep.

It was a trying occasion when the search-party returned one night with the sad news. The discharge of three guns signalised the catastrophe before they reached the shore,

A REVIVAL

and soon the bereaved families and their friends were wailing and weeping all through the encampment. As usual, foul play was suspected, for such an accident as this never happens without suspicion falling on others—an evidence that the evil surmisings which accompanied the deeds of the past have not yet been eradicated from the Indian mind.

The men who were lost were men of note in the community, one being a leading musician and organist in the church; another was our verger; whilst yet a third was a leading council man; and the youngest of the four, a most promising young man, was a member of the cornet band.

But this was not the only ill which befell our community from the Alaskan territory. There had been rumours of smallpox for some time from the other side of the boundary, and our Indians had been warned of its approach. But the unexpected manner in which it gained an entrance on the Canadian side leaves but little cause for accusation against any. Whilst at breakfast one morning a young woman rushed in on us, crying in an agitated manner, and declared that her husband had become demented, and that with much difficulty she had prevented him from carrying out the bed and blankets to lie down on the shore, where the tide was rising.

"And," she added, "he is covered with a strange eruption, which has broken out all over him, and it is appearing on me also."

As she concluded her complaint she burst into tears, crying out, "Oh, I am so ill, I fear I shall lose my senses."

We at once apprehended that it was the dreadful ailment. Simultaneously my wife and I sprang to our feet to examine our uninvited visitor. We at once concluded that it was indeed smallpox. Dismissing her instantly, she was instructed to return direct to her husband. I promised to follow her to examine him, which I did, and found him suffering from confluent smallpox, which accounted for the high fever and delirium which accompanied it.

I instructed him and his wife, together with all the inmates

A REVIVAL

of the house, not to leave their own premises, nor to enter any of the neighbouring houses. I promised also to return at once with such medicines as were necessary. My first act was to erect a temporary barrier across the street leading to the infected dwelling. In this I was not a moment too early, as I had no sooner completed it than a number of Indians assembled to enter, in order to manifest their sympathy. One or two of them asserted that it was not smallpox, as they had seen it in a former visitation. I had to warn them that any who attempted to pass the barrier I had erected would be deported with those suffering from the dreaded disease.

It happened to be Victoria Day (24th May), and a picnic had been arranged to be held in the valley behind the camp, to which I had been invited. I hastened thither and found them all assembled. Not one of those present suspected anything of the danger which had so suddenly broken out in their midst. When they had finished their feast, as usual they looked to me for a speech, but they little expected to hear such news as I was about to announce to them.

"You have heard me warn you," I said, "of the approach of the 'Haightly-lahaksh' from Alaska? Well, I regret to tell you it has come! It is in our midst now."

And then, having informed them of those whom it had seized upon, and of how I had established a quarantine which none might pass, I urged them to move away with their families.

"I advise you all to embark at once with your families and friends, and move off to your hunting-grounds until the infection has been overcome."

Had a bomb been dropped in their midst it could not have astonished them more. Before evening the encampment was almost deserted. They fled in all directions, for the Indian has urgent reasons for dreading the smallpox. The two preceding visitations had swept away thousands of them. But in the meantime vaccination had been introduced, and it had evidently decreased the ravages of the disease. For it not only proved a specific against the infection, but it also inspired the Indians with confidence, thus rendering them much less susceptible to the infection. This outbreak was caused by an infant which arrived with its parents one morning early by canoe from Tongass in Alaska. The parents must have suspected what this ailment was from which their child was suffering, as they landed at the last house in the camp. As the inmates were just about to breakfast, the new arrivals were invited to join them in accordance with Indian hospitality. Whilst they were eating their child cried unceasingly, and its face was covered with sores. The mother of the household inquired, "What has caused this?"

"Oh," replied the mother, "we encamped last night in a place where the mosquitoes were numerous, and our child is suffering from the effects of this."

The good woman of the house then took a blanket off her bed, in which she wrapped the child, and laid it on her bed until they had finished their meal. They then re-embarked and proceeded up the river to the next encampment, where they were again invited to eat. The hospitality of their unfortunate hosts both here and at the first encampment was rewarded, but not to their benefit. These visitors were sowing the seeds of disease and death. Nor did it fail to spring up. In less than a fortnight the infection had spread for over one hundred miles.

A party of the Nass Indians, just prepared to embark for the Skeena fishing camps, were amongst those with whom the infected party sat down to dinner.

This "Ginx's baby" affected the rest by its infection. Consequently the disease broke out simultaneously on the Nass and Skeena rivers. And this, too, when the fisheries were about to commence the season's operations. But by the detection of the disease at the first sign, and by establishing a strict quarantine by night and day, we were enabled to confine it to the quarter where it first broke out on both rivers. By disinfection and vaccination we succeeded in stamping out the infection, and I received the thanks of the Indian Department, which was publicly expressed in the Government Blue Book for the year.

The first Indian who contracted it was a young man who prided himself greatly on his personal appearance. He scorned all menial work, and had succeeded in learning photography, from which he derived sufficient means to support himself, with his wife and child. When returning up the coast a short time previously on a passenger steamer with his camera, several of the crew invited him to take a group photograph of three of their number. He wisely consented, but only on the condition that they should obtain the permission of the captain. This they succeeded in doing, and they proceeded forthwith to line up along the taffrail of the steamer for the photograph. Not satisfied, however, with their position, he requested them to change in order to place the tallest man in the centre. As the three sprang forward from the rail against which they had been leaning, it gave way, and with it the three men fell overboard directly in front of the immense paddle-wheel, which literally cut them to pieces instantly.

The astonished photographer was left standing by his camera to take the photograph of the men the subjects of which had been swept away in a moment. It was truly an unfinished picture. Well was it for him that he had refused to act without the permission of the captain, as otherwise the blame would most probably have rested on him. He was restored to health after his attack of smallpox, but he was so disfigured that he gave up photography and learned boatbuilding. He was himself drowned afterwards by falling from the wharf after dark on the Skeena, and he was greatly mourned by all his friends.

Probably the fact that we were compelled to disinfect all his photographic supplies, which were so injured by the

A REVIVAL

chemicals as to unfit them for use, tended to discourage him.

His old father, who had been named Heber, was standing by, with his wife, when his feather-bed was being burnt, which greatly irritated him. He probably remembered the many occasions when he had gone in pursuit of the seafowl along the coast in order to provide sufficient feathers for this luxury, and now to stand by while it was being consumed! "Who could endure it?" So, snatching his pipe from his mouth, he cast it into the fire, exclaiming, "There, burn me with it also." And then, pulling his tobacco from his pocket, he added it to the flames, crying, "What is there left for us to live for?"

He evidently included his wife in his sympathy, as she had but lately succeeded in re-covering the bed with new material. And though she said nothing as she sat watching its consumption, she evidently considered we were mad. I awaited an opportunity when their indignation had subsided, and then proved that we were taking all this trouble for their welfare. And if they were not convinced of my assurance then, they were afterwards, when we subjected them to a good bath by the river side, and then supplied them with new clothing, and permitted their return to the village and their friends in triumph. Here a new tent had been erected for their use, as their house had been burnt also. The Indian Department afterwards made a grant for the material for a new house, which was erected between the rocks at the end of the camp, reminding one of another Heber, the Kenite of whom it is written, "Strong is thy dwelling-place, and thou puttest thy nest in the rock."

Heber has passed away, having died in faith. He had been a great warrior in his day, and never fully recovered from a blow received in a fight from an assailant, who rushed upon him from behind and stabbed him with a double-edged dagger, which penetrated the lung. He passed through several trials with his family, as, in addition to that already stated, through the premature discharge of a cannon, his youngest son had his eyes blown out, and nearly lost his life. The young men of the tribe were engaged in a sham fight, in which the volunteers were pitted against the firemen.

A cannon belonging to the village had been placed on the shore, and a bag of powder had just been rammed into it, when this lad stooped down and looked into the mouth of the cannon. At this moment a spark from the pipe of the man who was placing the powder on the touchhole ignited the powder and discharged the cannon, which blew the lad some distance from its mouth. How he survived is a mystery. His face and neck were but a mangled mass of flesh and blood. The hair was blown off his head, as also most of his scalp, and his sight was destroyed. The Indian whose pipe had caused the mischief was also badly burnt, but the lad lingered between life and death for many months, and at length recovered, to be blind for life.

We had scarce recovered from the epidemic of the smallpox, when we were threatened by an evil of a different nature. This was the arrival of several liquor schooners in the river. These vessels had caused much trouble and quarrelling amongst the Indians in the early days of mission work on the coast, and it was believed that we had seen the last of them. But late one evening one of our young men came and informed me that, seeing a schooner anchored behind an island, he had approached her and was invited on board. Here he found two stalwart white men, who informed him that if he could induce his friends to purchase a keg of liquor or a case, they would reward him by giving him a bottle or two free.

I next learned that these men had succeeded in inducing the heathen Indians on the river to give them an order to purchase all their cargo. To this end they had instructed them to take the schooner, with cargo, up the river, and there await their arrival. This they did, and soon our

A REVIVAL

Indians, foreseeing the consequence of such a quantity of liquor falling into the possession of the heathen party, determined to seize the schooner themselves. I advised them to await the arrival of the Government agent and constables, to whom I had written, but they feared they could not arrive in time. Consequently a party proceeded up the river early on a Sunday morning in pursuit, and as the schooner men were well armed, I feared they would defend themselves and their schooner and cargo to the death.

But the Indians are masters of craft, and when they arrived near the place where the vessel was anchored, they sent forward a small canoe with two men, to reconnoitre. These went on board and engaged the owners in a bargain for the purchase of the whole cargo. To this end they stated that a number of their friends were coming. The others then approached in the large canoe, and whilst one of the liquor vendors was in the cabin and the other on deck endeavouring to effect a sale, instantly they were seized and bound, and conveyed with the schooner down the river to the Mission. Here they were placed in the lock-up, whilst their schooner was anchored off the village.

It was a clever capture, as the liquor vendors were well armed. Each of them had a revolver fully charged, whilst rifles and shot-guns were hung around the cabin. They sent for me shortly after their arrival and begged of me that I should go aboard the schooner and secure all their money and valuables, which I did. The schooner, which was named the *Vine*, was well filled with liquor in casks, boxes, and bottles. Brandy, rye, and other brands of whiskies, as also rum and gin, were packed closely on board. Had the heathen on the river succeeded in purchasing the entire cargo, as they had engaged to do, the results would most probably have been serious to themselves and others. As they are all possessed of firearms and do not hesitate to use them when intoxicated, it would have created a dangerous position both for themselves and the missionaries.

A REVIVAL

Fearing to leave such a cargo of liquor on the schooner lest the owners might effect their escape and carry it away again, or that some of the Indians might be tempted to make away with a quantity, I had the vessel beached and the cargo stowed away in one of the Mission buildings. I had despatched a special canoe with a letter to the Indian agent some fifty miles distant.

On his arrival a court was opened and the prisoners were tried. They pleaded guilty to the charge, but urged as their defence that they were only seeking to make a living. I pointed out to them that of all the Indians present in the court-room even the weakest had made some three hundred dollars by salmon fishing that season. I reminded them also of the manner in which they endangered the lives of the few white residents amongst the Indians, as there were no representatives or officers of the law to preserve order or to protect life amongst them. They were fined and their schooner confiscated and sold to pay the costs, whilst they were each sentenced to ten months' imprisonment. The cargo was all emptied into the sea in the presence of many of the Indians, and the prisoners afterwards threatened the Indian agent and myself. It was a salutary lesson to any others who might be inclined to engage in such a traffic to keep clear of it, and there has been no further attempt to break the law. The other schooners which had entered the river at the same time escaped, but never attempted to return.

The heathen Indians, however, though baffled in this attempt to purchase the cargo of liquor on the schooner *Vine*, were yet determined to obtain intoxicants. They, in common with all the tribes on the coast, had learned how to ferment and distil liquors. Before the advent of the whites they had no intoxicants. It was a soldier of the United States garrison at Fort Wrangle in Alaska, who had been dismissed the service for intemperance, who entered the Indian camp there and taught the Indians how to distil the "hoocheno," or fire-water, and also how to ferment the juice of the berries,

A REVIVAL

This discovery soon spread from camp to camp, and the tribes of South-Eastern Alaska, with the Haidas, Nishkas, and Tsimsheans, were amongst the first to engage in the illicit manufacture. Many were the casualties resulting from the indulgence in these intoxicants. Sometimes whole tribes were engaged in free fights from this cause, and numbers were killed on both sides. Both men and women, old and young, have fallen victims of this vice. It was soon evident that they had succeeded in their efforts to produce a strong intoxicant. One man died in delirium tremens after having been bound naked for several days to keep him from throwing himself on the fire. Another died whilst endeavouring to win a wager by drinking a large wassail-bowl full. A third, in a drunken condition when accompanied by his little son in a sleigh, staggered through an opening in the ice. The little boy had the presence of mind to disengage the rope from the sleigh and cast it to his father; but he was too intoxicated to lay hold of it, and was soon carried by the current under the ice and thus perished. Another drank himself blind, and would have died in delirium tremens had I not laboured hard to save his life. When called to see him, I found him in a wretched plight; he could scarcely be kept on the bed, crying out and struggling to escape from his tormentors. An incessant retching, which could not be controlled, threatened to terminate fatally; but by applying strong cataplasms of mustard, with suitable medicines, this distressing symptom was overcome, and he recovered to be blind for life.

At length our missionary, the Rev. J. B. McCullagh, who had received a commission as Justice of the Peace, decided to endeavour to discover the source of all the ills. Accordingly he sent a party of special constables, armed with a search-warrant, to search the village from which all the evils had arisen. Every lodge was searched, but in vain, and they were about to return unsuccessful, when one of them suddenly recalled to mind an incident which had occurred during a recent visit with the Church Army, when accompanied by my

A REVIVAL

son. The latter was desirous after their service there to take a walk into the forest, but was followed by one of the resident Indians, who informed him that he had best not follow that path, as the medicine men were performing their incantations there.

He returned, but his suspicions were aroused, and he mentioned the matter to one of their number. This man was now acting as one of the specials, and calling on two others he informed them of this, and together they entered on this same trail, and followed it.

They had not gone far till they reached a large spruce tree, to which the trail appeared to lead. Walking round it they detected a hollow sound, and soon they uncovered a pit or vault which was well filled with barrels, kegs, and casks, all full of fermented liquor. There were some twenty-three such packages in all, quite sufficient to supply them for months to come. As it was now dark, they returned to the village to call their partners to help them. These had given up the search, and the owners of the liquor depot were congratulating themselves on the failure of the searchers to find any intoxicants in their dwellings.

When the constables left they believed they had returned to their own village, whereas they had secured several sleighs, and made their way under cover of the darkness to the newly discovered depot. Here they loaded the entire stock on the sleighs, and carried it off to the Mission. Great was the consternation in the camp on the following morning, when they discovered their depot empty. A hasty council was called, at which it was decided to send a deputation at once to treat for terms. The deputation met the constables on their way to serve summonses and warrants on the lawbreakers. All obeyed, and found their stock of liquor piled up as silent witnesses against them in the court-room.

As each in turn stood forward, he pleaded guilty and was asked to point out his cask or barrel, which was done. At length but two casks remained, and to the ownership of these

A REVIVAL

no one responded. After looking at one another in expectation, a chief sprang to his feet and exclaimed, "Since there is no one sufficiently courageous to acknowledge his own property, I am willing to bear the blame. Charge it against me, and let the delinquent bear the shame." A fine, with costs, was imposed on all who thus pleaded guilty, which was at once paid, and all the offenders promised not to break the law again. In conclusion, chiefs and leaders, in short and vigorous speeches, confirmed the promises and advised all to adhere to them.

Thus the liquor conspiracy was broken up, and the way cleared for advancement. And an advance was made. Acting under the influence and advice of their fellow-tribesmen of the Christian community, many of them intimated their desire to be registered as catechumens, and after due preparation a large number were admitted to the membership of the Church by baptism.

CHAPTER XXVII

THE LAKGALZAP MISSION

> " Buried was the bloody hatchet,
> Buried was the dreadful war club,
> Buried were all warlike weapons,
> And the war cry was forgotten ;
> There was peace among the natives,
> Unmolested roved the hunters,
> Built the birch canoe for sailing,
> Caught the fish in lake and river,
> Shot the deer and trapped the beaver ;
> Unmolested worked the women,
> Gathered wild rice in the meadows,
> Dressed the skins of deer and beaver
> All around the happy village."
>
> LONGFELLOW (" Hiawatha ").

SHORTLY before this occurred, the Christian congregation of Indians belonging to the Methodist Mission at Lakgalzap were at their own earnest desire received into connection with the Anglican Missions on the Nass. They had long become discontented because of the too frequent change of missionaries. Their first missionary, the Rev. A. E. Green, had remained at his post for some fifteen or sixteen years, and drawn quite a congregation out of heathenism. But after his removal his successors came and went all too quickly for the adherents of the Mission. They had seen the missionaries of the Church Missionary Society at the two Missions, one at the mouth of the river and the other on the headwaters, remain at their posts for over twenty-five years, whereas they had had over twelve changes during the same period. This caused them to desire the same

THE LAKGALZAP MISSION

permanency of teachers, and hence their desire to join the Church.

We discouraged the movement, although urged to act, both by petition and by deputation. Instead of acceding to their request, we assured them that we should communicate with the leaders of the Methodist Missionary Society, and hasten the appointment of a missionary. But though a teacher was sent, he only remained a few months and then resigned, owing to the breakdown in the health of his young wife.

A long interim followed, during which the same desire was intimated in even a more intense form than before. At length when our missionary on the Upper Nass, the Rev. J. B. McCullagh, was returning up the river to his station he was compelled to encamp at Lakgalzap for the night. But he could not rest owing to a drunken brawl which was continued throughout the night. When preparing to depart in the morning some members of the village council waited on him, and begged him as a magistrate to issue summonses for the guilty parties, especially for those who brought in and supplied the liquor. This he did, and fined the offenders, leaving the council to deal with the minor cases, as he was anxious to proceed on his homeward journey.

But again he was compelled to postpone his departure, as he found there was an epidemic of autumnal fever amongst the young children in the camp, and the parents and friends begged him to visit them, and prescribe some remedy. He could not refuse to do this, and as he found several of them very serious cases, he consented to remain and prescribe for them until they were out of danger. But he requested, as the condition of his remaining longer, that they should not introduce the subject of their desire to be received into the Church. This they agreed to, but notwithstanding their promise, in a few days they commenced to hold meetings to discuss the situation.

Unable longer to conceal their desire, a deputation was

THE LAKGALZAP MISSION

instructed to wait on our missionary, to inform him that should the Church refuse to receive them, many of them would lapse to heathenism again. Fearing that such a movement, if taken, would injure our own Missions seriously, he consented to inform the leaders of the Methodist Church and also the Indian Department, giving due notice of their intention. And on St. Andrew's Day the entire community was received into the Church of England. I declined to be present, as I had already intimated that until one of the leaders of the Methodist Church had visited them, and had heard their decision and the causes which had led to it, I could not agree with the decision. This condition was fulfilled the following week by the arrival of the Rev. Thomas Crosby, who had been commissioned by the Methodist Church to visit the Mission, and inquire into the circumstances. A meeting was convened on his arrival at Lakgalzap, and several speakers were selected by themselves to inform Mr. Crosby of their decision and of the causes which had induced them to take the step.

The Rev. J. B. McCullagh declined to be present at the meeting lest it might be thought that he had influenced the speakers. It was evident to Mr. Crosby that they had taken action of themselves, owing to the lengthened intervals between the resignation of one teacher and the appointment of a successor. As this had occurred several times they had become dissatisfied, and decided on the change. I visited the Mission the following Sunday, and assisted Mr. McCullagh in the appointment of Church officers, and also of a branch of the Church Army.

Shortly after the Lakgalzap Mission had thus been taken over, the Methodist Missionary Society sent a deputation of three of their number to ascertain all particulars of the transfer, and it was agreed that a certain sum should be paid to the Methodist Church from the Diocesan Mission Fund for the church buildings and Mission-house on the Nass river. This and other particulars were arranged by the

THE LAKGALZAP MISSION

Bishop of the Diocese with the Superintendent of the Methodist Missions.

The Rev. J. B. McCullagh succeeded in finding a young man and his wife when in England on furlough, Mr. and Mrs. Laycock, who volunteered to come out and take charge of the Mission which had thus been taken over.

But they were confronted with many difficulties, not the least of which was that of the language, which led to misunderstandings. The Mission-house was accidentally destroyed by fire in the early winter, and with it all the furniture and effects of the missionaries which they had just brought out with them, many of them presents from friends which could not be replaced. At length Mr. and Mrs. Laycock decided to resign the Mission, but before doing so Mr. Laycock erected a new Mission-house and also procured a sawmill for the village. This latter was intended to prepare lumber for the erection of a new church, to which the congregation are now directing their efforts. Mr. Laycock then took duty under the Bishop at Prince Rupert, from which he proceeded to Atlin, where he held the Mission for a time.

Meantime the Lakgalzap Mission has had several teachers, none of whom have remained longer than the winter months. It is difficult to find teachers who will continue to reside there, as the Indians desert the station during the summer months and take up their abode at the salmon canneries and fisheries. Yet they are eager to have a missionary in full orders amongst them, to administer the sacraments and build them up in the faith.

But in the changing conditions of the country the churches find it difficult to meet the many calls from new centres of white settlers, and it is doubtful if either the Anglican Church or the Methodists can continue to supply ordained men to minister to such small communities. In such case more use must be made of the natives as teachers.

The advantage of a united church were seen shortly after

THE LAKGALZAP MISSION

the reception of the congregation of Lakgalzap. The Indians, who had adhered to the old heathen customs despite the efforts of the two Missions, surrendered to the Church Mission shortly after the union and were all baptized. Some sixty of them were thus received into the Church of Christ and baptized in a tent at a camp which had been the headquarters of heathenism; whilst at Fishery Bay a much larger number were received and baptized.

This number included three of the senior chiefs and the leading medicine man. A short time previously the latter had been committed for trial, accused of having caused the death of a woman by his incantations and witchcraft. The three chiefs had long been the champions of heathenism on the river, but Sgaden surpassed his brother chiefs in this respect. He was the head chief of the Giatlakdamiksh tribe on the Upper Nass, and believed himself to be the greatest chief on the river.

His great lodge was the centre of that citadel of heathenism, and though many an assault had been made on it in the early days of the Mission, and afterwards, yet this chief and his wife appeared to be impregnable against every effort to win them to the truth. This spirit of opposition arose from attachment to their own old customs more than from any hatred to the new way. It was in the practice of the potlatch that he, with many of his brother chiefs, had ascended the social ladder, and to turn his back on this would have resulted in social degradation and suicide.

And around this custom and accessary to it were the "halied" or Indian devilry, which in its hydra-headed divisions of cannibalistic, destructive, and necromantic practices kept the Indian camps in a continual turmoil, and made the medicine men a terror to their own tribes as well as to those outside. But Sgaden's surrender, though long delayed, came at length in a manner least expected.

At a feast given by the Christians of Kincolith, to which all the heathen chiefs of the lower river had been invited, a

THE LAKGALZAP MISSION

singular symbol of union had been devised. A long rope had been previously suspended from a beam in the feast-house, and when the feasting was over and speech-making had begun, one of the Christian chiefs explained the object for which the rope had been prepared. He then called on the Christian chiefs to lay hold on one end of the rope, whilst the heathen chiefs were directed to lay hold of the other end. Then bringing the two ends of the rope together they crossed them, and then tied them firmly together, each party still holding and pulling to tighten the knot thus made.

"As we have joined this rope," exclaimed the leading Christian chief, "even so we hereby consent and agree to be joined together."

To this the entire assembly expressed their approval with a cheer. A red banner, with the word "Peace" and other emblems embroidered on it, was then presented to the heathen party by the Christians. Some of the more consistent amongst the Christians demurred afterwards to such an agreement, and stated that they would not have been present had they known of the plan previously. It was an unholy alliance.

Shortly after the inauguration of the Church Army a great potlatch was being held at the heathen camp at Ankida, and the Church Army men proposed to pay the potlatchers a visit, and also other points on the river. The potlatchers resented their visit and offered them no hospitality, which is very unusual amongst gatherings of Indians. One of the evangelists, in speaking, referred to the agreement formerly made by the rope-knot, which he asserted they had now broken, and in the name of the Army demanded that the banner which had been given on that occasion should now be returned. This was done. The banner was handed back, and with it much bitter invective was heaped upon the Christians.

Chief Sgaden was seated in the centre of the heathen

THE LAKGALZAP MISSION

chiefs, but he remained taciturn throughout, and took no part in the tirade against the Church Army men. There was a reason for his attitude. His nephew was amongst them, and took a leading part in the severance of the unrighteous alliance.

When they were about to leave on their return down the river on the ice, this chief arose and quietly informed them that he should accompany them. It came upon the entire assembly, both heathen and Christian, as "a bolt from the blue." It was a great decision declared in a manner worthy of a chief. Anxious not to lose such a leader, a number of his friends decided to accompany him in the hope that they might induce him to return again. They followed him to the first halting-place on the ice. Here they begged him to return with them, and many were the arguments used to induce him to reconsider his action. He listened patiently till all had spoken. Then, rising to his feet, he stretched out his hand, and pointing to a mountain on the opposite side of the river he asked, "Do you see that mountain? If a land-slide took place and was rushing down its breast, could any of you arrest its progress or turn it back again?" To this there was no response. "Well," he added, "it is even so with me." It was sufficient. His friends left without another word and Sgaden continued his journey with the Christian escort.

They reached the Mission the next day. The following Sunday, after morning service, he made a public declaration of his decision to abandon heathenism and to follow in God's way. Two Christian chiefs stood on either hand as his witnesses. In a voice quivering with emotion he declared, in a few well-chosen words, how he had been led to take the decisive step. His witnesses then prayed that he might be enabled to stand firm, and then the whole congregation burst forth spontaneously in the strain

"Ring the bells of heaven, there is joy to-day,
For a soul returning from the wild."

THE LAKGALZAP MISSION

He was baptized afterwards at Fishery Bay at his own request, in order to witness a good confession before as many of his own tribe as might be present. It was one of the many triumphs by which heathenism was gradually overcome. Although many efforts were made to win him back to the old way, yet he remained faithful until his death a few years afterwards.

Heathenism died hard on the Nass. The Haidas surrendered to the truth much more quickly. They had all abandoned their heathen practices in a little more than a decade, whereas many of the Nishkas held fast to heathenism as long again.

Thus the Tsimsheans on the coast line between the Nass and Skeena Rivers, including the Kitkatlas on Ogden Channel, the Haidas of the Queen Charlotte Islands, the Nishkas of the Nass River, the Giatikshans of the Skeena River, as also the Tahltan tribe on the Upper Stikeen River, have all been evangelised and brought into the Church of Christ. It is worthy of note that a native teacher named Joshua Harvey, a member of the Kincolith congregation of native Christians, has been instrumental in evangelising the Gishgagass tribe of Giatikshans on the Upper Skeena. In addition, the Kitamaht Indians and the Indians of Bela-Bela on Milbank Sound to the south have been brought under the power of the truth by the missionaries of the Canadian Methodist Missionary Society, of whom the Rev. Thomas Crosby, the Rev. G. H. Raly, with Dr. Large and others, have laboured long and faithfully.

Among the Quagulth Indians to the north of Vancouver Island, where the Church Missionary Society took up the work abandoned by the French Roman Catholic Mission, much has been done by the Rev. A. J. Hall and Mr. A. W. Corker. The chief success of the former consisted in his mastery of the language, of which he prepared a Grammar and completed translations of the Gospels, portions of the Book of Common Prayer and Hymns, which will be of

THE LAKGALZAP MISSION

permanent benefit to the Mission. The Boys' Industrial School which Mr. A. W. Corker and his devoted wife have carried on and superintended for many years is effecting, by the influence of the pupils it has educated, a gradual change amongst not only the Quagulth Indians, but also other outlying tribes. A similar institution for girls under the same superintendence has lately been added, and will no doubt prove of immense benefit to the Indian girls, who are exposed to many and great dangers.

Northward, the numerous tribes of the great territory of Alaska have almost all been evangelised by the churches of the United States, each of the leading denominations having agreed to occupy its own sphere, thus avoiding friction and economising funds. To the Presbyterian Church must be accorded the honour of having been the pioneer of evangelisation in Alaska. And with the early efforts of this Church the name of Sheldon Jackson must ever be identified. It was largely owing to his labours that the harmonious division of the territory for mission work was arranged. And his success in the cause of education and in the introduction of the reindeer from Siberia will ever remain as a monument to his memory.

We were privileged, as has already been recorded, in first calling the attention of the Board of Missions to the needs of Alaska by a letter signed by the three missionaries then labouring on the north-west coast of British Columbia. And now we have the satisfaction of knowing that all along this coast line, from the Straits of Fuca to the Behring Straits, the Indian tribes have been evangelised. The Protestant Episcopal Church of the States, under the able and energetic leadership of Bishop Peter Rowe and Archdeacon Stuck, has been seeking and saving the lost sheep of the Alaskan tribes from Skagway to the Yukon; whilst to the south of the Alaskan boundary line, under the tactful and able leadership of Bishop Du Vernet, the Message of Salvation is being proclaimed to the incoming settlers along the line of the new

THE LAKGALZAP MISSION

trans-continental railway, whilst the Indian tribes are not forgotten.

Bishop Du Vernet was himself the pioneer clergyman at Prince Rupert, where he conducted the first religious services, and from this, the terminal city of the Grand Trunk Pacific Railway, he has extended the Church's work along the line into the interior. The white settlers on the Queen Charlotte Islands have not been overlooked, as there are two clergymen of the Anglican Church engaged in the work there. The other leading churches are also lengthening their cords and strengthening their stakes in these new fields of labour.

We rejoice that the evangelisation of the Indian tribes has been effected before the inrush of the white population. And the foundation has been laid, the only sure foundation, on which to build up a new nation in this fair land of promise. It is the foundation on which our fathers built up the great nation of which we are justly proud. It is the foundation, also, on which the Pilgrim Fathers began to build the mighty nation which is allied to us in blood and language, whose territory bounds us on both north and south.

It is a well-tried foundation of truth and righteousness.

And from this commanding and central position, where East and West unite, the influence of such a nation, stretching from ocean to ocean of Canada's great Dominion, shall roll in ceaseless waves and currents around the globe, to remind us of the King of Righteousness, whose subjects we are, and of His Kingdom, which shall never pass away nor be destroyed.

INDEX

ALASKAN Haidas, Mission to, 241
Ankida, origin of name, 277

BEARS, encounters with, 45, 313, 316
Bompas, Rt. Rev. Bishop, 229
Bonilla Isl. fur-seal hunters, 61
Burial, underground, introduced, 192

CANADIAN Methodists at Fort Simpson, 91
— — on Nass River, 85
Canoe travelling, difficulties of, 145, 235
— catastrophe, 154
Carving, Haida, 251
Chief's story, 281
Chinook trade jargon, 126
Church Missionary Society found Mission, 23
— — College, author enters, 36
— Army, introduction of, 325
Collison, Ven. Archdeacon, 38, 40, 43, 47, 231, 267, 268 294
— Rev. W. E., 262
Corker, Mr. A. W., 345
Cowhoe, Chief, 173, 257

Cridge, Very Rev. Dean, 42
Crosby, Rev. Thos., 345

DAWSON, Professor, visit of, 228
Dixon, Capt., 21
Duncan, Mr. Wm., 23, 25, 47, 258
Doolan, Rev. R. A., 28, 30
Du Vernet, Rt. Rev. Bishop, 346, 347

EDENSHEW, Chief, 109, 162, 166, 169, 175, 261, 264
Essington, Port, founding of, 290

FIELD, Rev. J., 302
Fort Simpson, Mr. Duncan lands at, 24
Fraser, Simon, explorer, 20
Funeral of chief, 279
Fur-seal hunting, 249

GAMBLING, how practised, 185
Giatkatla Indians, 18, 53
Giatlaub, visit to, 62
Gitikshan tribes visited, 292
Gitwinikshilk, 75
Gold, discovery of, on Queen Charlotte Islands, 113
Grand Trunk Pacific Railway, 302
Green, Rev. A. E., 338

INDEX

Gurd, Rev. R. W., 54
Gwaksho, Chief, fight with bear, 316

HAIDA Indians, 88, 89, 92
— — as hunters, 247
— — author's reception by, 102–106
— — crest system, 100, 101
— — opposition, 108, 123
— canoes, 162, 244
— carving, 251
— congregation, appearance of, 151
— feast described, 136
— language, difficulties of, 124–5
— mode of burial, 103
— music, 226, 250
— tattooing, 138
Haidas at Skidegate, 176
Halibut, fishing for, 209
Hall, Rev. A. J., at Alert Bay, 37, 43, 345
Harrison, Rev. C., 253, 257
Hazleton Mission, 307
Herber, the Warrior, 331
Hudson's Bay Company on Nass River, 272
— — at Fort Simpson, 273
Hunting, dangers of, 216

INDIANS *versus* whites, 58
Industrial training for Indians, 56
Intoxicants, trouble caused by, 164, 166, 334
Inverness founded, 55
"Iron People," 119

JACKSON, Sheldon, 210

KADONAH, Chief, 25
Keen, Rev. J. H., 36, 258, 260
Kinzadak, Chief, 80
Kinnanook, Chief, 148
Kincolith Mission Station, 31, 318
— burning of church, 319
Kishgagass Station, 301
Kishpiyouksh, 298
Klaitak, Chief, 278, 287

LAKGALZAP Mission, 338, 340
Large, Dr., 345
Law, introduction of, 215
Laycock, Mr. E. P., 341
Legaic, Chief, 35
Liberality, Indian, 322
Liquor vendors captured, 333
Lost in forest, 299

M'CULLAGH, Rev. J. B., 86, 335, 339
Mackenzie, Alex., the explorer, 17, 18
M'Kenzie, Alex., 218
Makai, of Massett, 198, 200
Massett, description of, 100, 150
— building at, 129, 154
— Church opening, 255
Meares, Capt., 118
Medicine men, 47
Methodists at Fort Simpson, 91
— on the Nass River, 85
Metlakathla, 33, 34, 50
Morice's History quoted, 274
Mosquitoes, fight with, 293

INDEX

Mountain, Chief, 304
Murderer, tracking a, 303
Music among Haidas, 226, 250

NAKADZOOT, the medicine man, 230
Nangsinwass, Chief of Skidegate, 179
Nass River tribes, 66
— — adventure on, 73
— — Methodists on, 85
— — Potlatch, 278
New Caledonia, 20
Nishkas and Tsimsheans at war, 82
— — as hunters, 315
— — manual skill, 278

OLACHAN fishery, 65-67
Otter, steamer, voyage in, 121
Otter, sea, hunting of, 247

PALGRAVE, Rev. F. M. T., 314
Peacemaker, missionary as, 131, 194
"Pene" or pseudo-revival, 274
Port Simpson, 146
Potlatch, 134, 141, 205, 342
Presbyterian Church of U.S. in Alaska, 149
Prevost, Captain J. C., 22
Prince Alfred, steamer, 42

QUADRA, Captain, 20
Quagulth Indians, 345
Queen Charlotte Islands, 78, 109, 113

Queen Charlotte Islands, voyage to, in canoe, 92-99
Quiyah, Chief of Zitz-Zaows, 310-312

RALY, Rev. G. H., 345
Religious fanaticism, 274
Revival, 325
Ridley, Rt. Rev. Bishop, 252, 262, 296
Robson, Hon. Jno., 304
Rowe, Rt. Rev. Bishop, 346

SAN Francisco, 41
Sanitary conditions enforced, 219
Satellite, H.M.S., 22
Sea-otter hunting, 247
Sebasha, Chief, 51, 55
Seegay, Chief, 90, 93
Sgaden, conversion of Chief, 344
Shakes, Chief, 50, 51
Sharks, dangers from, 207
Sheldon, Rev. H. A., tragic death of, 291
Sick, treatment of, 181
Simon Magus, a modern, 183
Skeena River Mission, 288
Skidegate visited, 175
Slaves rescued, 52, 78
Small-pox epidemic, 26, 202, 327
Sneath, Mr. Geo., at Massett, 233
Sparrowhawk, H.M.S., at Nass, 85
Stalactite cave discovered, 282
Steamer, first, on river Skeena, 305

INDEX

Steilta, Chief, 188
Stephenson, Rev. F. L., 50
Strong drink, trouble from, 332
Susan Sturges, captured by Haidas, 111

Tahltan tribe, 302
Takomash, Chief, 76
Takou Indians, 79
Tattooing among Haidas, 138
Thaimshim, mythical god, 298
Thorman, Rev. T. P., 314
Tomlinson, Rev. R., 31, 297
Totem, construction of, 137
Trade jargon, 126
Tsimshean tribes, 82, 289
Tugwell, Rev. F. L., 35

Typhoid, author's battle with, 132

Vaccination introduced, 202
Vancouver, Geo., discoverer, 17, 18, 229
— attacked by Haidas, 112
Virago, H.M.S., 22
Volcanic eruption on Nass, 270

Walbran, Capt., 273
War, Indian, 221–225
Weah, Chief, 121, 144
White settlers, influx of, 265

Zidahah, tragic death of, 285
Zitz-Zaow Indians, 302, 307

Printed in the United Kingdom by
Lightning Source UK Ltd., Milton Keynes
136604UK00001B/304-309/P